THE TUTTLE TWINS
and the
HYPERINFLATION DEVASTATION

CONNOR BOYACK

ILLUSTRATIONS BY ELIJAH STANFIELD

Libertas Press
2183 W Main Street, A102
Lehi, UT 84043

The Tuttle Twins and the Hyperinflation Devastation

Edited by Chris Jones

ISBN-13 978-1-943521-39-5 (paperback)

10 9 8 7 6 5 4 3 2

For bulk orders, send inquires to info@libertasutah.org.

Other titles by the author:

Skip College: Launch Your Career Without Debt, Distractions, or a Degree

Lessons from a Lemonade Stand: An Unconventional Guide to Government

Feardom: How Politicians Exploit Your Emotions and What You Can Do to Stop Them

The Tuttle Twins children's book series

"You made sure to pack a jacket, right?" Mom said. "You can't be too careful. You're going to be in strange situations and you never know."

"Yes, Mom," Ethan replied. "Two jackets. One light and one heavy. We have sixty-two different changes of clothes and extra underwear, too. You checked all that. More than once. We're fifteen years old, not six!" He rolled his eyes a little, but fifteen or not, he made sure Mom couldn't see.

Emily gazed out the window and watched the street—her street—slide by. Trees waved in the early morning breeze, as if saying goodbye. But that was silly. They'd be back. Of course they'd be back.

Ethan checked his waist pack, specially designed for travelers to make it almost impossible for pickpockets to access. In it he carried "the criticals": passport, cash, emergency contacts, a small map. Again and again, he unzipped it, dipped his fingers in, and zipped it closed. He did it every few minutes, like touching a talisman. Emily leaned against the glass. Dad looked back at them through the rearview mirror every chance he got, as if he were worried they wouldn't still be there.

"Nervous?" he finally said. Emily couldn't tell if that meant that he was, or he was wondering if they were.

But she was nervous. Her stomach wouldn't settle. "A little," she admitted.

"A lot," Ethan said.

"You'll like Jorge, I'm sure. His father Maita was a very good guide when we went to Ychurichuc. Showed us lots of stuff, even things that weren't on the tour."

"I'm not worried about the tour, Dad," Ethan said. "It's getting there that has me concerned."

Mom laughed a little. "Well, you planned it as well as anyone could. You've had this trip planned down to the minute for the last two years."

"Good thing, too," Emily said. "Or we wouldn't have known how much we needed to earn to get there. Ethan must have saved us hundreds getting deals on things."

"Eleven hundred seventy-two dollars and sixteen cents," Ethan said.

"Really?" Mom said, swiveling toward the back seat.

"No, not really," Ethan grinned. "I don't count *everything.*"

But he had been counting pretty much everything else. Ever since he'd seen their dad's old scrapbooks, Ethan had read everything he could get his hands on about the Inca, the ancient country Allqukilla, and the historical ruins at Ychurichuc.

And he wasn't the only one. None of the architecture, the step-sided pyramids, or the aqueducts had made much of an impression on Emily, but then Ethan had come across a mystery—the Inca *quipu*, the talking beads. Emily could never resist a mystery; from then on, she was just as hooked as he was.

And the endless Spanish lessons! Online, YouTube, and with Pedro, a pen pal who grew up in Chile. Ethan knew that when he woke up from a dream in which there hadn't been a word of English, they were getting well prepared to go.

The car passed the open field where they'd held their community carnival, one of a half dozen things the twins had done to raise money for the trip.

"I'll help you all you want," Dad had said, "but you have to earn the money."

In the end, the trip cost thousands of dollars, even with the discounts that Ethan had been able to get from booking the trip early and negotiating. It had been two and a half years of saving every penny.

All of her friends had talked seemingly nonstop about the clothing stores, the food court, the huge movie theater with the reclining seats. Emily hadn't seen much of those. She had babysat, cut lawns, baked cakes, organized fundraisers. She had done everything she could think of to put another few dollars into the account and bring them fractionally closer to seeing Ychurichuc for themselves.

And now they were in the car.

On the way to the airport.

Turn to the next page.

The ride to the airport never went so quickly. Ethan knew Emily was nervous, too, but she leaned against the window and let the city roll by as if she hadn't a care in the world.

Ethan thought he probably looked calm, too. No one else could feel his stomach doing loop-de-loops every time the car went over a bump. No one knew that he kept going over the flight information, the exchange rates, the money they had as a buffer in case things went wrong somehow. In his luggage he had a full printout of everything—the hotel's information, the bus route, and the map of the little town by the ruins. Just in case, he had duplicates in the backpack at his feet, and he had memorized as much of it as he could.

The blue sky stretched out ahead of them as they approached the airport, broken only by a lonely tower and the sleek bodies of aircraft waiting their turn.

Dad checked the rearview again, and his eyes sought Ethan's. Whatever he saw there, he cleared his throat and said, "Why don't you go over it again one more time, son."

Ethan nodded and said, "Okay. We're on flight 317, U.S. Southern Air to Mexico City. We change planes there and take AeroSud to Takewawa Municipal Airport. It's one hour ahead of us, so we need to move our watches once we get to Mexico."

"And that's where you'll exchange money, right?" Mom asked, as if they hadn't talked about it a dozen times already.

Ethan shook his head. "Not until we get there. The exchange rate is better for us the longer we wait."

Emily came alive next to him. "Fifty saladera to the dollar this morning," she said. "That's up six since Tuesday."

"You were paying attention," he said.

"Of course, silly. I'm always paying attention. Just not always to the same things you are."

Ethan turned back to Dad. "There are ATMs at the airport. Those are the best places to get cash from our debit cards. We'll exchange some money there and get supplies for the trip—stuff they won't let us take on the plane."

"I wish I could take some of our apples from our tree," Emily said, pulling one out of her sweater pocket and taking a huge bite.

"Emily!" Mom said. "Those apples are for the charity pies! You know they don't taste the same off any other tree."

"Sorry," Emily said around her mouthful. She chewed and swallowed. "I couldn't resist. And they won't let me take it into South America, will they? So I better eat it now."

Ethan snorted. "You could have left it on the tree at home."

Emily took a crunchy hunk out of the apple right in his ear. "But then," she said, "I wouldn't be able to eat one, would I?"

"Enough," Dad said. The car merged into the departure lane and coasted toward the curb. "After the supplies?"

"We get on the bus and head for Ychurichuc. It's a six-hour ride. When we get off, the hotel is just across the square from the bus station. We have two days at the hotel to play around and hike or whatever before the tour will be expecting us."

Mom said, "And then you come home to me."

"We have three days on site there at the ruins," Ethan said. "*Then* we come home to you."

"You have enough money?" Mom said.

Emily laughed and held up a small fistful. "I think we'll be okay."

"Emily!" Mom said. "What on earth?"

She laughed again and tucked the money into her waist pack. "It's a little extra I saved up. Plus a small gift from grandma."

"You should leave that here," Ethan said. "We have enough. We've counted it out, like, four times."

"I want to be able to buy something if I want," Emily said.

Dad parked the car and swung open the van's side door. Ethan and Emily looked at each other, each sensing the nervousness of the other. Things just got real.

Turn to page 70.

The three of them turned east and began to climb up the stairs to the cemetery.

"This is the oldest part of the site," Thon explained. "All of this other stuff was put here a century or so later," he motioned, waving his hand to the surrounding area. "Nobody really knows how long people had been burying their ancestors on this stretch of ground, but it certainly has been a very long time—thousands of years. As long as there have been people in this area."

"Those people would be your ancestors too," Emily said.

"Yes," he said, "they would. But they didn't have a written language, so it's very hard for us to know anything about them. Since the graves are unusual, stood on end, there may be hundreds more buried at this site that we don't know about."

They kept climbing the stairs. Ethan said, "I would think archaeologists would have done lots of digging here."

"They have," Thon replied. "No question about it. But getting permits from the government to do more digging is complicated. The government says that it needs to make sure that it preserves the natural site and the heritage of the people who bury their ancestors here."

"That doesn't sound unreasonable," Emily said. "A lot of desecration of native graves has been done in

America by people who didn't care that those sites were sacred to the native people."

"That's certainly true," Thon said. "But I *am* the native people, and we want those graves opened and looked at. The government isn't much interested in protecting our cultural heritage. They only seem to be interested in how much money they can extract from the people who want to dig those things up."

"It all comes back to money," Ethan said. "It always seems to come back to who has it and who can get it from other people."

"Like that guy back there, the tour guide."

"What?" Ethan said. "Jorge? What about him?"

Thon swept his arm over the whole of the ruin site. "You see a lot of other tour guides here?"

"One or two, yeah."

"And why aren't there fifty?" Thon said. "There's surely demand for it."

Ethan smacked his forehead. "The government gave them a contract, didn't they?"

Thon nodded. "It pays to know people in power, and guys like him end up getting paid a lot."

They reached the top of the staircase. The sun beat down on them full in the face but somehow the air was cooler here, and a light breeze blew across from the west. At the top of the stairs a flat, circular area, overgrown with grass and wildflowers, spread in front of them. Every few paces, an area was marked with a perfectly spherical rock. It looked like a marble ring on a school playground for giants.

"I've never seen graves like this anywhere else," Ethan said. "This is even more impressive than it looked like in the research that I did."

"Every one of these stones marks a grave," Thon said.

"But not every grave is marked by a stone," Emily said. "Is that right?"

Thon nodded. "We don't actually know how many of these stones were placed here until the Inca period, which is well after the original burials had begun."

Thon led them around the circular graveyard counter-clockwise. The entire graveyard sat at the bottom of a green bowl with scrub trees and vegetation running up the sides of the hills surrounding the gravesites. The trees on the east were taller, and the birds were thicker in the limbs of the trees on that side than in other places surrounding the bowl.

"The birds like it better on the cooler side," Thon explained, having seen Emily staring. "They'll move over to the west side in the afternoon. I think they like the berries and the fruit on the east side more. That's where the cave is that I want to show you."

They stayed out of the middle of the graveyard, but as they walked Emily could tell that the stones had not been laid in straight lines. Yet they weren't random, she didn't think. There was definitely a pattern there.

"It's the spiral design I read about," Ethan said, his voice full of wonder. Emily immediately saw the same.

"No one knows why it was laid out this way," Thon said. "Not even the oldest of my people knows."

"Some people think that it has to do with the stars," Ethan said.

"It's not the stars," Thon said. "We've charted it over and over. The legend is that the spiral represents a sliding down to the core of the earth, to Xibalba and the underworld. Laying the stones in a spiral allows the souls to travel from grave to grave as they move down into the lower levels of existence."

"I never read anything about that," Ethan said.

"No," Thon said. "And you probably never will. It's not even really archaeology; it's just a legend that my people tell." He moved off around the last of the circle and stopped, facing the jungle.

"Here we are," he said. "He stepped in between two scrub trees, reached his hand into a curtain of ropy vines and pulled them apart. There, in the center of a huge boulder laid into the side of the mountain, was a crack, dark against the bright foliage. It seemed far too narrow for anybody to squeeze through.

"There's no way I'm getting through that," Emily said, "I'm not sure that our *dog* could get through there."

Thon laughed. "You certainly can get through there. Watch." And he took a step forward, slid sideways, and disappeared.

Emily gasped. Ethan smiled broadly. "It's an optical illusion," he said. "The cleft only looks narrow because the rocks overlap one another. The way the shadows hit them, they look like they're much closer together than they actually are. Look!" And he slipped his arm into the crack and slid in after it.

Now Emily could see the trick. The front lip of the rock extended out toward them farther than the right side of the rock. Emily reached her hand in, and Ethan took hold of it and drew her inside. The way immediately opened much wider, and all three of them could stand easily.

It was a kind of foyer, an entryway into a much larger cave system.

"Bad luck," Emily said, "I didn't bring my flashlight." Ethan unzipped his belt pack. He drew out a large headband and flipped a switch, filling the area with light. Thon drew a flashlight from his pocket as well, one of the newer LED models.

In the interior of the cave, the temperature dropped by ten degrees. Every footstep echoed, and every noise was amplified by the surrounding rock. There was nothing to absorb the sound. Ethan couldn't tell how large the cave was or how far back it went, but as he shone his light around, the rock reflected the beam back at him in a thousand sparkles.

"It's beautiful," he said.

Thon put his hand on his shoulder. "Yes, I've often thought so," he said.

"Come back this way," Thon said. "There's some carvings on the wall that I think you will be interested in."

He led them off to the left a bit. It wasn't a path exactly, but the sloping hole in the mountain went to the back wall of this chamber of the cave. A small branch led off into the dark. The passage narrowed enough that they had to walk sideways for a short distance. Ethan's palms began to sweat, and even with the flashlight his vision spotted and the walls seemed to close in on him. For a moment his breathing sped up, but the passage soon broadened back out again into a wide chamber. Ethan pointed his flashlight upward, but it struck no stone above.

The walls were decorated with carvings.

"These don't look Incan," Ethan said, bending down to examine some of the closer ones.

"They're not," Thon said. "They predate the Incas by a couple of hundred years. Nobody really knows what happened to these people."

"Can you bring a light back here?" Emily called out behind them.

Ethan stepped back into the passageway. Emily's hand was raised, pointing at something. "Can you shine your light up there?" she said. "I thought I saw something when you walked by. I was looking at the ceiling. I think there's a ledge up here or something."

Ethan shined his light up toward the roof of the passage. The walls were narrow, only a couple of feet wide, but they went up twenty or thirty feet. Sure enough, there seemed to be a hole in the wall, where a ledge or some variety of passage led through, possibly into another room.

"I can't tell what it is," Ethan said.

"Maybe if you boosted me," Emily said. Ethan ducked his head, pulled the lamp off, and handed it to her. Emily strapped it to her head as Ethan laced his hands. She put her foot in his hand and stepped up.

"I can't quite see," she said. "Can I get on your shoulders?"

In answer, Ethan shifted and pushed her shoe up onto one shoulder. She brought the other shoe up and stood on him.

"That's good," she said. "I can see it now. There's some more carving on the wall, but there is something else, something on the floor. It might be cooking pots?" The light bobbed and pointed down. "It's amazing! There must be a way into this chamber, around the other side somewhere."

Thon said, "That's not for us to find. Still, I'm glad to know the chamber is there. I've been up and down this passageway several times, and I have never seen it before. I'll have to tell the archaeologists and come back here with some people who know the cave better than I do."

"Do you think you could boost me up?" Ethan said.

Thon got underneath him and Ethan scrambled up. "Em is right. There are several pots in here. They look intact, Thon! This could be a very interesting find!"

Then it was Thon's turn. He was very excited about what he saw in the chamber and couldn't wait to get back to his village to tell what he had seen.

Making sure they left nothing disturbed, the three of them exited the cave. They walked the rest of the way around the burial site. Emily took out her camera and snapped away at the burial site, noting that on many of the grave markers, there were also carvings of various kinds. The carvings looked Inca, but she would have to study them further to be sure.

"We should probably go back and link up with the rest of the group," Ethan said.

He looked back at the grave sites, reluctant to leave, wondering if he would ever see a place like this again. "So much history," he said. "So much to see and to learn."

Thon said, "It's nice to come here with someone who really appreciates the importance of history and what it means to my people."

"We appreciate it," Emily said. "That's why we came here. That's why we've always wanted to come here."

A sense of calm and peace settled on the twins as they exited the cave system and found Jorge and the group. And even though Jorge didn't look happy that they had left, Ethan didn't know how things could have turned out better. This was the perfect trip—just as he'd imagined it.

He didn't realize that part of the reason for the calm was that the animals had grown silent. Just then he felt, more than heard, the grinding of the earth, and watched the Great Obelisk, that had stood for two thousand years, topple slowly and thud massively to the ground.

Turn to page 335.

Night fell hard and early, with few city lights to illuminate things. Esmeralda had powerful beams, but Anibal judged it unwise to keep going without daylight to see by.

"I have blankets in the box in the back," Anibal said. "I hope they're not wet from the lake."

They were a bit damp, but the heat of the day dried them quickly. Emily and Ethan huddled in the back, looking up at the stars and hoping the mosquitoes had been shaken too much to be aggressive.

The sky got light at five the next morning. "Equator sun angle. Six to six, every day," Ethan said.

Emily pointed to herself. "US sun angle. I need more sleep." But she knew she wasn't getting any, so she got up and folded the blanket. Anibal was already awake, heating some water and making a thick chocolate on a portable stove. He offered the twins some, and they sipped at it, looking over the nearby streets. Soon enough, they were rolling forward again.

The devastation appeared to be in two major groups. Most of the very newest houses, the ones that had been built since the country began to become prosperous, had stood up pretty well to the earthquake's devastation. The very old houses, the ones that had been built three or four hundred years before, they also seemed almost impervious to the rumbling of the Earth.

But everything else had suffered tremendously. Glass littered the pavement, brick and plaster tumbled into the road from either side. Tall buildings lay broken open like piggy banks, with their facings slumped down in front of them. It was almost impossible to recognize this as the same city that they had been in only a few days before.

Anibal cruised slowly through the streets, rumbling over debris from ruined buildings and ruined lives, with tears streaming silently down his face. "We were warned," he said, "but what could we possibly do? Unless everyone decided they weren't going to live here anymore, what could men do against such power?"

"And where do we go now?" Emily said. "I don't even have my backpack. My passport is gone and most of my money. Our luggage is all back in the ruins of the Ychu hotel."

"I would think we would need to go to the embassy," Ethan said. "That seems to be the only place that will have the resources to help us."

"I can take you there," Anibal said, "but I think it will be difficult navigating through the city. I'm pretty sure the authorities are only going to want official traffic on the roads while they are trying to clean this up."

"Still," Emily said, "what else can we do? We can't very well try to walk across the entire city to get to the embassy."

"Even if we knew where it was," Ethan said. "Although," he said, a little sheepishly "I do have a map."

"You'll need one," Anibal said. "With the devastation this bad, I don't think we will be able to get cell phone reception or GPS."

A little bit at a time, the three of them and Esmeralda fought their way across town, guided by Ethan and his map. The situation was dire on the street. Not enough water, people queuing up in front of large semi trucks to receive handouts of bread and a few vegetables. The side of the trucks said "Takewawa General"—the insignia of the government.

Toward the center of town, they passed a large soccer stadium. Trucks and busses queued up outside, each one packed to the doors with people.

"This must be the main staging area," Anibal said. "It looks desperate."

"Not a bad place to go," Emily said. "Wide open space, nothing to fall on you in an aftershock."

"But the people packed in there—what must that be like? Just a few bathrooms, not much water, not much food—and the people there will have lost everything. It's a horror," Ethan said.

The grocery stores they passed had already been stripped bare, windows smashed and loose rice spilling into the street. No delivery truck could navigate the choked streets to deliver more goods, so the stores were limited to what they had on hand, which was never enough for a population that all of a sudden feared starving.

Twice they were stopped by official vehicles, asking them what they were doing on the street. When they explained, both times they were reluctantly let go, although the second time the policeman flagged them down a block later and asked them if they could pull a particular piece of concrete out of the road, unblocking it for other traffic. They were only too happy to help. Ethan hitched the chain to the back of Esmeralda while Emily spoke briefly with a group of locals in the area who were trying to clear enough debris to make progress toward getting out of the city, only to have to do it again another block down the road.

"They have friends up in the hills," she said, once they were back in the vehicle. "One lady said that the rumors are things are pretty good, or at least not nearly as bad, up in the hills. Most of the damage seems to have been done in the major cities."

"Which, unfortunately, is where everyone lives," Ethan said.

It took a couple of hours at Esmeralda's top speed, but finally they reached the place where the US Embassy was marked on the map. The embassy was still there, looking untouched. There were two Marines stationed at the gate, however, who shook their heads as Esmeralda approached.

"Keep moving," they said, waving the vehicle down the street.

"Excuse me," Ethan said, leaning out the window, "I'm an American. My sister and I are here on vacation, we're trying to get home now. We had hoped the embassy could help us to do that."

They stopped waving and the shorter one stepped forward. "I've heard that a lot the last few hours. The embassy personnel have been moved because the building is unsafe. You know how that can happen in an earthquake?'

"Oh, yes," Emily said, trying not to think of their ruined hotel. "We know that very well."

"Well, anyway," the Marine said, "they've been moved across town. Do you have a map?" Ethan produced his and handed it to the Marine. "Right here," he said, pointing to the map. "It's not too far away. They should be able to help you there."

It was, indeed, not very far from where they were. Esmeralda made the trip in about fifteen minutes and, in spite of the disasters that they had experienced together, or perhaps because of them, the three of them found that they were chattering away like old friends

Emily thought that of all the people that she had met on this trip, Anibal was the only one so far who she knew she would really miss when they got home.

On a vacant block down a street remarkably free of rubble, they saw a uniform they immediately recognized. Ethan felt a rush of homesickness but brushed it away.

Esmeralda ground to a halt in the street out front. The uniform guarded the front of a long, squat building like a silver tube half buried in the ground. Ethan recognized it from old World War II videos.

"It's a Quonset hut," he said. He consulted the map, just in case. "This is the right place."

The twins climbed down the ladder out onto the gritty pavement. "I guess this is where we say goodbye," Emily said.

Anibal flipped himself out of his pilot's seat and landed lithely on the ground. He took his baseball cap off and ran his hand through his thinning gray hair. "Yes, I guess it is."

On impulse, Emily reached up and threw her arms around his neck. "Thank you," she said. "I don't know what we would have done without you."

"Probably would have gotten on all right," Anibal said. But his face was buried in her shoulder when he said it.

Ethan settled for a manly handshake. "We'll miss you," he said. "Tell us how we can send you a postcard or something, to let you know that we're all right."

"And you send one to us," Emily said, "so that we know the same."

Anibal scribbled his address down on the map. "Now, don't lose this. Don't let it get stuck in an airport that's underwater, or a collapsing hotel, or get washed away by a disintegrating dam."

"No," Ethan said with a rueful little smile, "we promise."

With a wave, making sure that the twins had all of their gear, Anibal clambered back into Esmeralda and pushed the button to start her up. She chugged into life; he put her in gear. Away the two of them went, down the dusty street, crunching over broken glass and shattered brick.

Turn to page 398.

Emily looked around the hotel lobby with curious eyes. It wasn't as large as some she had seen, but everything was beautifully appointed. The staff were dressed in ornate costumes like those from an Inca ceremony. Rows of chairs lined two walls with an open space in the middle, broken only by an occasional coffee table as if they used this space for gatherings as well as for welcoming guests. Red, gold, and bright blue threads ran through the tapestries hanging on the walls which depicted scenes from the ancient past. And one wall was decorated with a panoramic view of the Ychurichuc.

Ethan took care of checking in and found that their room was in order. The porter took their bags up to their room, which had a balcony looking over the lake.

"This is exactly what I was hoping for," Emily said.

"Yeah," Ethan said. "Something is finally going right."

The twins were far too excited to stay in their room. They hung around long enough to watch the spectacular sunset across the lake from their balcony before heading to the beach. There they found that a huge fish barbecue had been laid out. They gorged themselves on delicacies from the lake and from the more distant ocean. There was music for dancing, some of it played on instruments the twins had never seen before, and Emily thought she had floated away and gone to heaven.

Turn to page 228.

It wasn't the distance so much as it was the very dry and dusty conditions that made the trip to Thon's village such a difficult one. More than anything, it was how steep and rocky it was. There was jungle everywhere, with thick, ropey vines twined around the trunks of trees. Once they climbed down through the valley at the end of the Yuchrichuc ruins, they began climbing again. The terrain changed dramatically.

"We are out of the rain shadow," Thon said, holding out his hand and grasping Emily's to haul her up over a particularly tricky patch. "On one side of the mountain, there is plenty of green because the water collects there from thunderstorms that shower down on it. But because the clouds drop their water here," he said, pointing to a nearby slope covered in jungle. "Then they have no more water in them to rain on this side of the mountain."

Emily nodded, sweat pouring down her face. Although they were up very high, the temperature was still hotter than she would have liked. She knew that she was sweating through her clothes and that finding new ones was going to be complicated. But after a mile or so of the trip, she stopped worrying about what she looked like, or smelled like, and started worrying about whether the others were going to be able to physically handle the rest of the journey.

Fortunately, Ethan was a good hiker, and Thon was more mountain goat than man. Emily had thought that she really enjoyed hiking, but the hikes that she was used to, the ones that she loved to take in and around the hills of home, had been significantly less steep, and always on some sort of a trail. Half the time this journey seemed to be just hacking through bush, through scrubby bushes and thorny weeds. Her cross-country running was good for endurance, but there wasn't any running here. And Ethan didn't even have that.

One minute they would be climbing through a rocky, pebbly patch, where the ground refused to stay still under her feet, and the next they would cross the hill and start down into a slick, jungly patch with vegetation that constantly defied her boots' attempts to get purchase.

After an hour by Ethan's watch, they stopped. Ethan unzipped his pack and withdrew some beef jerky. Without a word, Emily took it from him and began to eat. The protein almost immediately did her good, and her pace picked up.

Along the way, Thon told stories about the village, the people who lived there, and especially, given the circumstances with the earthquake, stories about why their village had withstood so many terrible disasters that had leveled more modern structures. "We build to last," Thon said. "Although, I didn't build anything, of course. It was our ancestors. But we maintained the buildings that they put together, and we have upgraded in many ways. We have invested in solar power, because the government power systems have a hard time reaching our village. We also take care of our roads, and see that they are clear of rocks. Big ones that could be dangerous in an earthquake are broken up so that even when we have some kind of natural disaster, like very heavy rains, which we get sometimes, or earthquakes, like this one, we always have a way into and out of our village."

"That sounds very sensible," Ethan said. "My question is, why don't the government roads get the same sort of attention?"

"We don't wait for the government to provide us with those services," Thon said. "We do it ourselves. The government doesn't come out here much. What would be the point? We don't vote. The road is narrow and in places very dangerous."

"That makes sense," Ethan said. "Those things make it expensive to maintain."

"Right," Emily said. "Even if they have to pay the workers the same. It's more gas to get here and harder on the equipment."

Ethan rubbed his jaw. "I bet the workers would demand more, anyway, to come work out here. And what sort of job will they do? They don't live here."

Thon nodded. "Our roads were built by our ancestors, not by a government official somewhere. The life of our village depends on those roads. We have to take care of them, we have to maintain them, for our village to thrive."

He struggled a little on a rocky patch, finally hauling himself up with a bush as a handhold. He reached back for Emily and helped her over the stretch, then she did the same for Ethan. Ethan wanted a break, but he was never going to ask for one until someone else did.

Thon went on, "A lot of people wonder if you can have a private road, or what you will do if the government doesn't maintain the streets into and out of your town. But our way seems to work. We all take care of the road, because we all depend on it."

"That wouldn't work in my neighborhood," Ethan said, puffing a little. Above him, the hill stretched up to Heaven. At least. Maybe beyond it. *It's the Mountain of Babel*, he thought. *Wish God would cut it down a bit.* His legs ached.

Thon sat down on a boulder for a second. "We should rest here a second. I'm sure you're tired."

"Not at all," Emily said, but her breathiness gave her away.

Thon smiled. "About the road thing, Ethan," he pronounced it without the "th," like *Etan*, "can I ask you, do you know everyone in your village?"

"We call it a 'neighborhood,'" Ethan said, finding his own boulder. It was cool and smooth under his legs, which blessed him for taking the load off them. "But no, not even close."

"We know the people next door and across the street. A few other people," Emily said.

Thon stared. "Really? That sounds horrible. Anyway," he said, shaking his head, "in my village I know everyone. Everyone knows me. When it's my turn to go out and work on the road, if I don't go, everyone in the village knows it."

"Can't have that," Ethan said.

"No, *claro*. No one wants to be the *gufan*."

The twins looked blank.

Thon laughed lightly. "I and my friends, we make this word. It is a person that does not do his best. A lazy person who takes but does not give to others?"

"Ah," Emily said. "A moocher."

Thon's face lit up. "That is a good word. Moocher. We all work very hard, but we know we are taking care of each other. It's what we do in my village."

"Sounds awesome," Emily said. "Did we even have a time like that back in the US?"

A moment later, Thon creaked to his feet, rubbing his back. Ethan was pretty sure he only did that to make the twins feel better, because he hadn't sweated or panted at all, even on the steep part of the climb.

At last, as the sun began to dip low on the horizon, they crested the last hill, thick with mist, and came down into a sheltered valley, with a small village, not more than 40 or 50 houses, surrounding a small church. It was nestled at the foot of two hills, in the V-shaped notch between them. But the hills had been terraced to provide flat land for planting crops. All over the hills people worked the terraces, cultivating grain, rice, and other foodstuffs.

Small animals, llamas, and even a few sheep clustered in herds in various places, and the entire scene was like a postcard.

"It's beautiful," Emily said, glancing over at Thon. His face was shining.

"It is," he said. "I have lived here all my life. I suspect that after I finish school, I will probably return here and take my place doing the work that's necessary to keep the village strong."

Turn to page 374.

"I don't know what to do," Emily said.

"I don't either," Ethan said.

"So let's choose one, since we have no way of knowing which is the right thing to do." Thon had still not reappeared.

That decided it for Emily. "Let's hide," she said.

They had descended far enough that there was some scrubby undergrowth. Their ponchos blended well with the dirt and greenery of the foliage. If they hide underneath, there was a decent chance that someone would charge right by them.

"Either side?" Ethan said.

"I think that's safest," Emily said. Each one of them chose a side of the trail and lay down, pulling their ponchos over them to hide. Ethan curled up tight to fit his entire body underneath. Emily tried to calm her breathing to make sure the poncho didn't move at all.

A few seconds went by with more shouting from above. A bullet pinged off a rock on the trail and went pweeing off into the foliage.

Emily could just make out Ethan's face across the trail, his eyes wide and worried.

In a shower of rocks, Thon came charging around the corner.

There was a pistol in his hand.

He turned and leveled the pistol back up the trail.

Emily hissed at him.

Thon looked around but didn't see her.

"Over here," Emily said.

He stepped over to the side of the trail.

Emily put her hand out and caught his pant leg. "We're hiding," she said. "We thought there might be an ambush below us."

Thon crouched, calm, keeping the pistol leveled back up the trail. "That's good thinking," he said. "I would have run right into it."

"If it's there at all," Emily said. "Hide with us."

"There's no time," he said. "I will run farther down the trail and find a place to hide there. Stay here and wait for me." And he charged away into the gathering gloom, sending fountains of sand and rock behind him.

Another crack, a heavier caliber weapon. Probably a rifle. The flash was just above Emily and lit the trail. Moments later, three of the bandits stampeded into view, carrying bolt action rifles. One of them also had a pistol. They stopped a few feet down the slope from Emily and Ethan and began to confer with each other rapidly.

"I only see one of them," the lead man said.

"Were there more?" The other two shrugged their shoulders. "The only one I see is that kid from the village. He won't have anything interesting on him. That village is a tiny little waste of space. They don't even have any decent technology there."

The first one smacked him in the head. "We can't let him get away and tell people that we're up here. That would ruin everything."

"And what happened to the other ones, the gringos?" one of them said. "Are they just super fast?"

They might have debated on this for some time, but just at that moment, from overhead came the unmistakable thump of the blades of a chopper.

Emily shifted her head fractionally to be able to see what was happening. From over the treetops, a decrepit World War II-era helicopter heaved into view.

"It is Jefe," the lead bandit said. "He's heading back to the camp."

"What are we going to do about these kids? He'll kill us if he knows we let them get away."

"We didn't see anything, did we?" said the leader. "Nothing has happened up here all morning, has it?

He looked significantly at the other two. "Not a thing," one of them said.

They turned to walk back up the trail toward the peak.

A moment later a voice sounded below them. "Hey, wait for me!"

Two more men strode up the path from below. They joined the three others and began the walk back up the hill. "Didn't I hear a couple of gunshots?" one of them said.

"Yes," the leader said. "It was just José here shooting at some wolves." They rounded the bend and disappeared above the twins. A few moments later, after all sound had ceased apart from the dripping of rain from the leaves, Ethan crawled out onto the path.

He took a tentative look upwards. "They're gone," he said.

Emily rose and dusted herself off. "Good thinking about the ambush," she said. "That was very lucky. We would have run right into them."

"Why didn't Thon?" Ethan said. "Did he turn invisible or something?"

"Hey," Thon said from below. "Let's get going."

The twins headed down, and fifty yards below them there he was, standing in the middle of the path with a goofy smile on his face. "That was an interesting way to end the morning," he said, stuffing the pistol into his backpack.

"How did you not run into those guys?" Emily said, a bright smile on her face.

He smiled back and wiped leaves from his front. "I dove straight into the bushes when I hit this corner. They missed me somehow."

"You brought a pistol," Ethan said. "You might've told us."

"I don't tell you everything," Thon said. "And I very much hoped I would not have to use it. But you never know what you're going to find in these hills." He reached out and took Emily's hand again. "You okay?"

"I am now," she said.

"That run has taken us to within about an hour of the village." He pointed over his shoulder. "You can see the top of the church from here."

Turn to page 206.

Emily tried to get to sleep but found herself lying awake. She thought about all the work, all the hundreds of hours they had spent working to earn the money to be able to make this trip. She thought about the dozens of books Ethan had checked out, all the study he had done on the Ychurichuc ruins. It just did not seem right that they would be leaving so soon without even having had an opportunity to go see the thing they had worked so hard for. She drifted off to sleep with the thought still on her mind that no matter what happened, they had come too far to turn back.

When the sun rose in the morning, slanting through a crack in the curtains, she felt even more strongly that there was no way going home was the right decision. She rolled over and found that Ethan had already gone into the bathroom to take a shower. When he came out, she was sitting at the small desk in the room writing a postcard to their parents.

Both of them said at the same time, "I don't feel good about going home." They laughed a little and Emily said, "I had a hard time sleeping. I'm not sure if this earthquake is a precursor to the big one, or if there ever will be a big one, but one way or the other I want to see those ruins."

Ethan said, "Probably a lot of people will leave, but I want to stay. I think we can handle it, and I know we've put too much work in to give up now." Emily nodded and finished writing her postcard.

Ethan squeezed himself into a bathing suit and said, "What I want to do right now is to go out on that water and ski."

Emily said, putting down her pen, "Give me five minutes and I'll be very happy to join you."

Ethan cut hard on his right ski, throwing up a fountain of water like a peacock's tail. *Maybe a big earthquake hits today, but if that happens I'm not even going to be sad*, he thought. *What a way to go!*

The sun beat down on Ychu Lake. The water was pleasantly cool. There was no breeze ruffling the water of the lake, which lay like plate glass except where the boat had passed, leaving a long, curving wake. The morning could not have gone better. They had a delicious breakfast. All the pipes and other appliances in the hotel seemed to have been fixed, if any of them had even been broken in the first place, and they had been able to go out for a short hike up into the hills.

There were some ruins there as well—nothing as spectacular as Ychurichuc, but some small village that had stone foundations. Emily had been especially entranced by that and wondered why it was not on the map or part of the tourist guide.

"It's a shame," she said to herself. "These people lived here thousands of years ago, and nobody seems to care." The ruins of their homes were right there, a couple of feet off the trail. Jungle vines twisted over the piles of stones where they lay in neat little circles.

Emily had wanted to climb through the foliage and get a better look at the ruins themselves. "Maybe even do a little digging," she said, but Ethan thought that would probably not be a good idea.

"We should leave that kind of thing to the experts," he said. "That way we're not disturbing something that we couldn't put right again."

Emily reluctantly agreed and they went on with their hike. The view from the top of the mountain down to the village of Ychu and the lake certainly rewarded their effort. It was spectacular, an afternoon that had only gotten better. As part of their hotel package, they had access to ATVs, jet skis, and now a pass to go out on the ski boat.

Emily watched Ethan from the stern of the boat as he carved another wave into the flat water of the lake. It had certainly been worth it to take this vacation and to stay, even when it looked like they might be chased off by the rumbling of the earth. Emily looked out on the water and to the surrounding buildings to see if there was any indication that there might be more, but the earth stood still, and everyone went about their business as if nothing had happened last night.

The next day was just as good. They even had a chance to go parasailing behind a boat. The amazing weather held, no breeze troubled them, and no more earthquakes disturbed their wonderful time.

Afternoon found Emily dangling from the end of a rappelling rope. Well, not precisely the *end* of the rope; there was probably more down there somewhere, touching the ground near where Ethan waited. She dangled from *rope*, though, off the side of a cliff, one hand pressed to the small of her back, the other up above her head as the rope wound down underneath her seat next to the face of a cliff. Below her spread the entire Ychu Valley, the small town nestled against the side of the lake. The gleaming water reflected the bright sky overhead. It was surely one of the best experiences she ever had.

She felt the tension in her legs and the slight burn in the palms of her hands where the heat of the rope had warmed up her gloves. Above her at the top of the cliff, a dark-headed man leaned over and smiled at her.

"You doing okay?" he asked.

"Fantastic," she said, and bounced a little off the side of the cliff, out into space and back as if she were hopping up and down on the floor. She supposed there could have been a more dangerous place to be—they *had* just had an earthquake—but she couldn't resist the temptation. The cliff face was just perfect. Below her spread a canopy of trees and below them, she knew, were soft banks of ferns and other tropical plants. Birds nervously zipped back and forth around her head as if trying to explain something to her.

"It's okay, little ones," she said. "I won't be here long." She let the rope slide through her fingers, dropping another fifteen feet or so, the wind whistling in her ears. Maybe there was a way to have more fun, but she couldn't think of it, and tomorrow they would finally get to go to the place they had waited so long to see.

That night the twins had seafood for dinner, and not long after that, they were both asleep shortly after the sun went down. It had been one of the best days of their lives, and although they were very excited about going to see the ruins in the morning, they were so tired they couldn't keep their eyes open.

Turn to page 150.

The tour group lay like scattered bowling pins next to the temple walls. Here, as elsewhere, the ruins themselves had held up well. Not a block seemed out of place. But the group was shaken and woozy, struggling to get up. Everyone was, locals and tourists alike.

Emily's cross-country training got her to the rescue first. She ran first to a small family and helped up their little girls, both of them bewildered but not crying. "Thank you," their mother said. Then she jogged over to an elderly couple, rolled over on their backs and tightly holding hands.

"Here you go," she said, getting them to a sitting position. "You stay here as long as you need to. I think it's over." She wove her way through the crowd and back to her brother.

"Wow," Jorge said, shaking his head and holding it as if it might come off, "That wasn't a drill, was it?"

"I don't think so," Ethan said. "They're calling everyone down to the parking lot so they can arrange transportation for them."

At this, most of the group staggered to their feet and started making their way down the stone steps toward the lower bowl.

"We should all go," Jorge said, ushering people off the hill. The twins and Thon began to follow. Jorge put his hand on Ethan's arm. "Hang on."

When the last of the other tourists had left the plateau, he said, "Look, I know we didn't make this work all that well today. You did a lot of work to get here, and now you hardly got to see anything. The least I can do is get you back to civilization so you can get home."

"We're listening," Ethan said.

"I have a vehicle that can handle pretty much anything," he said, making sure Emily was listening. "I'm going back down to Ychu anyway. I could take you."

"For free?" Emily said.

"For not a lot," he said. "Then we'll know how bad this is and whether you need more substantial help. I have friends there. You want to stick with me."

Thon stood back, his arms folded, shaking his head.

Ethan scratched his head, shook some more dirt out of his hair. "I guess we should," he said, checking with Emily. "It's not like we have other options."

Emily was looking at Thon. "What?" she said.

Thon said, "Can we talk for a minute?"

"Sure," Emily said, and waved away Ethan's protests. "Look, we have no cell service. No one does. That was a serious quake; there are going to be road and power outages, at least, and maybe worse. We should listen to every possible option, and I think Thon here has one."

Jorge scoffed. "Fine," he said. "I'm headed down to my truck. You want to ride with me, get your butts down there pronto. I don't have time for this." He jogged off.

Ethan's skepticism was all over his face. "What can you offer us?"

"I won't charge you money to get you to where you can get home, for one."

Emily said, "That would be refreshing."

"Over that hill there is my village. It's not too far. The roads will be okay, and we'll have food and shelter. We have friends and we can get you where you need to get home, no matter how bad things are."

"Back to the hotel?" Ethan asked.

"No," replied Thon, "*home*, home. Cell phone service is out. You think the roads are going to be intact? The buses running? How many thousand people will descend on the airport?"

"They'll put the infrastructure back together," Ethan said.

"Of course they will. But how long will that take? And in the meantime, who is taking care of you two? You think they have a lot of spare resources for that? We'll have a lot more to share with you than they will in Takewawa."

"We hardly know you," Emily said, but she was listening.

He shrugged. "What do you need to know?"

"What's in it for you?" Ethan said.

Thon looked back over the ruins toward the cemetery and the cave. "I just thought you seemed like good people," he suggested. "That's not really an answer. I don't have one. You have to decide whom to trust, I think, because this situation is going to get ugly fast."

If you think the twins should stay with Jorge, turn to page 391.

If you think the twins should trust Thon, turn to page 281.

Pietro threaded his way in between chairs and computer desks to a metal door directly at the back of the main area. He turned and gave them a wink, seeing that they were following him. Then he rapped on the door three times, then two times, then three more times. A panel slid open in the door, and the pinkish face of a young girl peered out.

"You and your secret knock," she said.

"Hey," Pietro said, shrugging. "We all have our little peccadilloes." She gave an elaborate and long-suffering sigh. From behind the door came the clacking of locks, then a buzz, deep and low, that seemed to come through the floorboards, and the door popped out half an inch.

"You have electromagnetic locks on everything?" Ethan said.

"Yep," Pietro said. "And a few other little surprises. But those are on a need-to-know basis, and you don't." He pulled the door wide and made a little bow, stretching his hand forward to indicate they should go ahead of him. Inside, the room was brightly lit with skylights above that opened up to let in the beautiful sunshine.

"This is my daughter," Pietro said, indicating the girl. She was about five feet tall, with riotous white hair, blue at the end, as if the tips had been dunked in blueberry Kool-Aid. "You can call her Pandora," Pietro said.

"Which is not her name?" Emily said.

Pietro made a face as if to say "don't be silly." Floor to ceiling, electronic equipment was stacked on every horizontal surface. Hanging in the air was the unmistakable smell of hot computer chips and cold sweat. Over against one wall, an entire bookshelf full of snacks stood to attention. It was not just the kind of snacks you would see at the airport at Takewawa, either, but good old American snacks: donuts, Twinkies, and energy drinks stocked six or eight deep.

"Looks like you're ready for any disaster," Ethan said.

"Pandora" choked back a laugh, almost gagging on her gum. She looked Emily and Ethan up and down and said, "I'm assuming you would be here to use the sat phone. Did he tell you how much he charges people to use it?"

Pietro said from behind a stack of computer equipment, "We haven't agreed on a price yet."

Pandora sneezed and wiped her nose on the back of her wrist. She appeared to be about twelve, maybe thirteen, and her English was native. Ethan would have thought she sounded just like somebody who might move in next door back home. "He always says that. Did you try to buy him already?"

"Of course we did," Emily said, staring at some rapidly scrolling code on a computer screen. "But $100 is apparently not enough."

Pandora sneezed again. "Sorry," she said, "it's the dust in the air."

Ethan looked up, "If your skylight wasn't open, I think your dust problem would be a lot better."

"It's not open," Pietro said. "It's just super clear. I go up and squeegee it off nearly every day."

Ethan looked up again. He couldn't see the glass at all, but if he said it was there, it was there. Emily ran her hand over the racks of computer equipment, touching each one lightly with a finger. She peered into the crack between a piece of shelf and what looked like a server. An iron strap wound its way around the back of the server, securing it to the shelves. All the shelving was thick wood, at least half an inch thick, bolted to a metal frame that went from floor to ceiling and disappeared into the rafters as if it was welded there. Which it probably was.

Under her breath, she said, "So this is why this place is still functional when everything else in the neighborhood fell over."

"Yes," said a voice in her ear. She jumped a little. Pandora was standing right behind her. "And that's why the building didn't fall down, too. We built this thing special when we came down here a few years ago."

Pietro yelled from over by the wall, "That's right, and it cost me almost everything I had. But it's worth it. When times like this come, oh yes, it's worth it."

He carried a box around and set it on a table by the door. He pulled out a black case, laid it on the table, and undid the locks. Flipping it open, he drew out a thick black square and set it on the table with some electrical jacks. He reached in with two hands and gingerly withdrew a slim black phone. Plugging one end of the cord into the phone and the other into the black box, he toggled a switch on the side of the phone and an orange rectangle lit up. Pietro smiled at the phone like a mother smiles at her newborn child.

"Now," he said softly, "We can do anything we want." He turned to Ethan and said, "You can talk to anyone in the world. Who would you like to call?"

Emily said, "I would like to talk to my mother and father."

"I can make that happen," Pietro said. "If I do, though, what guarantee do I have that I'm going to get paid for it?"

"You can have my hundred-dollar bill," Ethan said.

"Mmmmmm," Pietro said, rubbing his chin. "I don't know. That doesn't sound like quite enough security. Besides, how do I have any idea whether that money is going to be any good by the time I can use it?"

"You don't," Ethan said. "However, I'm not likely to be leaving here without it, so you can keep me here until I've done whatever you need me to do."

"Like Rumpelstiltskin," Emily said.

"It's the queen who does all the work," Pandora said.

"Not true," Pietro said. "*Rumpelstiltskin* does most of the work. He actually is the only sympathetic character in the entire story. But let's not talk about fairy tales

at a time like this. I assume you know your home phone number?" Ethan nodded. "Then hand me your hundred-dollar bill, and I will accept that as security. Although I'd much rather have your passport."

"I'm not handing over my passport to you," Ethan said. "It's the only one we have left."

Pietro flicked a glance over to Emily, who shrugged. "Bad timing," she said.

"Very well," Pietro said. "Follow me to the roof, and I shall connect you through the magic of this modern technology to the people who love you most in all the world." He started dialing, then stopped, and glanced over to Ethan. "These *are* the people who love you most in all the world, aren't they?"

Emily stared at Pietro. "Yes," she said. "These are the people who love us the most in all the world."

"Just making sure," Pietro said.

He picked up the phone and walked back to a door in the rear wall, which he opened to reveal a set of stairs. Two floors up, they stepped out onto a wide, flat patio at the top of the building. Bulbous skylights lay three in a row beside the door. Looking up, as if he could see the satellite, Pietro finished dialing.

"Can you put it on speaker?" Ethan said. Pietro tapped a button. There were some clicks from the phone, and then the unmistakable sound of a ring. It had hardly finished the very first full tone when there was another, louder click, and a voice that sounded somewhat frantic. "Hello? Hello?"

"Oh, Mom," Emily said. "Oh, Mom." Tears she hadn't known she was holding back began to burn behind her eyes. She didn't want to cry in front of these people, but it was such a relief to hear her mother's voice.

Ethan took up the conversation. "Mom, this is Ethan. Emily is here with me, and before you say anything, we're fine. We're just fine. The earthquake didn't hurt us at all."

"All we are is a little hungry and thirsty," Emily said. "But we're going to get that taken care of as well," she said, thinking of the snacks piled against the wall in the room downstairs. "We're here with some people who are letting us make a call on a satellite phone. But I think they want us to pay them, and the money we have is not what they're interested in." Pietro waved his hands at them as if to say no, no, go on ahead and talk.

"Thank you," Ethan said.

"Hang on," Mom said, "Dad wants to hear as well. I'm putting you on speaker." With dueling speakerphones over the next ten minutes Ethan and Emily told their parents all that had happened to them over the course of the last three days.

Here and there, their parents would say things like "how terrible." Mom gasped when they told her about the earthquake and the terrifying things that had happened since. It was almost surreal to speak about them in a quiet, calm location, away from any chaos and desperation, on a hypermodern piece of technology.

They heard Dad hum a little to himself when Emily talked about not having her passport any more, but other than that their parents said nothing.

"So, now what do you want to do?" Dad said when they were finished.

"Come home," Emily said without hesitation. "We want to come home."

"That's going to be a little difficult to manage," Ethan said. "The airport is completely wiped out." He looked over at Pietro, who nodded.

Pietro spoke up for the first time. "My understanding from my friends on the ground is that the dam that supplies power to the capital city burst and took out the power first of all, but then the water did the rest. The airport will probably be unusable for quite some time. And there's no other airport that you can fly out of that I can think of, at least not that these two will be able to use. I think their only hope is to get over the border into Ecuador and fly out of Quito."

"Do you have enough money to do that?" Dad said.

"I don't think so," Ethan said. He shrugged his shoulders, even though he knew they wouldn't be able to see him. "Almost certainly not." Ethan tapped his waist pack. "We made contact with the embassy people, but we don't really know whether they will be able to get us out of the country or how soon they would be able to pull that off."

"What are the embassy people saying?" Mom said. And the twins told them.

"But they can't magically make airplanes fly out of drowned airports," Ethan said. "They would have to get us into Quito as well."

Pietro spoke up again. "I think there will be a large number of refugees, probably several tens of thousands, trying to move north into Ecuador, or at least into the places where isn't so much damage. Emergency services are pretty thin on the ground here. And if I may say so, there's no way the embassy personnel are going to be able to do anything to help these guys. Not for quite some time anyway. They first will have to move official personnel, and then they will work on the rest of the people who are in the country. It could be, I don't know, as long as a month before they're able to work out how to transport all of the tourists to a place where they can get flights to go back home. It's the height of the tourist season. That isn't going to make things any easier."

"What would you recommend?" That was Mom, practical to the last.

"I have some recommendations," Pietro said, "But first, let's talk a little bit about payment. We've been having a short discussion about money here, and I think your twins understand the predicament I find myself in. The money here is inflating very fast, and practically no one in the city will take the national currency anymore. Which, of course, is making the situation even worse, but let's leave that alone for a moment. I'm also not enamored of dollars. They're difficult for me to spend, and I don't trust them because there's no independent control over the value of the money. I'd prefer to get paid in cryptocurrency. If you have a couple of minutes, I can walk you through how to set up an account, and we can get that transferred to me, which will allow me to be of more than just telephonic service to your children."

"I prefer a straightforward mercenary," Dad said. "I always know where I stand. I have the computer booted up, just tell me where to go." Over the next half an hour, which must have been terrible on the phone's battery life, Pietro walked their father through the process of setting up a cryptocurrency account capable of transferring money into it, and then talked him through transferring some of that money to an account that Pietro had set up for himself.

"That will take care of the phone call and food for the rest of the day." Pietro said, "I could be of additional service as well. I know the children think the embassy is probably their best bet, and that might be true, if I didn't have personal contacts with people who might be able to get them out of the country another way."

"Keep talking," Mother said, "We're listening."

"I came down here as a kind of refugee myself," Pietro said. "I used to live in the States. You can probably tell from my accent. I just thought that it might be a better idea to live somewhere else. I won't get into my thoughts on the global financial situation, in the interest of time. However, I have always known that preparedness meant more than just having a strong building and lots of snacks. It also means having the ability to escape if necessary. Now, personally, I think this situation here in Allqukilla is an interesting one, and I think there are opportunities here for an enterprising young man such as myself."

At this, Pandora snorted. Emily herself questioned the "young" part. Pietro tossed a dirty look over his shoulder before continuing. "Nevertheless, I have in place the ability to leave the country relatively quickly and get over the border without too much hassle. I would be willing to discuss the possibility of putting that network in play for your twins. It wouldn't be cheap, of course, but it would be much faster than any other way that the twins could get home."

Mother said, "Can you guarantee the safety of this method?"

Pietro laughed. "Of course I can't guarantee it. I can't guarantee *anything*, right down to the water supply to this building. I can, however, give you reasonable assurance that I think it's safer and quicker than any other method you could adopt. Going to the embassy is hardly a guarantee, either."

"Ethan, are you there?" Dad said.

"I'm here," Ethan said.

Dad said, "What do you think of this idea?"

Ethan looked at Emily, who was clearly thinking about this herself. On the one hand, Ethan thought it would be very risky to go outside of the official government channels, and he was pretty sure that's what Pietro was talking about doing. On the other hand, the idea of being able to get home in three or four days, rather than a month or a month and a half, was so enticing that he was having trouble containing his excitement.

"Let me talk with Emily a minute," Ethan said. Turning to Pietro, he asked, "Can we have a place where we can talk without being overheard?"

"Come with me," Pandora said, "I know just the place."

Pandora led the twins to the stair door and back down to the back room. There was another door in the far wall, heavy, made of wood, and although it didn't have a lock, the handle was brass and sturdy. She opened it up and inside was a closet filled with various kinds of supplies, from food to fire starters.

"In here," she said. "It's cramped, but there's only two of you." She ushered the twins inside, flicking on a light switch, and closed the door behind them. The bare bulb overhead showed rows and rows of shelves that rose fifteen feet high, crammed with various kinds of goods.

On Ethan's left hand was an entire shelf of different kinds of beef jerky. His stomach grumbled a little." Let's get this over with," Ethan said, "so we can get to eating and figure out what we're going to do. The first question is: do you trust this Pietro guy?"

Emily squinted and rubbed her chin. She sniffled a little and wiped her nose with a tissue from her pocket. "I don't know about trusting him," she said, "except that I do think he will keep his word once he gets paid."

"Unlike some others we won't name right now, yeah. That's the sort of the impression I get," Ethan said. "And I guess that's a sort of trust too, isn't it?"

Emily said, "Uncle Reginald says trust is the only currency. It's kind of like money all by itself."

Ethan licked his lips. "So I guess the question is, do we trust the embassy, or do we trust this semi-hippie ex-American who runs an internet cafe and acts like a libertarian prepper?"

"Yep, that's the question," Emily said, and smiled. "And the answer to me is kind of obvious."

If you think the twins should return to the embassy, turn to page 249.

If you think they should continue to work with Pietro, turn to page 95.

Ethan looked at Emily but she offered no help; her face was blank and drawn. This was the worst-case scenario of their trip. It was so bad they hadn't even imagined it as a possibility. To have this happen, caused by an earthquake they couldn't have foreseen, was almost more than either of them could stand.

"What do you think we should do?" Ethan said.

Emily shrugged. "If we're going to go, let's go," she said. "If we stay here any longer, I'm afraid that we will change our minds again and decide to stay."

Ethan was miserable, but it was the only thing to do. He turned to the counter agent and said, "We'll take the flight now."

The woman seem to understand that the twins were feeling some distress. Then again, who wasn't?

She printed the tickets and handed them to Ethan and Emily. "You have your luggage?" she asked. They nodded dumbly and handed the suitcases over. "The plane will be boarding in fifteen minutes, so you will have to hurry."

Security was manageable going this direction, except for one thing: saladera.

"I'm sorry, you can't take it out of the country," a security guard said. The flight board flashed "Final Boarding." They could see the gate from there.

"There is a form to fill out, and then we can exchange your saladera for dollars." He reached in his pocket and pulled out a form. It was three pages long.

The attendants turned off the light and began to close the door.

Emily threw handfuls of saladera at the guard. "Here! Take it. Take all of it! Come on, Ethan! Run!"

Ethan reached into his pack and handed a thick sheaf of saladera to the guard. His hand came up mechanically. He stared down at the pile in his hand, the leaves fluttering in the air.

"Guess we can't take time for the form. Keep the change," Ethan said, and bolted after his sister.

The three-leg plane ride took them a day and a half. The twins said very little to each other. They tried to get a little sleep on the airplane, but both of them seemed to feel that there was no rest to be had. They would doze off, then wake up minutes later, still looking at the seat back in front of them, still wondering whether they were doing the right thing but not feeling that they had any other choice.

Once at the airport for their first layover, they called home and left a message explaining what they had decided to do. When they got off the plane in Mexico City, they called again, even though it was the middle of the night.

Dad answered the phone, "I got your message," he said. "I'm very sorry, but you made the right decision."

"You sure, Dad?" Ethan asked. There was a catch in his voice. Ethan looked at Emily, but Emily would not meet his eyes. "We both feel pretty awful about it."

"I'm sure you do," Dad said. "There's no way you could not feel terrible about it, but sometimes being a grown-up means you have to make tough decisions. We will be waiting for you at the airport when you get home."

Hours later, Ethan and Emily staggered off the airplane, jet-lagged and feeling worse than they ever had before. It would be a couple of days before they felt like themselves again.

As they walked through the terminal, Ethan saw several shocked people staring up at a TV screen and paused to see what had happened.

"What—it happened!" Ethan announced in a bit of panic and amazement. "The earthquake!"

Emily walked back to look at the screen, where she saw a reporter talking about a major earthquake in Allqukilla. They had dodged it. They had made the right decision. But what was happening to all the people who were there? What would life be like for the locals?

There wasn't much news in the days ahead, mostly because the communications infrastructure had been damaged, and so had the roads and runways, making travel inaccessible.

But Ethan did find one souvenir—his secret stash, still filled to the brim with saladera. "Forgot about this," he said, handing some to his sister. And his dad. And mom. And any friends that came over to play. They watched the news and wondered what might have been.

"Lesson learned," Emily said later the next day. "Maybe we should plan our next trip somewhere safer."

THE END

At first the way sloped up gently and the path was good: firm and dry, well-marked and wide. But within a few hundred yards, the climb began to get much steeper. Trees grew at odd angles out of the hillside. The trail was quite good; the places where it got especially steep had rocks placed like steps, allowing their boots to get good purchase. They made good time despite the difficulty of the route.

Thon led the way, his head constantly on a swivel, as if he expected someone—or something—else to show up. This unnerved Ethan and he asked Thon about it more than once. But Thon's only response was to shrug his shoulders and say, "I'm sure we'll be fine." The clouds continued to thicken overhead, and the chatter of the birds quieted down.

Once or twice, Emily caught sight of long, lean shapes slinking through the underbrush, as if they were following the path of the trail. "You don't have wolves in these hills, do you?" she said.

"We do," Thon said. "There's a pack of them not far off this trail, following us. But during the daylight they won't do anything."

"What about if it rains?" Ethan said. "What if the clouds get thicker and it appears to be night?"

"That would be very bad," Thon said, his voice flat, almost uninterested, as if he were discussing a move in chess. "So we will pray that doesn't happen."

Higher and higher they went, zigzagging back and forth on the narrow trail, waiting for the patter of rain to begin to fall on them from above.

Just before they reached the crest of the hill, there was an especially steep section where they had to take up hands and haul on each other.

Their breath came in ragged puffs. The temperature dropped. They could see the condensation of their breath in the air, as if they were dragons. With a low, distant rumble, the skies opened up, and the rain began to fall steadily. Worse, the clouds descended until the top of the peak above them was bathed in mist.

"I would think this was beautiful if I didn't have to be out in it," Emily said. She threw a poncho over her head, one of the supplies furnished by Thon's village, and it kept the worst of the water off her. The three of them looked rather like brightly colored claymation figures in their rain gear. But it kept them dry, and they kept stolidly on, keeping a wary eye out for wolves.

Ethan made as much noise as he could, beating on his backpack and even whistling a little bit, remembering from his Boy Scout days that most animals are afraid of strange noises. Whether it worked or not, no wolves harassed them, and eventually they stopped seeing the dark shadows in the brush.

Their way leveled out and became easier.

"We're almost at the top. Come on," said Thon, his face letting a small smile leak through the tension.

Ethan noticed that he hadn't let go of Emily's hand, nor that she had demanded it. *Let them have a moment here. We'll be down soon enough, and that will be the end of that.* But he was a little jealous, and wished that his sister and their guide hadn't become quite so friendly.

The path across the plateau was long and straight, with very little vegetation on either side. One section, right across the peak, wound between two boulders that stuck out of the earth like the legs of a giant. For some reason, Ethan felt that this was a place that demanded as little noise as possible. Perhaps it was because it reminded him of the statues at Osgiliath in *Lord of the Rings*. Surely this was a place that deserved his respect.

"Is this a sacred place?" he asked Thon.

Thon nodded, pausing to look at the rock pillars. "There once was a great statue here," he said. "It was built even before my people came to this area. No one knows anything about it. But I have always felt that this place was one of ancient power."

How long they might have stood there, rain or no, they would never know, because a shout from behind them broke the stillness.

"Hey! Stop!" The voice followed this by rapidly shouting something in a foreign language.

Thon's head came up quickly and his eyes widened. "Run!" he said.

This is what he's been expecting and looking out for. I thought it was the wolves, but it was this. The twins merely stood there, surprised and confused.

"Run!" Thon said, a little more urgently, adding a shove. "Bandits!"

They had to be told twice, but not three times. The twins burst into full motion. Emily had thought she was tired, but as it turned out she had plenty left in the tank to run madly down the path.

It was more of a scramble. The path switched back, descending rapidly. Scree shot out from under her boots. She would run a few steps, put the brakes on, slide in a shower of loose rock and sand, shift direction, and charge back the other way, only to repeat the process a few seconds later. Emily threw a glance back over her shoulder to see if she could see Thon, but he was nowhere in sight. A shot cracked across the face of the mountain. Emily couldn't tell where the bullet went.

Ethan reached out and snagged hold of her backpack, hauling her to a stop.

She whirled on him. "We have to run!" she panted.

"What if that's what they want us to do?" Ethan said. "What if the shot from behind us was to scare us forward into a trap?"

"What if it *wasn't*?" Emily said. "What if they're chasing us, and stopping here means they'll catch us?"

If you think the twins should hide, turn to page 35.

If you think it would be better for them to run, turn to page 296.

Ethan and Emily dragged their luggage into the line at the counter and waited their turn with Mom. Dad parked the car and joined them. The twins had been to the airport before, but Emily marveled at how unfamiliar everything was. The rubbery smell from the conveyor belts. The click of luggage being locked. Mom's hand on Emily's arm, gentle and steady.

Sure, she was nervous. This was their first trip by themselves. But Emily couldn't wait to get started.

The bags weighed in at 49 pounds each, one pound under the limit. No surprise. Ethan had weighed them both several times. They showed their passports to the attendant and got their boarding passes. Their luggage went behind the counter and rolled off toward security.

And then it was their turn.

Mom's eyes glistened as she hugged them. "You be careful," she said. "Come back to me."

"Mom," Ethan said, not quite rolling his eyes, "Of course we're coming back. It's going to be a great trip. We've planned everything."

Dad hugged Emily. "We love you. Have the time of your lives!"

"We will, Dad. It's the most exciting thing ever," Emily said, hiding her nerves behind a big smile.

The straps of Emily's backpack dug into her shoulders as she leaned over to give Mom a kiss. She might have overpacked a little, but she couldn't decide what books to take, and reading on her phone just wasn't the same.

The security line was short this morning—just a few others ahead of the twins.

"Ethan Tuttle," Ethan said, holding out his boarding pass and his passport to the security agent. She barely glanced up at him. Her gloved hands flicked through his passport pages. She saw many stamps and formed a tight smile. She took a pen and ticked his boarding pass.

"Next," she said.

"Emily Tuttle." The agent went through the same process, without the smallest change in expression. What would that be like, sitting there for hours, checking papers that were almost guaranteed to match? What's the point? Emily thought she'd prefer to work someplace else.

"Worst job *ever*," she whispered to Ethan as they emptied their pockets, took off their shoes, and prepared to walk through the large X-ray machine.

Emily couldn't bear to be cooped up in a place like that. She'd much rather become a tour guide. Or better, a famous archaeologist! She could solve the mystery of the *quipu*, the Incan message beads, then everyone would want her to come and work on their mysteries, too.

After arriving at their gate with an hour to spare, Emily grabbed one of her books to pass the time. Their parents wanted them to arrive plenty early in case the security screening took a while. "Bureaucrats aren't known for their speed," Dad had said. Ethan unzipped his backpack and drew out the waterproof folder that held their travel plans. He didn't really read them, Emily noticed. He was just holding them in his hands as if it would make all their work real, finally real.

But she felt a strange vibe, as if their careful plans would soon be tossed aside. Shrugging off the creeping feeling, Emily dove into her book.

Turn to page 117.

Ethan stood on the stairs, looking at the river of people pushing toward the two machines, trying to decide whether to get sucked in by it.

"Might as well," a voice said as a hand clamped down on his arm. A girl, blonde, thin, taller than he was. Strong, too. He went along.

She waded into the stream, fording it like a horse, and got them as close to the machines as physically possible before the crush became too heavy.

"You speak Spanish?" the girl said.

She didn't look like she would herself, but Ethan responded anyway. "Más o menos."

She laughed and switched languages. "I didn't want to say this in English. Spanish is a little safer with the lobby full of tourists. This reminds me of those movies about the 1930s, where everyone goes crazy and tries to get all the cash they can. It's stupid, and people even know it, but they can't help themselves."

"So why are we doing it if it's stupid?" Ethan said. Her eyes were very blue.

"Because we can. And because otherwise we go back to bed and that's boring."

"There are other things to do besides going back to bed," he said, although that was exactly what he was thinking of doing. "And what do you mean about the movies? I thought they ran out of cash in the Depression."

"They did. Or some people did. The big problem was the banks failed. I read about it in history class."

She had an accent, even in Spanish. Something European. Nordic? She looked like every famous poster of a Swedish woman. She wasn't much older than he was.

Unconsciously, he raised up to his full height and bounced a little on his toes. "I know about banks failing," he said. "I know about why they failed, too; they lent out too much money and kept too little on hand."

She cocked her head. "You do know about that. I thought Americans didn't study that stuff."

"I'm not your usual American."

"Apparently."

"Anyway, this isn't a run on the bank. It's just a single ATM."

She laughed. "What do you think this is? You think the machine prints money?"

Ethan was embarrassed. They moved a couple steps closer. "No, I mean, obviously not. It's..." He thought for a moment. "It's a *bank*. I mean, not the whole thing, just a part of one. It's a branch."

"And?" she said, eyes twinkling. She shouldered ahead of a dark-haired man, pulling Ethan with her.

"And there are hundreds of these things all over the country. They all network back to the main bank. If we're doing this here, then probably every ATM in the country is getting hit, too. And if that's true…"

"It had better not be," she said. "Things could get really bad."

"But we can use credit cards, other kinds of money. We'll have money."

"Will everyone?"

Ethan said, thinking fast, "Most people, yes. But not everyone. And there are other problems, too, because too much money is a problem just like not enough."

"Inflation."

"Inflation," Ethan said. "We don't think it can happen because it's always in the movies from a long time ago. Like those movies about the 1930s." He watched her face break into a smile. "But it can happen. It's getting out of control here in Allqukilla already."

"And this? What is this ATM going to do to it?" she said. They'd reached the machine.

"Guess we should find out," Ethan replied.

"After you," his new friend said.

As Ethan approached, his thoughts were running a mile a minute: was he contributing to a problem? Did he really need the money now, or would it have been better to have saved it in the bank for a later time? And why was it so easy to get ahead in line all of a sudden?

He soon had the answer: the ATM was empty. No more saladeras.

Not only had the money disappeared, so had his new friend, who was gone as quickly as she had arrived. So much for that.

Turn to page 40.

Jorge said, "I think I'll come along, keep you guys company."

Ethan glanced at Emily. What was the point of his coming with them on a fifteen-hour trip? But there wasn't any reason Ethan could think of to object, even though a part of him really did not want Jorge to come along.

He had a much better feeling about their new driver. Anibal seemed open, genuine. Ethan wanted to ask him about payment, to see if Jorge was stealing the money, but the situation never seemed like it was right to bring that up.

Anibal climbed around to the driver's side and got in via a short metal ladder. "Why don't the two of you sit in the front," he said.

Jorge said, "I can climb in back."

The cabin featured two doors at the front and rear, with long vinyl bench seats, somewhat cracked with age. The green vinyl looked like something from a school bus from the 1970s. Anibal saw Ethan examining it and patted the seat with a fatherly gesture. "They're the best that no money can buy. These babies have been comfy for the last 20 years in this vehicle, and probably for at least 30 years before in a junkyard somewhere. The glory of them is they never get wet, and cleaning off is a snap. All I do is hook up the hose and wash her down."

Emily laughed and pushed Ethan to climb and slide over next to Anibal. The interior smelled as if it had just been freshly washed with some lemon-scented cleaner. At least they wouldn't be holding their noses the whole way. Everyone seated, Anibal pressed a button and the old machine roared to life. It had to be loud enough for everyone in town to hear it. Anibal threw the gear shift forward, and the machine lurched ahead in the direction of the lake.

Jorge leaned forward over Anibal's shoulder, his eyes locked on the windshield. "Any report of rock slides on the southern side of the lake?" he said.

"Haven't heard of anything," Anibal said, "but there hasn't been a whole lot of communication with that part of the town. Not that there was ever that much of the town in that direction anyhow."

The huge dirt caterpillar chugged out of town, and started down the winding road that led around the south side of Lake Ychu.

In contrast to the carnage and chaos of town, the scenery in the wilderness was pristine. It looked just the same as it had earlier that week when the twins went rock climbing and boating on the lake.

The trees were unaffected by the earthquake, and the sun beat down on the road with its usual cheerfulness.

"It just seems impossible," Ethan said, "the things we just saw, people hurt, buildings collapsing, and then we get out here and it seems as if nothing has changed at all."

"That's nature," Anibal said. "Nature doesn't care. Everything goes on, and it's only the humans who are affected by these things."

Up ahead, a couple of miles away, the curve of the dam held back the water of Lake Ychu.

"That's the main power supply for the capital city, isn't it?" Emily said.

"It is," Anibal said. "I remember when they built that dam 25 years ago. It caused a lot of heartburn for archaeologists up here, people who were digging out Inca ruins. They were pretty sure that there were ruins underneath the water line and after the lake filled up no one would ever get to see them."

"That's quite a loss," Ethan said.

Jorge snorted in the backseat. "It's not as big a loss as it would be if we didn't build this dam and provide power for Takewawa," he said. "The real tragedy would be if they weren't able to build more houses or lay more infrastructure because they didn't have the power necessary to handle the demand. Besides, I bet you guys enjoyed some time on this lake here. There wasn't anything like that before."

"I suppose you're right," Ethan said, "but it still seems a shame that we have to choose between the two."

"Even up at Ychurichuc," Jorge said, "you have to make trade-offs. There are lots of local tribes that want to claim ownership of the site, but the truth is that it belongs to everyone, and without the government stepping in and promoting the place, not very many people would get to see it."

"You mean nobody went up there to the ruins before the government took them over?" Ethan said. He tried to keep his voice as neutral as possible, but he was all too conscious of Jorge's hot breath on his neck.

"He's got you there," Anibal said.

"No, he doesn't," Jorge shot back. "Of course some people went up there, but nothing like the crowds you have now. The site is much better promoted than it ever was before."

"Because the people who owned it before didn't actually want to have fifty thousand people a year crawling all over it," Anibal mumbled, though Ethan could still hear him.

"Now that we have solid, licensed people doing the guiding, it's all a lot better for the tourists than it was," Jorge said, as if Anibal hadn't spoken.

"Licensed? How do you get a license to be a tour guide?" Emily said, her voice all innocence, though she was pretty sure she knew the answer.

Jorge fixed her with a glare. "It's a process," he said. "There are top men who qualify us."

"What men?" Ethan said.

"Top. Men." Jorge sat back in his seat. "We can't let just anyone go up there and pretend to be a tour guide."

"By all means no," Emily said, her soft voice right in Ethan's ear. "Not without paying someone in Takewawa a fat fee. That wouldn't be right."

Ethan laughed into his hand and tried to turn it into a cough.

The track vehicle rumbled down the road, seeming to take the pavement at exactly the same speed whether they were going uphill or downhill. In truth, the way was rather flat, and there wasn't a whole lot of up-and-down anyway. The road ran in a complete ring all the way around the lake, about sixteen miles, all told. They were only going part of the way, to where the road split off after they crossed the dam and went down the steep mountainside into the Takewawa valley where the capital city is located.

It seemed an age, as the ancient vehicle ground its way along the road, and never once did they see another vehicle coming the other direction or following them along their way. They reached the extreme Southwestern end, and Anibal ground the vehicle to a halt at the edge of the long, curving road leading across the top of the dam.

Jorge said, "What are you waiting for? There's no traffic, we can just go right across. The road down to Takewawa is just past the end of the dam. Then it's only another 3 or 4 hours before we reach the capital city itself. Seems we didn't need this vehicle after all."

"Never say never," Anibal said, brightly. "We have no idea what the road down to the capital city looks like. We may be glad of the old girl yet."

He ground the gears and started Esmeralda forward. The differing heights of the landscape gave Ethan an odd sense of vertigo. To his right, the dark blue of the lake stretched out all the way to the town at the far eastern end. To his left, a 150-foot drop threatened to suck them into space.

The vehicle, however, had no such romantic problems or difficulties and simply ground its way forward at its same stolid pace.

Halfway across, Emily said, "What's that?" Along the top of the dam, a dark jagged line ran from the cliffside, across the top of the concrete structure, to the lake, and it appeared that some water had pooled onto the roadway.

"Don't know," Anibal said. "I've never seen anything like that in all the years of crossing this bridge."

"I'm sure it's nothing," Jorge said. "Let's keep moving."

"I don't know," Ethan said "That looks suspiciously like a crack."

"In this dam?" Jorge said. "Not a chance. They built this thing to stand up to far worse than any earthquake we've had so far."

They ground on slower, Anibal shifting down and looking anxiously out the front window at the line in the pavement. At first, the rumbling of the engine masked any other feeling they might have had, but as the waves whipped up lakeside, the vibration grew to the point where they could tell that it wasn't coming from anything mechanical. Esmeralda began to practically bounce up and down on the bridge.

Anibal set his mouth in a hard line and downshifted, increasing their speed. "It's an aftershock," he said. And the crack in front of them, for it was indeed a crack in the concrete, began to widen.

Waves, generated by the shifting ground beneath the lake, lapped over the right-hand edge of the dam and pushed against the crack as if trying to escape. A chunk of concrete fell off into the abyss to their left. Then they had reached the crack, but even in the last 30 seconds it had grown wider, and it widened steadily as they watched. Lake water poured through the crack and carried away pieces of concrete.

"Hang on," Anibal said, and threw the ancient machine into high gear. The engine thundered into the gap and tried to pull the metal body across against the torrent of water that slammed into the side of the track vehicle like a mountainside. The vehicle slewed sideways, its rear end still generating forward force, pushing the front end of the vehicle along the now jagged curve of the remaining part of the dam.

"We're never going to make it," Jorge said. "I knew this was a terrible idea."

"Probably so," Anibal said shouting over the roar of the water and the cracking of the concrete, "but we're here now and we're going through."

The water reached the top of the track and started coming in the doors. Still Esmeralda chugged gamely on, as if all the powers of earth and sky could do nothing to stop her. But then a mighty wave came from the lake and slammed into the side of the vehicle, carrying away the concrete from underneath the rear tread.

Emily could feel it going. She could feel the tracker sliding off the concrete, lifting up to bob in the water.

Anibal's forehead perspired as he cranked on the wheel and shifted gears trying to keep the treads working, trying to keep Esmeralda from sliding off the cliff. But it wasn't going to work. The water was too strong, and even Esmeralda's enormous bulk and heavy treads could not keep her on the top of the dam. The dam itself fractured and water rushed through. Esmeralda slewed sideways and lodged against the rail looking out over the abyss into the Takewawa River Valley. For a moment she hung there, using the metal of the barrier and the remaining concrete wall to wedge in place, but it wouldn't be long before those would give way and they would all go down into the raging torrent.

"Help me hold the wheel," Anibal said, throwing a terrified glance over his shoulder at Jorge.

"Every man for himself," Jorge said, and opened his door, climbing out onto the concrete barrier and dragging himself away from Esmeralda and toward the sound part of the dam.

"No," cried Anibal, "you'll never make it!" But Jorge was already out and scrambling away down the dam.

Emily craned her neck back to see if it might be smart to follow him when a concrete chunk tore itself from the lake side of the dam and swept Jorge and the rest of the guardrail off into the tumbling cascade of water. As it dragged itself across the top of the dam, the concrete struck Esmeralda in the rear and shoved the great vehicle forward. The front treads grabbed hold of the remaining concrete at the edge of the dam and traction hauled the entire vehicle forward two feet, five feet, ten feet, and then the rear tread grabbed hold as well. They were moving.

"We're not dead yet," Anibal said. "There's still a chance. We'll never give up!" Water slashed through the cabin, tugging on the twins and Anibal, threatening to wash them out of the cab. Their backpacks, placed in the backseat, sloshed toward the door left open by the departing Jorge. Emily reached back and tried to snag her pack, but she missed, grabbing only a strap of Ethan's. Her own went tumbling out and down the face of the dam.

Esmeralda roared forward, chugging for safety. The dam behind them finally cracked and began to give way under the onslaught of the water. The face of the huge concrete structure seemed to crumble like sugar

dissolving into a cup of tea, and with a titanic roar, the entire dam gave way. Lurching forward, treads spinning at their top speed, Esmeralda dug into the dirt road at the side of the dam. Inch by precious inch, she hauled herself, the twins, and Anibal up the short rise and into the forest on the northwest side of the dam.

Water poured from the vehicle back down the slope, and the greedy lake devoured what was left of the concrete. But the vehicle was safe, and so were they.

The twins climbed from the vehicle, legs trembling. Ethan felt as if he had been thrown in a clothes washer and spun. Water dripped from their pants.

Emily stared with red-rimmed eyes over the raging torrent as the lake emptied itself into the river valley. "Jorge," she said.

Ethan said, "Not just Jorge. Think of all the people who are downstream from the dam. I hope there's a warning system, some way for them to get out."

Anibal shook his head, "I don't know if there's a warning system," he said, "but I do know that the closest houses downstream from here are several miles away. They should certainly hear the roar and have a chance to get to high ground. The problem is, the power for most of the city depends on this dam. Without it, the city will be mostly dark. The other problem is, if you were expecting to get out via the airport, that's not going to work anymore."

"Why not?" Ethan said.

"Because the airport is directly downstream from the dam. The Takewawa River runs right along the southern edge of the airport. This much water, it's going to slam into the airport and wash out the runways. Besides, without power, no one is flying out anyway."

The twins stared at the disaster of the dam and realized their plans—their hopes of getting home—had been washed away just as violently.

It was a somber trip the rest of the way down off the mountain side and into the valley. No one wanted to talk much about what they had seen, and there were plenty of things to occupy their attention as well, as they surveyed the damage to the countryside from the earthquakes and the collapse of the dam.

In contrast to the calm scene by the lake, on this side of the mountain range, everywhere were uprooted trees, boulders, debris of various kinds. They saw a couple of cabins that had been torn from their foundations and carried along in the flood. The road they traveled wended generally downward. It was far enough up the side of the valley that it had been unaffected by the flood, but that didn't mean they could have made it down without Esmeralda. The huge engine and great tracks of the vehicle kept crawling like a tank over downed trees, mudslides, washed-out road. In the hands of someone less skilled than Anibal, they probably wouldn't have made it even with the prodigious strength of Esmeralda helping them down the hillside.

At one point, Ethan did manage to say, "I'm sure Jorge got swept away with all of your money, too."

Anibal cast him a glance, returning immediately to the task of driving. "All my money? What makes you say a thing like that?"

"Well," Ethan said, "not *all* your money, just the money that we paid for you to take us down to Takewawa."

This time the look from Anibal lasted a fraction longer. Then Anibal began a slow chuckle, shaking his head. "That greedy son of a gun," he said. "Grasping right to the last. I've known Jorge since he was a little kid," he said. "He was always after money. He always thought he could do a little better than what he was doing, make a little more money than what he was making. Not that there's anything wrong with that, but Jorge would bribe the policemen and the licensing people to keep his competition down. He had his fingers in half the scams in town. Still, I remember his father—there was a good man—and I tried to help him when I could. He wasn't a bad guy, really. Just got his priorities mixed up. Poor dude."

Anibal reached over and patted Ethan on the leg. "I wondered why he wanted to come on this trip. He never wanted to do a minute's work that he didn't have to. I suspect he had some sort of plan for getting some more money out of you guys before it was over with. No, son, I didn't ask for a dime for this. I was going this way, anyway, and this was an opportune time."

Emily said, "Not to speak ill of the dead, but I felt like there was something wrong the minute we met him."

"Just a little greedy. It's a fault a lot of people have, don't you think?"

"Certainly is," Emily said. "We've had plenty of experience with that ourselves." She took a few minutes to tell Anibal about some of the experiences they had had organizing a rally for food truck vendors and their investigation into the road to Surfdom.

"Wow," Anibal said. "You guys have seen quite a bit."

"We've seen a lot more the last couple days," Ethan said. "I wish it had been a little more pleasant."

For now, they were coming down into the valley floor and could really see the damage the earthquake and the flood had done to the valley and the city that lay inside it.

The main road that led down to Takewawa had disappeared. Anibal braked Esmeralda to a stop, the engine still chugging, and rubbed his chin. He pointed out to his left, where fresh dirt covered a clearing in the trees. "That's not supposed to be there," he said. "There was a road here the last time I came down. This is the main track into the city."

But it was not the main track into the city any longer. The road has been completely erased by broken trees, new mud, and boulders. If there had been a road there, underneath all that, no one could see it. "We'll have to continue on this one-lane track," Anibal said. "It goes the same place eventually, but the main road was built so that we wouldn't have to stay on this old goat track any longer."

Down below them, the ravine was choked with brush, smashed rock, and glistening mud. Water continued to flow over the face of the dam, bringing further debris down from above. Huge slabs of concrete the size of a city block lay with rebar sticking out as if futilely reaching for the sky.

Ethan whistled. "And to think," he said, "we were almost caught up in that."

Far off in the distance, they could see haze from the city, with a few buildings sticking up out of it. Off to the left, on the southern edge of town, was the airport. Or had been. Ethan was pretty sure they should be able to see it from their vantage point, but he had no idea what he was looking at. "Isn't the airport supposed to be right down there?" Ethan said.

"It was," Anibal said. "You should be able to see it." He pointed to an area smudged with brown and green as if it were a patch of camouflage. "There should be two runways right there, and the flight tower." Nothing at all showed in the debris field.

"And to think," Emily said, "we could have been in *that*!"

"Yeah," Ethan said, "it doesn't seem to have made much difference where we went, or what we did. We were going to run into this earthquake."

Anibal said, shaking his head, "I feel horrible for my country. This is going to take forever to clean up. I just don't know where we will find the money." He put Esmeralda in gear and started her down the half-paved goat track.

"We noticed," Ethan said, "that the saladera was losing value. This is only going to make that process worse, isn't it?"

Anibal said, "I'm no great wizard with money, but it will for sure. The problem is, much of the devastation here has destroyed government projects. The dam, the airport, many of the large public buildings, all of them are owned by the government. They will have to be replaced by the same people who built them. In order to get the money to pay the workers to do the cleaning up of the debris, and then the even harder work of rebuilding everything, they're going to have to come up with a great deal of money. Normally, they get that money from taxing people."

Here Emily broke in. "We know quite a bit about that, actually."

Anibal looked over at her and nodded. "Yes, you told me. So you already understand how all that works.

Unfortunately, when the government runs out of money and can no longer tax the people enough to get more, there's only one solution."

"Print more of it," Ethan said. "Yes, we heard about this from our grandpa. I guess we're going to get to see it up close."

"The longer you're here, the more of it you will see," Anibal said. "I don't have to be any kind of economic genius to understand that when a huge expenditure needs to be made by the government, what they usually do is print more currency."

"Right," Emily said. "Then that currency gets into the economy, and the value of all of the other currency declines. The denomination on the bills get larger and larger, but they buy less and less."

"That's how inflation works," Ethan said. "We've experienced that a little bit."

"Nothing like this," Anibal said, and frowned. "It's going to make things much more difficult. The value of pretty much all of our money will fall off a cliff starting right now. It won't just affect us on the ground here, but internationally as well." Anibal ground into a higher gear, as the road started to level out towards the bottom of the hill.

"Not only that," Ethan said, "I was just thinking about the town of Ychu. That's a major source of tourist revenue, money coming in from outside the country, which Allqukilla is going to need desperately. But the town depends on the lake. And most of the lake," he said, "is right down there."

"And heading for the ocean," Anibal said as if he had lost an old friend. And perhaps he had, Ethan thought. He must have lived by that lake for a very long time.

Anibal said, "Now that beautiful lake where you were water skiing a couple of days ago is just a hole, half empty, with mud at the bottom. The devastation will be horrible not just here, below the dam, but also above it. So many people depend on Ychu for their livelihood. I have no idea what my province is going to do."

And with that somber thought, they came down out of the trees and onto the flat land that led to the capital city.

Turn to page 18.

Emily whipped the door open as if she thought someone might be on the other side with their ear pressed to it. Pandora was there but she was standing a few paces off, her arms folded and a look on her face like this really shouldn't be taking them this long.

"So, your father," Emily said. Pandora's eyebrow twitched upward, but she made no comment. "Is he a man of his word?" Emily said.

"If you pay him," Pandora said. "He calculates everything by what profit there is in it, and whether it will keep him alive."

Emily nodded. "That's what we figured."

"Let's go talk to him," Ethan said.

As they opened the door to the roof, Pietro said, "And that's why I ended up down here. I told you it wasn't much of a story."

"It's enough of the story for me to know that it was worthwhile for our children to come and find you." It was Mom's voice.

And Dad said, "When the kids come back, you can tell them that we will trust whatever decision they make and do everything we can to support it."

"You just told them yourself," Pietro said, looking up at the children. "So what have you decided?"

"A couple of things," Ethan said. "First off, is there a bath or a shower in this building?"

Pandora laughed. Pietro nodded. "Spared no expense," he said. "Anything else."

"Yes," Emily said. "I see your beef jerky and your potato chips. I see your Gatorade and your cans of peanuts. Please tell me that you have the means of making *real* food. And by real food," she said, "I mean something with meat in it, that's warmer than body temperature."

This time Pietro laughed. "You're full of demands, aren't you?"

"We are indeed," Ethan said. "But I'm told you're a man of your word if you get paid. We're prepared to pay you and to take our chances that your network for getting out of the country is going to be better than anything other people cobble together at the last minute." Ethan extended his hand and Pietro looked at it for a moment, looked up at Ethan's face, and finally stuck out his own hand and shook.

"All right," he said. "I will treat you as if you were my own children."

Emily said, "I think, for my peace of mind, I'd ask you to do just a little bit better than that."

Pandora laughed again.

Emily expected Pietro would take them all the way down until they were below ground, but instead he led them through a door opposite the one where they had had their short conference and up a flight of concrete steps to the second floor of the building.

The door at the top of the stairs creaked open, and again Pietro made the sweeping bow to tell them to go ahead of him. They stepped into a room that spanned the entire building right and left, front and back. Each wall featured wide windows with a funny kind of tinting to them. In the center of the room were pillars of glass for the skylights that supplied light to the room below, sort of like an elevator shaft in the middle of the building. It also provided illumination to this floor, although Emily could see lights set into the ceiling of the room, too.

The room smelled pleasant, as if some kind of air freshener had been used in the place recently. There were two beds off to one side, along the wall, and when Emily looked closely, she could see a couple of walls. Over in one corner were two doors leading into a small room that stuck out a few feet from the wall in either direction.

Pietro let the door swing shut behind him with a clack. He pointed toward the beds. "Beds," he said unnecessarily. He pointed to the far corner where the odd doors were. "Showers," he said. "I'm sorry I don't have many more of the conveniences of home."

"That's okay," Ethan said. "I think this will be just fine. If I can get the grime off my body I'll be very happy to fend for myself for all the rest."

"No need for that," Pietro said. "You're now guests of the state. The state is me." And he laughed uproariously.

"I take it that's some sort of quotation," Emily said.

"Louis XIV," Pietro said.

The shower was real. No hot water ever felt so good. Forty-five minutes later, the twins came back downstairs and spent a few minutes on the internet finding out what all was going on in the world. The news was pretty dire for the country of Allqukilla. The news was showing footage of the aftereffects of the dam burst. The aerial footage was hideous, and it meant that two or three million people in the country were without power. Most of the arterial highways in the country were blocked by rubble and debris, and there were tens of thousands of tourists who were cut off in the village of Ychu and other places in the surrounding areas.

"Exactly what we were worried about," Ethan said. "We're lucky we're not trapped there now."

Rescue missions had been mounted by the country's army and all manner of support services, and there were relief missions on the way from other countries, but it was still a horrific mess. The estimates were that somewhere around 50,000 people had been killed, a number that was increasing by the hour. A few villages had managed to keep power, most of them ones that had already been generating their own. The capital city appeared to be the hardest hit.

"We're pretty lucky," Ethan said, "all things considered."

"Yeah," Emily said. "It kind of makes the loss of my clothes and my passport seem kind of trivial. I even got a new backpack out of the deal." She held it up. "Most expensive backpack I've ever owned."

That night, around mouthfuls of some of the best hamburger the twins ever had in their lives, Pietro explained how the next couple of days were going to go. "You'll stay here tonight," he said. "In the morning, I expect to hear from my transport friend, Travis, who carries supplies back and forth from here to other places in the region. We've done some, uhh, work together, and Travis has the wherewithal to get people out of the country in difficult situations."

"That might be an issue," Emily said. "Seeing as I have no passport."

"It's only going to be an issue at the Ecuadorian border if you actually have to present an ID," he said. "Lots of people will not have documentation. And if that looks to be a serious problem, there are ways around the official channels."

When he saw the twins look dubious, he said, "Now look. The truth is that you really are from America, and that you really are just trying to get home. How that comes about seems largely irrelevant. The embassy in Quito will be only too happy to make sure that you get taken care of and get back to the States where you belong. The problem is getting there. But Travis can get you there."

That night, when Emily and Ethan were lying in bed staring at the ceiling, Ethan said, "Do you really think this is a good idea?"

Emily said, "I was about to ask you the same question. I don't mind doing everything that we can to get where we need to go, but I'm not entirely sure about breaking the law to do it."

"You can think of it this way," Ethan said. "Nearly everybody pouring over the border into Ecuador will be lacking a passport or other identification. A lot of that stuff is going to be buried under the rubble of the city here."

"That's true," Emily said, "and that *is* sort of what happened to me as well."

"And it isn't as if we're trying to do something wrong," Ethan said. "We're trying to do what they want us to do anyway. They want us to get out of their country, and they want us to go home. It seems like the best thing we can do is to do that."

Emily said, "But is this the best way to do it? It seems we have a decision to make."

"Yep," Ethan said. "Even though Dad has already paid for the services of this Travis dude, I don't think he had fully explained to him what his services would entail. Now that we know, what's our decision?"

If you think the twins should return to the embassy, turn to page 198.

If you think they should carry on with Pietro's plan, turn to page 322.

A few days later, a small group gathered outside the church.

A large, brand-new truck, sleek and white, sat in front of the stone chapel, its nose pointed north.

"It's very nice of you to allow us to borrow your truck for this expedition," Ethan said.

The father waved his finger at Ethan. "Not an expedition," he said. "This is a mission of mercy. There will be no adventures with bandits. There will be no earthquakes. There will be no excitement at all. Samuel here is a good driver. The truck is brand new, and the road north is clear. I have made contact with my counterparts in Ecuador, and they have arranged with the embassy to make sure that everything will be in order when you reach the border. This is one trip that will not add much to your adventures."

Emily stepped up and threw her arms around the priest. He staggered back in some surprise. "Why child," he said, "I don't think our parting deserves all this display."

"But I do," Emily said, her face buried in his cassock. "You have been so kind to us, you and the entire town. We will never forget you."

The priest chuckled and patted her back. "I am sure you will not," he said. "Allow me to apologize again on behalf of the people of the town for the terrible time you had in the mountains getting here."

"That's all behind us," Ethan said.

"I understand why they did what they did. I'm just glad that you won't have to worry about them anymore."

"I can promise you that," Father Augustin said. "Our ambassador Consuela was most persuasive." This pronouncement was greeted with laughter from the townspeople.

"And we will be back," Emily said, stepping back a little and wiping her nose. Her eyes were red, and not just from lack of sleep or out of excitement to be leaving. "Your town has become a part of our lives."

"There are people like us everywhere in the world," Father Augustin said. "You can find them in every town you go to."

He shook hands with Ethan. Then other villagers came forward—the ladies organizing the relief for the town, doctors, nurses, regular folk that had shared meals with the young Americans.

And then of course, Thon.

For all that he had become like a brother to the twins, he seemed shy about coming forward and saying goodbye to them.

Emily shook his hand demurely and then pulled him forward for a hug.

"I wish you could come with us," she said.

"I know," he said, "and so do I, but my village still needs me, and there is a lot of work left to be done."

"Another time," Ethan said, shaking his hand. "You know, for a couple of days, it was really nice to have a brother." Thon beamed.

He held out a glass bottle corked at the top. "This is from my village," he said. "We know that drinking alcohol is forbidden in the States for people as young as you, so this is just grape juice, but it is our very best grape juice from vines of this year. I think you will find that it is delicious."

Emily held onto the bottle as if it were a child, her eyes shining. "I remember this from dinner up at your village," she said. "It *is* delicious. That will be a wonderful refreshment on our trip."

Samuel climbed into the driver's seat of the truck and gunned the engine. The truck roared to life like an animal waking up. And then it was time to go.

They climbed into the powerful vehicle, put their few supplies and their satchels in the back seat, and started off.

Father Augustin turned out to be a prophet with regard to the trip. It was uneventful in the extreme. The roads were peaceful, and the countryside was beautiful with tall trees and wide lakes dotting the landscape, unlike anywhere else in the country. It reminded the twins of home. Now that they were actually leaving the country, they could not get to the border fast enough.

Ethan wondered if things would really go smoothly at the crossing, considering that they really had no proof of identity and no paperwork at all. But he needn't have worried.

Father Augustin was as good as his word and had things arranged: a priest met them at the border, clutching in his hands a manila envelope stuffed with paperwork.

The officials there, harried and stressed with all the work that they had had to do with refugees over the previous few weeks, looked with relief on a problem so easy to solve. They stamped the forms and the twins were cleared to cross the border.

They hugged Samuel goodbye and watched as he took the white truck with its beautiful cross on each door back toward Sapallu.

There was one more surprise, though. The priest drove them sedately in his black sedan directly to the airport in Quito.

"I should go find a phone," Ethan said when they arrived, "and see if I can call Mom and Dad. We should let them know we're at the airport and on our way back."

"I don't think you're going to need to do that," Emily said, and began to run.

There at the gate were their mother and father.

They wrapped each of the twins up in giant hugs.

"We were so worried," Mom said. "You have no idea. We just couldn't wait another day to see you."

"And you have no idea what's been happening to us," Ethan said. "Good thing the plane ride home is a long one, because we're going to need every minute of it to tell you what we've been through."

THE END

Ethan sat in the middle seat of the bench at the front of the truck and stared at the hotel.

It really did look like it was in pretty good shape, but he knew that looks could be deceiving. The last thing they needed was to get some kind of an injury or get trapped in a collapsing hotel.

"We're not going in," he said. "They have people posted at the door to stop us anyway, and I don't think they would do that if the building was safe."

"I'm sure you're right about that," Emily said. "I just wish that I had a change of clothes somewhere. These are already getting kind of gritty and heaven knows when I'll be able to get a shower."

"Yeah," Ethan said, "I think a lot of the things we used to take for granted are going to be much more appreciated from now on."

The time ticked by. Ethan fought the urge to start punching buttons on the dashboard to see if the radio would come on so maybe they could get some news or at least listen to some music to pass the time.

Emily said, "That was cool up at the ruins, though. At least we got to see them. The whole trip wasn't totally for nothing."

The scene in front of them continued without much variation, except for the cast of characters. Medical personnel scurried back and forth like water striders on a creek.

People continue to trickle out of the front of the hotel. The emergency personnel concentrated most of their attention on the ruined wing, where there were clearly still people trapped inside.

Ethan's hand itched. He wished he could do something to be useful, but he knew that if he went over there all he would be doing would be getting in the way.

"That's horrible," Emily said, watching as a small child came staggering out of the rubble. "The earthquake really did a number on this poor town."

Away from the hotel, around the square, other buildings had fared better, it appeared. Of course they were lower, not a multi-story building like the hotel. None of them had power though, as far as they could tell.

"I can't sit in this truck anymore," Ethan said. "I've got to at least get some air."

"I'll join you," Emily said, and she opened the door. The noise struck them immediately and assaulted them with cries of wounded people, emergency personnel yelling back and forth at one another to allocate resources. And over all of it was a kind of sighing, as if the land itself were depressed about what had happened.

Ethan stood with his back against the car, feeling helpless and lost. Eventually he went around and sat down on the front bumper. Emily stood there for a while with her hand on his shoulder.

"It's not your fault," she said.

"I know that," Ethan said, "but I can't help feeling like I'm trapped and I should have a way out, but I don't."

"We have a way out," Emily said. "That's why we're here with Jorge. He'll be back any minute, and then we'll go."

"But go where?" Ethan said. "It's not like we're going to get back to the capital city and all of a sudden they're going to teleport us home."

"Scotty would come in real handy about right now, wouldn't he?" Emily said.

"I guess we'll have to dedicate our lives to producing teleportation technology, so nobody gets trapped in situations like this anymore," Ethan said.

Emily smiled. "Well, if you're back to Star Trek references, I guess things are looking up."

Turn to page 217.

The bus was nothing like the twins had expected it to be. It creaked to a stop in front of the airport with a squeal of brakes and a sigh that sounded like it came from a geyser at Yellowstone. People speaking a dozen different languages lined up at the front and back doors. The twins tried to decide where they would most likely be able to get a seat, but they needn't have bothered. It quickly became obvious that they weren't going to get a seat at all. The bus was going to be more than full, with people standing in the aisles.

"This is a really long bus ride," Emily said. "I don't know if it's a good idea for us to try to stand for the whole thing."

"Good thing we can sit on our luggage," Ethan said. "At least we will have a way to sit down a little, even if we don't get a seat."

They waited their turn to clamber aboard. Lots of people seemed to have brought packages, and even cages holding live animals, as if this was a trip they didn't want to take without their household pets. For a while it seemed as if they wouldn't be able to get everyone on board, but with some pushing and shoving, everyone managed to get inside. The doors creaked closed.

Emily and Ethan stood in the aisle in the middle of the bus, surrounded by people in colorful serapes, one of them with a crate of live chickens in his lap. Within a few moments they had left the concrete roads behind and were trundling along on a dusty, semi-paved road that wasn't quite wide enough for two cars to pass side by side. The bus pushed its way up into the mountains driving in the center of the road. Every time they hit a pothole or some kind of a rut in the road, the bus creaked and groaned as if it would fall apart.

Emily rolled her suitcase into the tiny space in between a woman with chickens and a man who carried a small pig on his lap. She looked up and down the aisle at other people who were in a similar predicament. Most of those who hadn't gotten a seat appeared to be tourists like herself. She smiled tentatively at a lady just down the aisle from her. The lady didn't smile back, but looked disgustedly from side to side. Emily wheeled her suitcase underneath her and prepared to sit down. She turned, and behind her stood a giant of a man with a bald head and a beard. He had his hand wrapped through a strap attached to the roof of the bus. She bent her knees and his face broke into a wide smile, as if he wanted her to sit down.

If you think Emily should sit on her suitcases, turn to page 333.

If you think she should continue to stand, turn to page 148.

The pat came again, and Emily shifted her hand underneath whatever it was. Smooth, round, with a slick coating. It might be...

The big van rounded a corner, shifting the massed crowd. Cries came from the edge, where people were being squished. Emily found herself with a couple of clear feet beside her. She crouched, and put out her hands. The van steadied and the crowd rocked back. Emily found herself with an armful of child.

Her—Emily knew the child as *her* without having to think about it—head only came up to about Emily's waist. The girl was coated in a fine, gray dust, but a cut at her forehead had formed a stream of vibrant blood down her face. Emily took a closer look and saw that the cut had stopped bleeding. The child struggled against her like a wounded bird.

Softly, Emily said, "Are you lost?" She realized she had spoken in English. The child's only reaction was to go perfectly still, stiff, like a wood carving. Emily tried again in Spanish.

"Are you lost? Do you know where your parents are?"

The child relaxed a fraction. She said in halting Spanish, "No, I don't know where they are."

"Did you get on the bus with them?" Emily asked.

"No," said the child. "I lost them in the airport." And she began to cry.

She was far from the only one. The van was filled with the soft sounds of human misery. Emily felt her eyes burn as well. But what good was that going to do anyone?

"Do you need someone to hold onto?" Emily asked.

"I need my mama." More urgent. Bordering on desperate. There was no room in the cargo bus for desperation.

"I'm not your mama," Emily replied, "but I'm someone you can hold onto if you want to."

In the darkness she could not see the child, but presently two small arms threaded their way around her neck, and a soft wet cheek pressed softly against her own.

Her legs were beginning to cramp from crouching, so she stood up, lifting the child with her. The child wrapped its legs around her waist.

"My name is Emily," she said. "What's your name?"

"Maya," said the child, and laid her head on Emily's shoulder.

Ethan bumped against them as the van took another curve. His hands came up to feel out what Emily was holding. "What have you done now?" he said.

"Tried to make the world a slightly better place," Emily said. "You should try it. This is Maya."

Ethan said into the general direction of where the child's head would be, "Hello, Maya. My name is Ethan. I'm Emily's brother. We're lost, too."

Turn to page 319.

Ethan was worried the flight would take forever, but the anticipation of what was to come made the whole thing fly by. Just when the twins were starting to get antsy, the plane's engines changed pitch and they were landing in Allqukilla. They got their luggage and rolled them over to the line for customs.

Emily adjusted Ethan's pack, then Ethan adjusted Emily's, shifting their weights and trying to get their backpacks into a comfortable position. Ethan had tried his out, of course, before they left and it had been fine. But he hadn't really expected to stand with it strapped to his back for so long. The customs line moved at a snail's pace. But there was no getting around it.

In front of the twins, an obese man with a sweat-stained dress shirt lugged a huge briefcase and slid his brown suitcase forward a foot or so every couple of minutes. Behind him, a mother tried to keep her small son quiet as he cried softly and kept saying over and over that he was hungry. Emily unzipped her backpack and handed the boy an apple.

Ethan just shook his head at her. She winked and zipped her bag back up. "That's the last one," she said. "So I won't actually be lying when I tell them I don't have any produce to bring into their country."

He had begun to doubt that they'd ever get to tell anyone anything. Dad was right about bureaucrats.

The obese man waddled up to the counter. He had a rapid-fire conversation with the customs officer, and she waved him over to a pair of armed men in uniform who stood by a dirty wooden table. He hefted his suitcase to the tabletop and unlocked it, spreading it open. Ethan was mildly curious as to what it might contain, but he had no time to look. An available customs officer waved them forward—finally!

Ethan and Emily handed over their passports. The officer snorted and glared at them. "Tourist?" she said.

"Sí," Ethan said, and she snorted again at the gringos practicing their Spanish. The woman picked up a stamp, whacked it onto their passports, and handed them back.

"Welcome to Allqukilla," she said flatly and bellowed out to the next person in line.

That was it?

"That's it?" Emily said.

"I guess it is," Ethan said, rolling his bag forward. "We're official now, whatever that means."

In front of them, glass doors beckoned, and the bright light of the afternoon sun poured through to the tiled interior. Off to the right stood a bank of telephones, and to the left there was a row of lockers with a brightly lit ATM in the middle.

"We need cash," Ethan said, but Emily was already entranced by the TV screen on a nearby wall. The broadcast was in Spanish, but the graphic made it all too clear what the subject of the report was.

"Earthquake," Emily said, pointing.

"Looks like it's just a warning," Ethan said. "This is an active fault area here, you know. They haven't had a major earthquake in sixty years."

"Sounds like one is due any time."

"Sounds like there's no reason to think one is ever going to happen again. Come on."

Ethan dragged his suitcase over to the ATM and unzipped his waist pack, withdrawing the card. The ATM cheerfully sucked it in, and he had a momentary flash of fear that it would never come out again.

"Look," Ethan said. "The saladera is down again, or the dollar is up. We can get an extra ten since when we looked at the rate yesterday." Ethan has been fascinated by how poorly the local currency was doing—each day brought new news of inflation. It must be awful to have to use saladeras as your money, he thought to himself.

But Emily wasn't thinking about any of that. She was still captivated by the TV program. A man was talking, showing a graph he'd made, like a seismograph. The reporter kept asking him a question, and he nodded finally, with a little shrug.

"You going to exchange?" Ethan said.

Emily tore herself away from the screen. "I guess so. I have a bunch of dollars, so I could go over there to the booth, but everyone says the best way is to get money from the ATM. What's the rate there?"

"Sixty-one fifty to the dollar."

Emily squinted, reading the booth marquee. "Fifty-five over there. I'll pull money from the account at home and keep my dollars. They might come in handy later."

She produced her card and went through the same process Ethan had, tucking a large sheaf of brightly-colored bills into her own pack.

Now Ethan was watching the TV. "My Spanish isn't very good for geology, but I think they're saying that scientists are warning there could be a major quake soon. Their graphs seem to say that there have recently been a series of micro shocks along the fault line. I think... I can't understand their accent very well."

"What do we do, Ethan?" Emily said. Her face was drawn and colorless. "A big earthquake down here would be terrible. What if we couldn't get home?"

If you think it would be best for the twins to get on the next flight home, turn to page 186.

If you feel like the twins should stay, turn to page 146.

"It's very important that we make sure that we get out of here as quickly as we can," Ethan said, his voice urgent but low. His eyes went to the surrounding mob, as if trying to make sure he wasn't overheard. He spoke in English, though there were plenty of tourists about who would understand them.

"Where are they taking us?" Emily asked. "I have to get my bag."

"I don't think we're going to be able to get our bags," Ethan said. "I don't think they're going to let us. But it's okay. I'm sure they'll store them, and we'll be able to get them later. Right now we need to get away from the airport."

"Why?" She looked at Ethan's face, and he knew that she could tell that he was concerned.

"It's the dam," he finally said, nodding in the direction of the first responders. "They're worried that the dam might be about to burst."

"The big dam over the river?" she asked.

Ethan nodded and kept her moving towards the van, which had now replaced the buses at the side of the road. They were using every available vehicle to move as many people as possible. But where were they going?

As they passed one of the guards, Ethan called out, "Where are you taking us?" The man only shrugged and kept people moving forward. Probably he didn't know, much less care, but even if he did, he wasn't going to tell.

They reached the front of the mass of people and were shoved onto a long, low cargo bus clearly made for luggage and not for humans. It must have been the only thing available.

They climbed aboard. The ceiling was low, but Ethan and Emily were just able to stand upright. If the ride was long it was going to be hard on them. More came through the doors until they were packed in so tightly there was no room to sit. Dust was everywhere and clogged their eyes and ran down their throats. Coughing came from every side of the bus.

Then the door closed and the bus rumbled off. The cargo bus had no windows—baggage doesn't need to look out and check the scenery—but it prevented anyone inside from seeing where they were going; the darkness was disconcerting. Passengers slumped into each other, saying "excuse me" in various languages, sniffling, coughing, a mass of humanity in the worst and most destitute circumstances. Ethan kept his hand firmly clamped over his belly pack, where his cash, passport, and all his identification resided. Every chance they had to get out of here was riding around his middle.

Something wet squished against Emily's hand in the dark. The windowless van rocked, and it happened again, a pat of damp stickiness. Gone again.

Emily put her hand to her nose. It smelled of iron, the unmistakable sweet reek of blood.

If you think Emily should try to figure out where the blood is coming from, turn to page 114.

If you think she should keep it to herself so as not to alarm the others, turn to page 367.

"I feel like we have taken an unconventional route almost the whole way here," Emily said. "Here's another opportunity for us to take the road less traveled and, to be perfectly frank, I don't think that's worked out all that well for us."

Ethan frowned. "It does seem as if every time we try to make the smart but unconventional choice, it gets away from us. Maybe this time we should just stick it out with the way we had originally intended to go."

Travis said, "You mean stick with the plan, even when the plan appears to be falling apart?"

"Yeah," Ethan said. "Something like that."

"It's bold," Travis said. "It's innovative. I like it."

"All we have to do is figure out whether we're the idiots that can't see that we're just doing the same thing over and over hoping for different results or the geniuses who persisted until they succeeded." Ethan rolled his eyes.

Emily said, "My only fear is that we're going to run out of gas sitting here on the freeway."

Travis turned and looked her in the face. "That's not something you should worry about," she said. "Remember how there wasn't very much cargo space in the trunk?"

"Yeah," Emily said.

"That extra cargo space that used to belong to the trunk is now converted to additional fuel space. We have probably something on the order of fifty-five gallons of fuel on board. We can idle here or cruise back and forth on the freeway at ten miles an hour for a month before we run out of fuel."

"Clever," Ethan said.

"Necessary," Travis said. "I do a lot of long-distance work. A lot of the places I go, there isn't exactly a gas station handy."

That was the beginning of the longest trip Ethan and Emily could remember having taken in their lives. The freeway was not completely stopped. Not quite. Every five minutes or so they could move forward twenty yards, thirty yards. Once they even got into second gear.

Ethan pored over his map, and when they ran off the edge of it, he took one of Travis's and began to follow their route on that, looking for any way that they could get off the well-beaten track and actually make some time.

One stretch, however, was so slow that Travis finally just turned off the engine. "I'm going to take a little walk," she said. "You guys might want to do the same."

The cars ahead of them hadn't moved for more than thirty minutes. A lot of people got out of their vehicles and lay on their hoods, chatted with their neighbors, and even shared food.

Ethan said, "At least this isn't the worst part of our trip."

"Not the worst," Emily said, "but not as much fun as I was hoping. At this rate, how long will it be before we are able to get out of the country?"

"At this rate," Ethan said, "we'll be here until Christmas."

"What are we averaging?" Emily said.

"About seven miles an hour," Ethan said. Emily looked dubious. Ethan wagged his finger. "Remember? There was that one stretch where we got up to almost thirty."

"Oh, yes," Emily said. "That was the best quarter-mile of my life."

There wasn't anything to do but laugh about it.

Turn to page 136.

Turn to page 136.

"We can't risk it. This guy could be anyone," Ethan said.

Emily nodded. "We have to be careful. I think the bus is our best bet."

Ethan trudged over to the taxi driver—if that's who he was—and shrugged. "I'm sorry," he said. "I think we had better just wait for the bus to get fixed."

A shadow passed over the man's face. "Okay. That's your choice." He transferred his gaze to a couple over Ethan's shoulder, and his smile suddenly reappeared, setting the bait out for another potential victim.

The twins rolled their bags back to the bus and clambered aboard. Several groups of tourists had debarked, leaving bare stretches of aisle to stand in. Emily even had a seat about two-thirds of the way back, though she gave it up when a pair of small dogs yapped at her.

The stink was powerful, and the heat showed no signs of abating. From the front, the sounds of metal clanking and soft Spanish swearing kept up a steady beat. It looked like a long wait.

Turn to page 362.

Ahead of them stood the interior door into the main hotel. Inside on the left, a flight of stairs led upward and connected to the end of the second floor hallway where their room was.

Dust drifted down the stairwell. The carpet of the stairs was coated with it, a thick grey powder, the color of broken drywall and plaster. A large crack ran up the wall above the second step and disappeared into the ceiling. It was wide enough that Emily thought she could probably stick her finger into it.

Ethan noticed as well. "What other cracks are there that we *can't* see?" he said. "This is not a good idea."

Emily put her foot on the lowermost step. She bounced up and down on it, checking for stability. It didn't give in at all. It felt like a normal stair, like regular concrete.

"I think it's fine," she said. "The stairs feel pretty solid." She started up the first couple, testing each one gingerly.

Ethan stayed on the landing below. "Did you see the other wing of the hotel? The entire structure could give way any time," he said.

"Seriously, Ethan, it doesn't feel like that. Come on up." She took three or four more steps until she was at the bend in the staircase. There was no creaking, or any sort of audible weakness.

But the air smelled like someone had dumped out the inside of a vacuum cleaner. Ethan felt like he needed to brush it away from his face. He started up the stairs after her. From somewhere far into the hotel, behind the closed main-floor door, came a rumbling crunch, as if something very heavy had fallen. They felt the impact through their feet and more dust drifted down from the ceiling.

"That didn't sound very solid," Ethan said. "Come on, we need to leave now."

"I'm not leaving without my stuff," Emily said, from the stairs above him. "We're almost there, I can see the door to our floor."

In a moment she had taken the remainder of the stairs and was standing in front of the second-floor door. It sagged a little on its hinges, as if the frame wasn't quite true to square any more. An inch of space showed between the door and the frame.

She tugged on it, but it wouldn't open. "Come and help me," she said. "It's already part-way open."

Ethan trudged up the remaining couple of stairs to where she stood and put his hand into the crack between the door frame and the door. He pulled while Emily tugged on the door handle. The door creaked open. A couple of feet and that was all. It wouldn't go any farther. It made a little arc in the dust on the floor.

"Our room is only five doors down," Emily said. "I can almost see it from here."

Looking into the interior of the hotel, things seemed almost normal. There was less dust here, and no visible cracks in the wall or other structural damage. In fact it looked as if this part of the hotel had escaped damage all together.

"See?" Emily said, "there's nothing to be worried about." And she stepped into the hall.

Ethan followed after her, padding on the soft red carpet. On either side, the hotel room doors gaped open, propped wide.

They paused at the first room, and Emily took a peek inside. On the bed several bags sat open, filled with clothing, books, and even some jewelry.

"Look at that," Emily said. "We could pay for the whole trip just by taking a handful of that jewelry right there."

"We're not stealing someone's jewelry," Ethan said.

"Oh, I know that," Emily said, "I'm thinking of what would happen if somebody who wasn't as honest as we were got up here."

Just then, from down the hallway, a figure stepped into the light, as if he had materialized in the hall. As soon as he saw the twins, he ducked back into one of the rooms.

"Someone like *that*," Emily said, "We better hurry."

They made their way down the five doors to their room. The door stood open as well, like the others in the hall.

"Looks like we got here too late," Emily said. "Somebody's already been through our room looking for something to steal."

"Or maybe the staff opened the doors to make sure that they had everyone out of the hotel," Ethan said. "And now they don't. This is stupid."

Their luggage had been set on the floor behind the second of the two beds. Emily thought she could see it back there, robed in dust. She stepped cautiously into the room. Before she could get there, however, the entire structure gave a groaning crumple, and the floor shook beneath her.

"Aftershock!" cried Ethan, "Get in the doorway!" But the floor was already in motion, and there was no time for her to get there.

Instead, Emily threw herself on the floor next to the bed, wedging herself into the space right next to it. A piece of ceiling broke loose and smashed across the beds. But Emily's quick thinking left her in a pocket of space beneath it.

"Emily!" shouted Ethan. Another rumble came from somewhere else in the hotel. The vibration of it buzzed in his feet. "Emily! Are you all right?" Ethan shouted from the doorway. He kept his hands on the doorposts, feeling the aftershocks rolling through the building. They only had moments to get out of there.

"I'm . . . I'm okay," Emily said, her voice a little shaken. A poster-sized piece of plaster humped up and flipped over onto the nightstand. Emily's hand came up onto the bed from underneath. "I'm sure glad we took that emergency preparedness course," she said, poking her head out from under the remains of the ceiling.

"Yeah," Ethan said, "although I was hoping that it wouldn't come in quite so handy."

"I think I can reach our luggage," Emily said.

"Not a chance," Ethan said. "We're getting out of here right this second. No luggage is worth losing our lives over." He reached across the bed, and grabbed Emily's wrist, pulling her to her feet.

She cast a longing glance back toward the far side of the room where their luggage was now buried under half a foot of broken wood and crumbling plaster. Nothing to do about it now. They stumbled through the debris out into the hall.

A man sprinted by, his face drawn. He snagged a fistful of Ethan's shirt and hauled the both of them along with him, throwing them forward down the hall. "Run!" he shouted in Spanish. "The whole place is coming down!"

The twins didn't need to be told twice. Without hesitation, they both turned and sprinted for the door.

Behind them wallpaper tore from the wall. Doors fell off their hinges, falling into the hallway like funhouse dominoes. The three of them crashed into the door at the end of the hall, forcing it open another couple inches. Ethan and Emily pelted down the stairway with the other man hot behind them.

They reached the bottom floor. The crack in the wall was now almost six inches wide. A rending groan tore the ceiling above them. Ethan yelled, "Jump!" They threw themselves through the door to the outside just as the upper stairway gave way and crashed down behind them. Dust rolled out in a great cloud, blanketing them as they lay on the grass outside.

The guard stared at them open-mouthed. Ethan coughed and slapped dust from his clothing. Emily tossed her hair and brushed crumbles of plaster out of her eyes.

Standing over them, the guard said, "That was very stupid."

"You're not kidding," Ethan said.

The guard took in the concrete stairwell spilling out the door and shrugged. "I guess I don't need to guard this entrance anymore."

Emily might not have been killed, but she hadn't escaped unscathed. She staggered to her feet, her right leg buckling. Her pants were torn from the knee down to the ankle and underneath a ragged cut dripped blood into her shoe.

Ethan lay on the ground and stared at her leg. "That looks nasty," Ethan said. "We've got to get that washed out and bound up."

"Too bad we're not in a disaster area," Emily said, eyeballing the emergency responders all around them. "Where will we ever find emergency supplies?"

Ethan chuckled a little bit. "You can't be hurt too bad if you're still cracking jokes," he said.

"You know me better than that," Emily said. "I think I'd be cracking jokes at the gates of disaster."

"Hey look," Ethan said, "there's some gates over there with a sign that says 'It's a Disaster.'"

The two of them laughed together a little, releasing tension. Ethan rose to his feet and put his arm around his sister to support her. Together they limped around to the front of the building, where there was a pavilion set up, under which people with Red Cross armbands were distributing bandages to the wounded.

"My sister's hurt," Ethan said when they arrived there.

"It's just my leg," Emily said. "There's a cut, but I don't think it's too deep."

A distressed-looking nurse moved efficiently around the table with a roll of bandages. She looked at Emily's leg and pulled a bottle of solution from her belt. She sprayed the legs with the solution. Emily hissed in a breath.

"That hurts," she said to Ethan.

"It should," he said. "Going up in that building was really stupid."

"For once," she said, "I'm not arguing with you."

In a few minutes the nurse had the leg bound up, and the bleeding mostly stopped.

She handed Ethan the remainder of the roll of gauze. "You're going to want to change this in about an hour," she said. "Then, if you can, you want to change it again at least every day for a couple of weeks. If you don't, it could easily get infected. We don't exactly have sanitary conditions here."

"Or water to wash things out with," Ethan said, "but, thank you, we'll make do."

Emily felt like she could walk a little better on it now and was able to limp along holding on to Ethan's hand. They crossed back to the truck. Jorge was still nowhere to be seen.

"Maybe we should go over to the bar," Ethan said. "See if we can find them."

"I've had enough of walking around and going into strange places," Emily said. "No, thank you."

Ethan sighed and sat down on the bumper. "Then we'll wait. That doesn't sound too bad to me either. It's already been kind of a long day." He glanced up at the sun. It was well past its zenith and down the other side.

"And this started off as such a nice day," Emily said, "Now here we are."

"Yes," Ethan said. "Here we are. And don't we both wish we were somewhere else."

Turn to page 217.

The border crossing took forever. Cars lined up for miles, refugees of all kinds. Many people looked destitute, exactly as Ethan would have expected refugees to look. But others looked more like the twins did, with cars that worked well, clearly packed with goods, and some of them were downright prosperous, with fancy vehicles like he would have expected to see in any Western big city.

No matter how long the wait was, Travis never seemed to get frustrated by it. "Used to it," Travis said. "Along with planning ahead, the ability to be patient in difficult circumstances, to never assume you're going to be able to get where you want to go quickly, is about the best thing that you can have in your emergency preparedness backpack. So to speak."

Taking everything in stride, her calm never wavered as they inched their way forward to the border. "I will say this, though," she said, "the border crossing here is a breeze under ordinary circumstances. Usually, there are a few dozen vehicles ahead of me, and it's sort of like a toll booth would be back in the States. This jam must mean that they're doing much more investigating of the vehicles that are crossing the border."

"Only to be expected," Emily said. "They couldn't very well just open their borders and let in anyone who wanted to go."

"Well," Travis said, "it seems that way, but I don't know if this is actually improving anything. What exactly are they going to be looking for? Drugs? Undoubtedly there will be drugs in some of these cars, but will they find them? People are carrying so much luggage; are they making them unload all of it before they let them across the border?"

"What about documentation?" Ethan said. "You know that we have a little bit of a problem when it comes to that."

Travis looked back at Emily. "Yes, I heard that. I will be surprised if it's a significant issue. More than likely there will be a holding area for refugees who don't have the appropriate permissions. Ordinarily, one does not need a visa to go from Allqukilla to Ecuador."

"So this should be a very simple border crossing, and it should be easy to get across as long as you have a passport. Which I don't," Emily said.

"Which it isn't, and you don't," Travis echoed. "But again, you'll hardly be the only one in this line who has problems relating to documentation. I'm sure there will be a provision for that as well. Ultimately, you have to look at it from their point of view. What do the Ecuadorians want? Ordinarily, they want border control, the ability to know who is coming into their country. But since most of the people in this line are leaving the country, from the Allqukillan standpoint, the more the merrier. Right now there is a huge drain on their emergency response capacity, and on their ability to provide services to people. The more people who leave the country, the less problem they have with that. So they will do everything they can to help people get out of the country, whether they have documentation or not."

"Not their problem anymore," Ethan said.

"Exactly. However, let's look at it from the Ecuadorian side. What do they want?"

Ethan rubbed his chin. "I think Ecuador wants to make sure that they don't have a bunch of criminals coming into their country."

"Almost certainly," Travis said.

"But they still need people to come in," Emily said. "There's surely quite a bit of trade in workers and goods and services coming across the border all the time," she said.

"And I can tell you that there are," Travis said.

"They'll need those to continue, won't they?" Emily said.

Travis nodded. "Yep. So how do they organize their system so that they keep the bad people out and let the good people through?"

"That's what passports are for," Ethan said.

Travis rolled down her window and let the slightly fresher breeze from outside come through. The area of the border was quite beautiful, with tall, palm-like trees lining the road, but right now, choked with cars, and the smog that they generated, it smelled rather more like a garage.

"Okay," Travis said, "is the passport going to do the job?"

Ethan thought for a moment. "Not necessarily," he said. "A passport doesn't mean that you're a good person, only that you're a citizen of a particular country."

"That's right," Travis said.

"In my case," Emily said. "I don't even have a passport to prove that I am from where I say I am."

"Another excellent point," Travis said. She dangled her arm out the window. "So what would you do?"

"I don't know," Ethan said. "It seems like there are two good options here, or possibly two bad options. You can let traffic flow through, which helps to boost your economy and the livelihood of people who depend on traffic across the border, but if you do that you risk a large number of people who are going to do terrible things to your country."

"On the other hand," Emily says, picking up the thread, "if you lock down the border to keep out the bad people, you choke off the flow of money and goods that is helping your economy to thrive."

"Not simple, is it?" Travis said. "Regardless of what *you* would do," she said, "what do you think *they* will do?"

Emily chuckled a bit. "If our experience with government is any indication," Emily said, "they'll do some mixture of both, that will do nothing to restrict bad people from coming into the country, but will be an almighty hassle to people who are legitimately trying to do business."

Travis laughed and threw her an appraising glance. "You two have had some very interesting experiences, haven't you?"

"You don't know the half of it," Ethan said.

Travis said, "I suspect Emily is right. I bet when we get ourselves to the border and find out, what we will find is that they are checking passports, but not much else, and pushing people who have difficulties with their paperwork or who don't have a specific place to go in the country, into camps just over the border. That seems to be what everybody does in these kinds of circumstances."

One particularly long stop seemed to stretch forever. Travis, hunched over the steering wheel, patted her hand on it once and said, "That's it, I'm going for another walk."

"We're getting close to the border," Ethan said. "Is that a good idea?"

"How long have we been sitting here without moving?" she said.

Emily immediately said, "Nine minutes and 23 seconds."

Travis laughed. "That's long enough for me. I need to stretch my legs, and this looks like a rest stop to me." She opened the driver's door—Emily noted that Ethan kept his eyes glued to her as she did—and then, like a cat stretching in the sunshine, sauntered off up the freeway.

"You don't have to gawk," Emily said.

Ethan whipped his eyes back to the interior of the car. "What?" he said, though his innocence was forced.

Travis wasn't the only one taking the opportunity. Lots of the other drivers had exited their vehicles and in some places it almost looked like an open-air market again.

Emily turned around in her seat and took in the scene through the back window. "You know," she said, "back there it looks like someone has food."

"We have food," Ethan said, holding up the bag of beef jerky.

Emily scowled. "That's not what I'm talking about. I mean *actual* food. I think those are burritos or tamales."

Ethan regarded the bag of beef jerky for a moment and said, "That sounds good to me." He tossed the beef jerky into the back seat. "Let's go check it out."

The twins exited the vehicle, stepping out onto the pitted concrete of the main road. Emily glanced up ahead. As far as she could tell, none of the cars up there were moving either. They had at least a few minutes to investigate the scene.

"Come on," Ethan said, his eyes locked on the group a few cars back. "Those are tamales. I can see the corn husks."

Fifty yards or so behind the Sentra, a small group of people stood around on the concrete, chatting amiably with each other, and periodically handing various items back and forth.

The twins approached cautiously, having been cooped up for a long time, and worried about what they might find in a refugee train.

On the edge of the group of about twenty or so, one of the women turned to the twins and said, "Good afternoon. I would ask where you were headed in your vehicle, but that seems pretty obvious." Her Spanish was accented with an unfamiliar cadence.

"Yep," Ethan said, "we got trapped in Takewawa like a lot of other people."

"You made it farther out than most tourists," the woman said. She extended her hand. "I am Rosalia," she said. "We live in the highlands outside of Takewawa."

"The highlands?" Emily said.

"Yes," she said. Seeing the look on Emily's face, she shook her head a little. "No," she said, "we didn't have too much damage. My house will probably be fine, but we have no water, and no power, and no idea when we will get those. The local stores have been completely stripped of food, so we have few options but to travel north. My family is from Ecuador," she said. "I know they will take me in for a few weeks until things get sorted out in Allqukilla."

Ethan eyed the tamales hungrily.

Rosalia caught the direction of his gaze. "Oh," she said, "you want one of these?"

"We sure would," Ethan said. "I can pay for them."

Rosalia burst out in laughter and shouted something to the women in the group behind her. They all laughed as well. "What will I do with your money?" she said.

"Money can be pretty useful," Emily said, "but I guess if you're leaving the country, saladera won't do you much good there."

"That's right," Rosalia said, "but even if I weren't leaving the country, right now what matters to me much more than money is variety in my diet, or even just curiosity. We're not sure how long we will be stuck on this road, which means that we need to make sure that we have the necessities of life."

"It's a barter system," Ethan said. "I know about that."

Rosalia nodded. "I happen to make really good tamales. But I've already eaten all I can stand, and I have even more in the car that I'm keeping in reserve. You wouldn't happen to have some roast pork, or possibly a bite of spiced rice and beans, would you?"

Ethan and Emily looked at one another sadly. "I'm sorry," he said, "we don't have anything like that."

"Too bad," Rosalia said "I would love to have shared my tamales, but I can't let them go for nothing. They're too valuable."

Emily scanned the group, looking at the things that they were trading, and noticed something. "I'll be right back," she said.

Ethan gave her a quizzical glance, but she ran back up the road to the Sentra, got into the cabin, and pulled out a small cooler they had taken from the storeroom at the internet cafe. She jogged back on the road, the cooler dangling at her side.

When she arrived, Ethan's face broke into a wide grin. "That's a great idea," he said.

"Thought you'd like it," Emily said.

Rosalia looked on with interest. Emily popped the top of the cooler, reached inside, and pulled out two bottles of Coca-Cola, condensation still dripping down their sides.

Rosalia's eyes widened. "Oh, that's a good thing," she said. She turned to let the others know, but she need not have bothered. As soon as Emily held up the iconic glass bottles, every eye had turned to her. Conversation stopped as if Emily had turned it off with a faucet.

"They're still ice cold. I have ten of these," she said.

Ethan cocked an eyebrow. She said to him, in English, "I kept two for ourselves."

"Make it three," Ethan said, kicking at a stone on the road. "Don't forget about Travis."

Emily almost said, "It's a sure thing you never forget about Travis," but instead she just nodded. "We have nine of these, now," she said.

"That should get you quite a bit here," Rosalia said. "I'll give you two tamales for each bottle of Coke."

"Done," Emily said, and handed over two bottles of Coke for four tamales.

Ethan picked up a couple of bottles and wandered over to the other side, where a woman had a bag full of juicy red apples. "Coca-Cola?" he said.

"*Sí, claro,*" the woman said, and handed a peck of apples to Ethan.

She took the Coke, twisted the cap off, and tipped it back. That was like a moth to a flame. People came jogging over from all over the highway.

Soon, the twins were having difficulty deciding what to take in exchange for their bottles of Coke. "Here," Ethan said, to Rosalia. "Here's another bottle. Can I have two more tamales?"

"Sure," said Rosalia. "I'll make that trade all day."

Emily didn't understand. "We already have tamales," she said. "Why do we need more?"

"We don't," Ethan said, "but there is a hungry-looking man who just walked up, and it looks to me like he has some *brazo de reina.* I've always wanted to try that. I'll bet he'll trade a handful of slices for a couple of tamales."

Rosalia laughed. "That's how barter works," she said. "You guys are into the swing of it very quickly."

Turn to page 389.

They stowed their suitcases in one of the big lockers, dropping a coin into the slot and taking the key. Emily unzipped her bag and drew out a folded bag, big and heavy, that they could pack with food and other things they thought they would need for the trip. Pushing the locker closed, Emily unfolded the bag and draped it over her arm. The twins crossed the checkerboard tile to the front doors of the airport, the gateway to the beginning of the true adventure.

Ethan paused with his hand on the door, as if taking a breath on the verge of a major decision. Emily breezed past him, pirouetting into the bright sunshine.

It was the same sun in the sky, the same expanse of blue, but somehow it was different, even alien. She felt a part of her come alive, a part that she hadn't even known she had in her. She sucked in deep lungfuls of air, separating each new smell as best she could. The air was filled with spice and sweat, the tang of some kind of fruit she could only guess at, diesel smoke, and a hundred other things she couldn't identify.

The front of the airport sat at the bottom of a wide circle of asphalt, with a floral garden in the center. Exotic reds, blues, and yellows bloomed in competition with one another, doubtless sending forth some of the fragrance she was smelling. On the far side of the circle, traffic passed in a steady stream of honks and clouds of smoke. A large walkway spanned the road, and on the far side a sign said "Mercado Libre."

"I think there's a market over there," Ethan said, consulting his map. "But just down the street is an ABC market, a big grocery store. I'm sure we can get everything we need there."

If you think the twins should explore the hustle and bustle of the Mercado Libre, turn to page 247.

If you think ABC Market sounds like their safest bet, turn to page 394.

Thinking there was something odd about the man's smile, Emily decided to remain standing instead. She imitated the man's example and wrapped her hand through the leather strap that dangled from a metal bar running the length of the bus. She set her feet wide and cushioned her knees against the shock of the bus jouncing up and down. Ahead of her, toward the front of the bus, a blonde woman in a flowery dress sat on her luggage and tried to keep from being thrown from side to side. Abruptly the bus banked around a sharp corner, and she was flung sideways into a woman with a basket of chickens. Thick white bird poop splashed all down the front of her dress. She shrieked in horror as the woman cackled even louder than her chickens. Above her, Emily heard the rumbling laugh of the man behind her.

He leaned over and told her, "We don't get much entertainment on this bus. It's kind of fun to see what happens when clueless tourists decide that they should sit down on their luggage instead of stand up and hold on."

"You wanted *me* to sit down right here, didn't you?" Emily cast a sidelong glance at the pig on the neighboring woman's lap.

"Of course I did. It would give me something to laugh about. But I guess you were too smart for that."

Emily didn't think she'd have called it smarts, exactly, but she was very glad she'd looked up at the man when she did. Her feet were getting a bit tired, but at least she wasn't covered in bird poop.

Turn to page 265.

The morning dawned bright and clear, and the twins were up almost the moment the sun crested the hills to the east.

"The bus to the ruins leaves from right in front of the hotel," Ethan said. "I want to make sure that we're on the earliest one."

Emily was already headed for the bathroom. "I'll only be a minute in the shower. Do you want to go down to breakfast?"

"I don't know if I can eat," Ethan said. "I'm too excited."

"You *must* really be excited," Emily said. "I've never known you to be unable to eat."

"Well," Ethan said, rubbing his hand over his hair and smiling a little bit, "maybe I could choke something down."

Emily laughed, and less than half an hour later, they were downstairs in the dining room tucking into a hearty breakfast. They kept an eye on the front windows of the hotel to watch for the bus to pull up.

"I better exchange some money," Ethan said. He had looked at his supply of saladera and found he was getting a little bit low, even with his secret stash.

They *had* spent a lot of money just buying postcards and little things like that at the hotel gift shop, but it seemed that the money just didn't go very far. At the gift shop there were even places where they had crossed out the price of an item and then written in a higher price above it. It was almost like watching the price rise while you stood there.

Ethan went to the ATM while Emily was drinking her mango juice, and when he came back, he had a quizzical expression on his face.

"What?" Emily said.

"It's nothing," Ethan said. "At least, it's what I expected, but it's still funny to see it actually happen."

He handed over a pair of thousand saladera bills.

"Two thousand?" she said.

"Today when I went to pull money out of the ATM, we got an extra ten percent. It's kind of amazing how fast inflation is eating up the value of the currency. I'm glad that's not happening to the dollar."

Emily took a bite of toast, but then she set it to the side as if remembering something. "But it *is* happening, isn't it?"

"I suppose it is," he said. "Although here we can actually watch it happen. Anyway, I kind of don't want to exchange any more of our dollars. They're holding their value much better than the saladera."

Emily frowned at this. "It's tricky, though. If something were to happen, I don't know where we would get another ATM out in the countryside."

"Good thing we're not likely to be out in the countryside. I mean, not more than a bus ride away from the hotel."

"We're not supposed to be, but you always like to be prepared." Emily laughed and finished off her mango juice. It was much thicker than American juice, more like syrup than the juice she was used to. The flavor burst on her tongue like fireworks. She had never tasted anything quite like it. "Your level of preparation is always amazing to me," she said. "It's one of the things that makes you so much fun to travel with."

"Well, it *has* been fun. I'm always amazed at the number of interesting things you can find to do that weren't a part a part of the original plan."

"That's what I'm here for," Emily said, and stood up, wiping her mouth on a napkin. "But I think it's time for us to follow the *original* plan. Right now, I can't wait to get to those ruins. It's as if I've been standing outside them all my life, and I'm finally going to get to enter the promised land."

Ychurichuc, when they finally reached the promised land, was not exactly what Emily had expected from the travel brochures. She knew that the ruins were not particularly large or even terribly impressive, especially when seen from below, but as the bus from the hotel trundled its way up the mountain side, greenery slapping against the windows as they passed, she had at least been expecting something to appear on the hillside in front of them, to loom out of the mist in impressive, ancient fashion. Instead, the bus pulled into a parking lot surrounded by several shops selling obviously Chinese-made kitsch.

She cast a glance at Ethan. He shrugged.

"Not surprising," he said. "This isn't the part that would have made the travel brochures."

She laughed a little but couldn't shake the disappointment. The bus ground to a stop and the twenty-five or thirty tourists from the hotel debarked. Despite the lack of rain over the last few days, the parking lot was slightly muddy. Thick mist covered the hillside, blanketing the countryside in every direction. That part, at least, was just as she had pictured it.

Ahead of them an archway of faux stone led to a grassy area and the staircase of ancient stone the twins knew almost as well as their own front steps. To the left of the arch stood a small ticket kiosk.

"We should be meeting the guide right there," Ethan said, pointing at the ticket booth. No one looked likely. Emily scanned the area for someone who fit the description they had been given. Finally a small knot of tourists moved off toward the entrance gate, revealing a stocky man with matching khaki shorts and shirt, with a safari-style hat hovering over a soul patch and neat mustache.

"I'll bet that's him," she said. At the same moment he saw the two young Americans and flashed them a smile.

They made their way over to him. Ethan said, "Are you Jorge?"

"I am," he said in perfect English.

Emily immediately wondered if they had made a terrible mistake. Something about the smile struck her like a note off-key. Still, she said, "My father and your father were good friends."

Ethan stuck out his hand and Jorge took it. Emily decided she should probably shake hands with him as well. She found his hands greasy and damp.

"I'm glad you're here," he said. "I wondered if the earthquake would scare you off."

"We were worried, but we figured we'd come too far to turn back now."

There was that smile again, and Emily had the same tingle up her spine, like someone scraping a nail on a chalkboard. "Quite right, my friends!" he said. "It's a once-in-a-lifetime opportunity. We'll see some things in the next two days that most people have never seen before.

Ethan's face lit up. "I can't wait to get started." He moved toward the arch as if nothing could restrain him.

Jorge's smile faltered a little. "Before we do, though, there is the matter of buying the tickets and paying for the tour."

Ethan smacked his palm to his forehead. "Oh, I forgot! I'm sorry." He withdrew from his pouch a fair-sized stack of saladera.

Jorge licked his lips, but his face twisted into a grimace, through which the smile could not quite make itself seen. "Of course that will work, but, um, if you happen to have something else—dollars, perhaps—I could give you a better deal."

Emily gave Ethan a tiny shake of the head and hoped he saw it.

Whether he did or not, Ethan held out the saladera once more. "This is all we have," he told him.

"That's too bad," Jorge said, as he reached out and pocketed the big portion of the stack. "I will see to the tickets in just a moment. But before we do that, I should tell you I have been a guide here for many years, just like my father before me. I practically grew up on this hill," he said, waving his arm at the ruins on the hillside. "I know many of the secrets of the ruins, and I would be happy to share them with you, especially as our families are friends, and you have clearly done much study to prepare for this trip. I can show you things no other tour guide can."

"That sounds wonderful," Ethan said.

Emily thought there must be a catch—a "but" just waiting to come out. A moment later she was proven right.

"Of course, I can show you those things," he said, "but I will need some additional money. This is an add-on to the basic tour and costs a little more."

Ethan turned to Emily. "Can I talk to you a minute?"

"That's a good idea," she said, and they went back toward the bus, where Jorge couldn't overhear. Emily watched him turn to the kiosk and begin to negotiate for the tickets before she said anything.

"He's already overcharged us," Emily said. "Didn't you give him more than we agreed?"

Ethan nodded. "It wasn't very much more, and in dollars it adds up to be about the same amount. I thought he was just taking his fee adjusted for inflation. I don't think he was robbing us."

"Still," Emily said, "I wonder about him. We have this extra tour offer all of a sudden. Why not tell us about it when we were exchanging email the last six months? Why spring it on us now?"

"I'm sure it's just a matter of him using his expertise to make more money. There's nothing wrong with that."

"No," said Emily, "But there's something about it I don't like."

Ethan turned toward the arch, the gateway to the ruins. "We ought to consider it. We did come here to get more than a basic tour, didn't we?"

If you think the private tour sounds fun, turn to page 210.

If you think Jorge is trying to take advantage, turn to page 181.

Emily lay on her back with the impossible blue of the sky above her and let the sun creep along her body from her head down towards her middle. Truth was, she didn't feel like she would ever get up again. How could she have let her bag go? How could she have let her important documents, the critical things that she needed, out of her immediate possession?

She knew better. Had known better. But the earthquake came so quickly and the order to evacuate followed so irresistibly that she had been swept along by it. Now she was useless, without hope, stuck in a city with no food, no water, just hoping she and her brother could figure out some way to get out of this situation. The stadium rang with shouts, cries of stress, and here and there even a joyful reunion. Emily just felt empty. She knew she had made a terrible mistake. What she didn't know was how to fix it.

The stadium itself was a large one, probably the largest in the city. Around the edge of the upper concourse hung banners representing various champions. There were not too many of those. It appeared that Takewawa's soccer team had not been overly successful.

The stadium itself did not appear to be much damaged. The stands were still perfectly oval, no sagging anywhere, and there were no cracks in the concrete that she could see. Every half hour or so the ground would rumble, but nothing like the horrible shaking that had engulfed them at the airport.

Government officials of various kinds milled around on the track setting up tables and preparing to take people's names. Around her people attempted to call on cell phones but there was no cell service; at least, no one that she saw had had any success at all in finding reception. They tried repeatedly until their batteries ran out, but got nothing but frustration.

Ethan had wandered off toward the north end of the stadium to try to find water, as he said he was getting very thirsty. Truthfully, Emily was getting thirsty too, but she would rather have died than admit it. She had caused enough trouble already.

Alone, with nothing to do, Emily picked out officials and watched them to see what their jobs were. If the twins were going to get help, it would come from there. One of the officials over on the south end had a walkie-talkie into which he spoke periodically. He was the only one she had seen with any outside communication. After fifteen minutes or so of watching, Emily got up, making sure she knew exactly where her spot on the grass was—she had begun thinking of it as "home"—and threaded her way through the crowd in that direction.

When she reached the official, he was just talking on the walkie-talkie again. He said, "Yes. We have about five thousand people here. They need water, food, and medical supplies." He let go of the transmit button and listened for a reply.

The walkie-talkie squawked at him and a voice came out the other end but the Spanish was so fast and so garbled from the walkie-talkie's tinny speaker she couldn't make out what it said. It wasn't good, though, judging by the frown on the face of the official. He punched the button again in some anger, "And then what am I supposed to tell these people?" he said.

The walkie-talkie squawked at him again, and a flurry of Spanish erupted from it. He clicked it off in disgust and clipped it to his belt.

"Excuse me," Emily said.

He picked his head up slightly and looked at her out of the corner of his eye. When he saw a blonde, obviously American girl standing there he just shook his head. "I'm sorry, Miss. There's nothing I can do to help."

"I'm not looking for help," Emily said. "I just want to ask a question."

"Yes?" he said, dubious.

"Is the American Embassy working to help Americans get home?" she said.

"At some point," he said, "they probably will be, but not today. The embassy was heavily damaged by the earthquake. They have a temporary location, I'm sure, but no one has told me where that is. I'm afraid you'll have to stay here."

"Thank you," Emily said. "I know you're doing your best." And she turned to walk away.

"Wait," the man said. He glanced down to the radio on his belt, and back to her. Something in his face softened. "I do have a contact that might be able to get a hold of the embassy personnel, if you would like me to try."

"Yes," Emily said. "I would very much. But if you have more important things to do I understand."

"No, no," the man said, and spat onto the track. The dust and loose grass swallowed it up. "It would be nice to be able to solve someone's problem today. I fear it will be a long time before we are able to solve very many."

"I'll be right over there, almost inside the center circle," Emily said, pointing.

The man nodded, fiddled with the dial on his walkie-talkie, and punched the button again.

Toward the middle of the afternoon, the officials got themselves sorted out and began to call groups of people over. They took their names and addresses, had them show whatever ID they had—very few people actually had any—and wrote their names down on a long list.

"Why are they not using computers?" Emily said.

"It wouldn't do any good," Ethan said. "There's no cell reception so there's no internet. The computers can't talk to each other. Power has to be spotty at best. Paper will be a lot easier to carry back and forth from place to place." And indeed, a large number of cars and buses kept coming in and out of the stadium, mostly dropping people off, but also exchanging groups of officials and security personnel. There were a fair number of gun-toting security guards around the outside of the track around the camp.

It was getting on towards six o'clock by Ethan's watch when they got around to calling for their group. They lined up in front of a table. Standing behind it was the security official that she had spoken to earlier. When they had reached the front of the table, Ethan handed over his passport, "I am Ethan Tuttle," he said. "This is my sister Emily Tuttle, and we're here on vacation."

"Some vacation," Emily muttered under her breath.

The official behind the table recognized Emily. "Ah," he said. "I've spoken to the American Embassy. They would like to help you, but just now they are very short-staffed, as you might imagine. The embassy itself was hit hard by the earthquake, but they do have a temporary embassy for American refugees, and they will be moving people there in the next couple of days. We will get you on the bus to their location as soon as we can." He held out his hand for Emily's ID.

She turned her hand over, palm up, empty. "I'm sorry," she said. "My ID is still in the airport. I don't have it with me."

He frowned a little and shook his head, but more like he was sad than angry. "That's a very common story," he said. "I have been hearing it a lot today. We'll do what we can to help you."

Turn to page 236.

Ethan and Emily walked a short distance to talk privately. "We could wait for the bus to get fixed, but I'm looking at this inn here," Ethan said, half-turning, "and this row of cars," turning back, "and thinking it's awfully convenient that the breakdown happened to come exactly where it did. I think it's possible—no, I think it's *likely*—that this happens all the time." He eyed the taxi driver suspiciously.

Emily said, "It does seem awfully convenient. Why would they be here if this wasn't something they knew they could count on?"

"But think about this—that also probably means that they are legitimate taxi drivers," Ethan said. "The policeman seemed to know them, and he left them alone. I think if we're careful, it will be okay."

Emily said, "If you're game, I am," and together they dragged their suitcases across the parking lot to the driver's car. His face lit up in a smile again.

"I see you've decided. Let me put your luggage in the back of the car." He popped the trunk and the twins wheeled their luggage around to the rear where he put their suitcases in the trunk and closed it with a thump.

"You won't regret this," he said. "This will be much faster."

"Also more expensive," Ethan said.

The taxi driver waved this away. "Only if you didn't spend any money to get to Allqukilla. You did, didn't you?"

"Of course."

"Well, then. How much of that money did you want to waste standing in the aisle of a stinking country bus?" He eyed Ethan for a moment, then nodded. "That's what I thought."

"You still haven't told us how much this trip is going to be," Emily said.

He considered them a moment, his hand on his chin. "Tell you what. You give me 2400 saladera, and I'll take you wherever you need to go in Ychu."

Emily thought for a moment. Ethan was a bit faster with the math. "That's around thirty-five dollars. I think that works."

Emily took a look back at the bus, and shrugged. "Okay. You're paying, though," she said to Ethan. "You're the one that has the extra local currency."

The taxi driver started the car, and they were on their way.

Once they were pulling out of the parking lot, Ethan said, "Will you tell me the truth if I ask you a question?"

The driver looked up from the road, surprised. "Sure," he said.

"Are you parked out here by accident, or did you know the bus was going to break down?"

The man's eyes widened in astonishment and then he began to chuckle until he was finally laughing heartily. The car swerved a little as he got control of himself again. "You're pretty smart kids," he said. "Most people don't figure that out for a long time, if they ever figure it out at all."

"We were suspicious," Ethan said.

"And you should be," the man said. "We have an arrangement with the bus driver to have that bus breakdown a couple of times a month. You just happened to draw the lucky ride."

"Now I suppose you're going to take us somewhere in the wilderness and rob us," Ethan said.

The man began laughing again and this time he was laughing so hard he had to pull the car over to the side and stop. When he got control of himself tears were streaming down his face, "Boy, you Americans are so funny," he said. "If I did something like that, do you think the bus driver, or the other taxi drivers, or the policeman at the inn would let me keep running the route? There is no way I could do that, cutting into their business like that, and scaring tourists away." After a second he pulled out again and kept going, but every few seconds he'd break into another chuckle.

As the car wended its way, the rocky dry terrain gave way to greener, lusher scenery with canopies of trees, vines, and undergrowth. A mist began to collect above them in the hills. Then they rounded a curve, and there below them was Ychu.

It sat in a large bowl, in a crescent of emerald around the east shore of a sapphire lake. At the far western edge, a mirror crescent of alabaster marked the Takewawa Dam, the source of power for the capital city and the reason Ychu Lake existed in the first place. The sun glinted off the lake into their eyes, as if the whole valley shimmered.

In the back seat, Emily gasped.

The driver gave a knowing smile. "I never get tired of the view."

"How much farther to Ychu?" Ethan asked him, his face pressed to the glass on the passenger's side.

"About a half an hour," the driver said. "We can go much quicker in the car than you would have in the bus."

"Is the bus really broken down?" Ethan said.

"Well," he said, "with that old clunker, there's sure to be some sort of mechanical problem Luis can be working on. Maybe he will decide it's working again, or maybe another bus will come along. Either way, you will be in Ychu sooner than they will be."

The car made the pitted road significantly less bumpy. Ethan and Emily found that they were sincerely enjoying the ride. In addition, the driver had interesting knowledge of things that were happening in the countryside. "You will love the village of Ychu. The resort town is very nice and the people at the hotel are quite friendly. The lake is beautiful this time of year."

"What about the ruins?" Ethan said. "Those are the things we care most about."

"The ruins will talk to you themselves," the man said. "I don't need to tell you anything about them. If you've come all this way by yourselves, then you've studied, and nothing I can say will make them any more magical than you will find them when you get there."

After a moment, he added, "I should warn you, the exchange rate at the hotel is not very good. You should make sure you use the ATMs when you want saladera."

"I think that's our hotel!" Ethan said, pointing. Right on the lake shore perched a building of white stone with an inlaid roof of red and blue tile. It was one of the most beautiful buildings she had ever seen. Out on the lake, boats swished back and forth, some with water skiers trailing behind them.

The driver turned to them and said, "You are very lucky to be coming at this time of year. This is the perfect time to visit Ychu; the weather is outstanding. The only difficulty is if the earthquake finally happens, but they are always predicting earthquakes in this part of the mountains, and we never get any. I'm sure you will be fine."

The car swiftly descended into the valley. The road got much better the closer they got to town.

"What direction are the Ychurichuc ruins?" Emily said. The driver pointed off to the left, to a thin ribbon of asphalt leading east up into the mountains through a narrow canyon.

"The ruins are that way, about fifteen miles," he said. "It is an easy bus trip, and the bus goes directly from the hotel. You will have no problems."

Moments later the car pulled up in front of the hotel. Ethan turned his back, drew out some of his secret stash, and began to count out saladera.

"Or dollars," the driver said. "Those are fine as well."

"Really?" Emily said. "Why is it that people are so interested in taking U.S. money instead of the currency of the country they live in?"

"Well," said the driver, "your government is not very fiscally responsible, but our government is much worse. Your money has a better chance of holding its value than ours does. In fact, ours is losing about twenty to thirty percent a month."

"That much!" Ethan said.

"That seems like an awfully high rate of inflation," Emily said. "We learned about inflation from our dad and grandpa."

"Yes," the man said, "it is losing value that fast. The government has decided to print money in order to pay its large debt. For example, I have to buy gas every time I drive from the inn to Ychu. Monday this week, I filled the car up for 1800 saladera. Wednesday, it cost 1850. Today? Probably 1950 or so."

"That's awful!" Emily said. "It's like the money in your wallet is disappearing."

"That's exactly what it's like. As if someone were reaching into my wallet every day and taking money out of it. And it's not just gasoline, either. It's bread, and potatoes, and rent. Things people need."

"I'll pay you in dollars, then," Ethan said. "And you keep them as long as you can to save the value." Ethan handed over a small pile of bills.

"That will be plenty," the man said, smiling. "Let me get your bags out of the trunk."

Turn to page 27.

The cordial part of the interview ended. Ethan and Emily were told to step outside and wait for transportation to the American-only camp.

"That wasn't very encouraging," Ethan said once they were through the doors and standing in the smoky sunshine. "I don't think they're very pleased that we're here."

"That makes two of us," Emily said.

"I sure wish we could get a message to Mom and Dad," Ethan said. "But I don't suppose there's much hope of that."

"We have the freedom of the town, don't we?" Emily asked. "I mean, we're not like prisoners or anything. We can go wherever we want to go."

"Ye-es," Ethan said, doubtfully. "I would think we would want to stay here by the embassy as much as possible. What if the transport comes and we're not here?"

"This isn't really much of an embassy," Emily said. "It's more like a temp agency. A temp-bassy." Ethan smothered a laugh.

Emily continued. "They're just trying to scrape by and figure out what to do with all these people who landed on their doorstep. They don't have a whole lot of resources, and they're not going to be inclined to help us more than the minimum." She tipped her head at the guard, who gazed out across the ruined city with no more expression on his face than a Greek statue. "No offense," she said.

"None taken," the guard said, with the barest twitch of a smile.

"I think they're doing the best they can," Ethan said.

"That's actually what I'm afraid of," Emily said, "that this is the best they can do. It's possible we could do better if we did some things ourselves."

Ethan shaded his eyes a little against the sun. The embassy sat on a small rise, and he could see down the street a little ways in each direction. What he could see was not at all encouraging. "There isn't likely to be a whole lot of help out there," Ethan said, waving his arm at a road leading off to the north.

Down the street on one block, half of an apartment building had fallen into the street. Dirty-looking people picked through the rubble, looking for who knows what.

"I mean," Ethan said, "look at that." Down another street to their left, the pavement had been cleaved in two by a wide crack in the earth. "We're not going to get very far if the whole city looks like this."

"No," Emily said, "but the truth is if *we* can't get very far, *they* can't get very far, either." She pointed at the temp-bassy. "Especially when it comes to getting a message to Mom and Dad, they're not going to go out of their way to help us. There has to be a way for us to do that. The entire city can't be completely cut off from communication with the outside world."

Ethan frowned. "What do you suggest?"

"What's in your emergency battle plan? I know you have one, you always do. What did you plan to do if everything went completely to pieces around us, it was just the two of us, and there was no one to help?"

Ethan though for a moment. Acrid smoke, not thick, but in the smell of every breath, burned the back of his throat. Fires burned in several places, as if the entire city were sitting on top of an active volcano. Sulfur stench mingled with the odor of diesel fuel and burning wood.

"The plan would be to find a place to get a message to the outside world, some sort of internet establishment or place that has a satellite phone," Ethan said.

"I bet they have one in there," Emily said, jerking her thumb back toward the door of the embassy. "But I don't suppose they're going to let us use it to call Mom. We'll have to find one of those on our own. There has to be someplace in town where we can do that."

"I guess there would be," Ethan said, "if we could get there. If we even knew where to go."

"We can work this out," Emily said. "We're smart people. I know we've never been through anything like this before, but that's one of the things that makes it fun."

"Fun?" Ethan said, arching an eyebrow. "You're not seriously using that word for this situation, are you?"

"Of course I am," Emily said. "It may not be the kind of fun that we would have at Disneyland, but it's still fun." She didn't have to say that there was another kind of fun they had been planning to have on this trip that hadn't come about exactly the way they had expected. "At least," she said, "I'm going to try to have as much fun as I possibly can. Come on! This is another one of those puzzles that you love so much. Where would we find a satellite phone?"

Ethan turned a slow 360-degree swivel, looking down each street as far as he could see. After a while, he stopped, facing southwest. He pointed. "Do you see that?" Ethan said. "A few blocks down."

Emily shaded her eyes and peered in that direction. "Is there something on top of that building? I can't quite tell what it is."

"I think those are solar panels."

Emily shot him a glance. "That's genius," she said. "If there's any place in town that still has power, it will be one of the places that doesn't have to run on a city grid."

Ethan nodded. "That's what I was thinking," he said. "The only place we could find power will be someplace that can produce it on its own. That kind of place may have other sorts of benefits that we can appreciate in this particular situation."

Emily's stomach rumbled. She placed a hand over it and grimaced. "What time is it?"

"It's a little after 11," Ethan said. "I'm hungry, too. A taco truck would sure come in handy about now, no matter what kind of government regulations it has to obey."

Emily grinned, remembering one of their adventures back when they were younger. "That *was* pretty cool, wasn't it? Those guys were in a tight spot!"

"I also would really like to check out any place that has a solar panel and what looks like a bunch of electronic equipment bristling from the top of the building. We can wander down there, and if it doesn't check out, wander back here. It won't take us very long to do that."

A few people milled about at the entrance to the embassy, but the bus was gone and the line had been processed. The guard went inside and brought out a crate of water bottles. He tossed one to each of the twins, who thanked him and drank deeply.

"If we go, we might miss something. Even though it's only a few blocks, who knows what could happen? It might be safer to stay here," Ethan said.

He looked at Emily to see what her response would be.

If you think they should wait at the embassy, turn to page 350.

If you think they should check out the Internet Cafe, turn to page 260.

The refugee camp was better than Emily expected. Yes, it was dirty and dusty. Yes, it was placed on a stretch of ground that was about the worst in this part of the world. Yes, it was cramped and there were thousands of people crammed into it. But there was enough food to go around, though bland, and there were facilities both for taking in food and for eliminating it later on.

The Ecuadorian guards treated them with respect, not as if they were invading the country, but as if they were people who simply had nowhere else to go. Since that was what Emily though the definition of a refugee was, she felt like that was not too much to ask.

"Not that we have refugee camps in the States," she said to Ethan as they lay in their tent the first night. "But if we did, I would expect them to be like this."

"We *have* had something similar," Ethan said. "They were called internment camps, or concentration camps, and it's been a little while. But they weren't too much different than this, although I think accommodations were slightly better."

They had said an awkward farewell to Travis a few hours before. Travis had skillfully negotiated the border crossing, but hadn't been able to do anything, even with her mysterious Doctor Who-style magic paperwork, to eliminate the difficulty of Emily not having a passport.

"I'm sorry," Travis said, looking a little down in the mouth, "they're being very strict about passport control. Although it's pretty obvious that a fifteen-year-old blonde who speaks perfect English and middling Spanish is almost certainly not an Allqukillan citizen and everyone in their right mind knows you hail from the States, the fact is you don't have the paperwork to prove it, so they are going shunt you aside into the refugee camp, instead of allowing you to go on to Quito and get a flight out of the country."

Emily was crestfallen. Ethan seemed a little unhappy himself.

"You can still go," Travis said to Ethan, "although it would shock me if you wanted to."

"Of course I don't," Ethan said. "Wherever Emily is, that's where I need to be as well."

"I expected you would say that," Travis said. "Which is why I already told them that both of you will be going to the camp."

Ethan's mouth dropped open a little, and he looked as he was about to protest, perhaps because he didn't like to be taken for granted, but then he seemed to realize that being taken for granted for being a gentleman who did noble things to protect others was probably a good thing, and he clamped his mouth shut again.

Emily could see the difficulty that he had in saying goodbye to Travis, and she had to admit that Travis had been a terrific traveling companion. "If we ever get back this way again," Emily said, "we'll be sure to look you up."

"I would look forward to that," Travis said, "although I don't know what we would do together, since you're unlikely to need my particular brand of services, and I don't spend a lot of time sightseeing."

"Still," Ethan said as if he were scrambling to come up with something, "you never know. Maybe there are some things we could do that would at least allow us to see one another."

Even Travis couldn't miss the open desire on his face to make that happen, and she smiled kindly at him and gave him a hug. "That sounds nice," she said. "Maybe we can do something like that. I think it will be quite a while before anybody comes to Allqukilla for tourist activities, however. They have quite a mess to clean up down there."

She saw them safely to the front of the refugee camp, put them in the hands of the two Ecuadorian guards at the front of the camp, and drove off, waving out the side window of the Sentra. Emily and Ethan hefted their backpacks and trudged into the camp where they were assigned a tent on the far northern edge.

"It could be worse," Ethan said, "we could be in the middle, where all of the smell of collected humanity would descend on us."

"It's thick enough here," Emily said. "Although I'm sure we're contributing to it."

"Hey," Ethan said, "I don't smell yet. I had a shower less than 24 hours ago."

"You will be in the morning," Emily said, and she was right.

They had only been in the camp a day or so when personnel from the American Embassy in Quito arrived in the camp to start trying to identify and process Americans who were stranded there. As it turned out, there weren't very many Americans in the camp at all. Emily and Ethan got an audience very quickly, and an efficient caseworker named Pam promised to be able to do something to help them out within a couple of days.

Best, she was able to connect them to a satellite phone so that they could call home and let their parents know where they were and what was going on.

"They say we'll be able to get out of here in less than a week," Ethan said.

"What's the food like?" Mom said.

"It's bland, mostly rice and beans, but sometimes we get a little chicken. If you could order us a pizza, that would be really great."

"I think the pizza will have to wait until you get home," Dad said, "but we will surely be waiting with one at the airport."

Three days later, the tickets were arranged, and the permission was granted for them to fly out of the country. On a plane packed with Americans, most of whom had migrated north out of Allqukilla, Emily and Ethan were finally able to head home.

It hadn't been the adventure that they had expected. They had learned a tremendous amount about money, about inflation, and about how easy it is for people to lose trust in the currency that has always been their medium of exchange. They had found good people, bad people, and a whole lot of people in between.

"It's weird," Ethan said, "In the end, I don't feel like I got ripped off at all."

"I know what you mean," Emily said, "It wasn't the trip we were expecting, but it certainly was something that we'll be able to talk about for a long time."

"And who knows," Ethan said. "Maybe one day we'll have a chance to come back."

Emily knew what, and whom, he was thinking of, and smiled a little. Their plane taxied down the runway. "I look forward to planning another trip with you as soon as you feel up to it," she said.

Ethan chuckled a little bit. "Maybe we could wait on that one a while."

THE END

"I just don't trust this guy to show us anything," Emily said.

"That's that, then. We shouldn't take his offer," Ethan replied. "Besides, he's just going to want dollars, and I want to keep as many of those as possible."

"Okay," Emily said, "but he's waiting. It looks like he's got our tickets."

Across the parking lot Jorge flashed them one of his toothy grins.

The day lay beautiful around them, bright sunshine with a clear blue sky. Exotic birds flitted back and forth in the trees to the side of the parking lot. Gray in the sunshine, the staircase led up into the ruins themselves.

They stepped across the parking lot towards Jorge.

"We decided not to take your offer," Ethan said, and as an afterthought, "Although, thank you very much. We appreciate it."

Jorge's mouth dropped into a tight line. "All right. I was expecting something a little more adventurous from someone whose family came so highly recommended."

"I guess we're just not the adventurous types," Emily said, meeting his gaze levelly.

Jorge turned without a word and walked over to the arch at the gate to the ruins. "We have to wait for just a minute for a couple other people to get here," he said.

"We have another couple of families who will be coming on the tour with us."

"Just a minute" turned into ten, then fifteen, and still they stood there in the sunshine, slowly baking into the gravel and mud of the parking lot. The humidity felt like they needed scuba gear just to breathe. Animals, unseen, made their harsh calls in the bush. Fronds waved as beasts passed by in the underbrush. Eventually a small knot of additional tourists arrived and met up with Jorge. They seemed unsure of themselves and kept looking around as if they didn't really want to be there.

One of the families, with a shifting cloud of children, was clearly Latino, with an accent that sounded Mexican to Ethan's untrained ears. He introduced himself and his sister and the group shook hands, the littlest boy hiding shyly behind his mother. One father and mother were joined by their two daughters, both of them not yet ten years old. Possibly twins, Ethan thought, but he didn't ask.

"We have one more family due to arrive," Jorge announced, and a few minutes later they did—an older couple in their 60s, from Guatemala. With them came a younger man—not much more than a boy, really, eighteen years old or so—who Ethan thought must be a grandson.

A round of introductions were made, and money flowed into Jorge's hands. He did not offer the special tour to the other groups, which surprised Ethan. After the tickets were purchased, they stood in line for a moment. Then they were inside.

As soon as they passed through the gates, it seemed as if the air was cleaner, brighter. The sun shone clearer. All the colors seemed more vibrant as well. The grass under their feet took on a deeper shade of emerald. The calling of the birds and other animals from the jungle became louder and more insistent, as if they had stepped into another world.

Ethan glanced at Emily. Her face shone as if she couldn't believe where she was or what she was doing. And ahead of them, the great staircase leading up to the ruins.

"Now, these are not the original stairs," Jorge said, assuming a tour-guide stance and voice. "These are replicas. The originals were destroyed by the Spanish when the conquistadors eliminated most traces of Inca civilization, especially religious sites such as this one."

Ethan was only half paying attention, but he couldn't help thinking that governments these days were still doing similar things, only in modern times religion was less important. Now the government made sure it controlled the thing most people wanted and worshipped instead: money.

Ethan took in every detail—the shapes of the carvings and the green of the moss as it grew between the flagstones of the stairs as they ascended the side of the hill. The group made its way up with other small groups ahead of and behind them. Jorge spoke softly enough that the words were too low for Ethan to be able to make them out.

"He's very quiet," the young boy said, leaning against one of the stone blocks at the side of the staircase. "That is quite refreshing. Usually the tour guides bellow like cattle." He spoke English well, although with a thick accent—exotic, not Allqukillan, Ethan thought.

"You come here a lot? You have experience with this?" Emily said, without looking up from the stones.

"Some," he said.

Emily stood and brushed the dirt from her pants. "Well, this Jorge guy has been guiding here for several years now, and…" She stopped as she caught sight of the boy she was addressing.

He wasn't tall, not any taller than she was, with dark hair and eyes. His jeans were worn, but his shirt—it wasn't really a shirt, but some sort of tunic—was new, and possibly homespun. Who wore homespun clothes these days?

"I'm sure he has been," the boy said. "I've seen him around. He's better than the others, though there's something about him I don't entirely trust."

"Who are you?" Ethan said. The tour group moved up a couple more steps. Jorge kept up a running chatter but paid the twins no attention at all.

"Just a kid from over the hill," he said.

"I'm Ethan."

"Thon."

"That's an unusual name," Emily said.

"Not among my people."

"My name's Emily."

Thon nodded at her, just once. "I like that name." He smiled. Ethan saw her ears grow red.

"Are you just here for the tour?" Thon asked.

"We actually wanted to see everything," Ethan said, "Not just the stuff everyone gets to see."

"Everything?"

"Well, yeah," Emily said. "We studied and planned for this trip for years. It took us every cent we saved just to get here. This is a dream."

"My sister means that we feel like we couldn't come all this way and just see the stuff we could have watched on YouTube."

Thon gazed at the tour group, now cresting the stairs. "You want to go with them? Because I can show you other things. Even things he can't," he said, pointing at Jorge.

"How much?" Ethan said.

"How much what?"

"Money. You want us to pay you, don't you?"

Thon's face was priceless. He stood there like a codfish, his mouth agape. "Pay me? What for?"

Emily smiled, and caught Ethan's eye. "That decides it for me. How about you?"

If you think the twins should take the opportunity to hang out with a local, turn to page 8.

If you think the twins should stay with Jorge, turn to page 335.

The line at the counter stretched out to infinity. Apparently they weren't the only ones who thought it might be better to get out of town quickly. Ethan and Emily found themselves sandwiched between a nervous businessman and three teenagers in battle fatigues. None of them seemed to believe that patience was a virtue.

The three fatigue-wearing teens were talking in a hectic mix of Spanish, English, and a language Emily didn't recognize. Their conversation seemed to consist mainly of insults to the country in general and the airport in particular. The businessman in front of them checked his watch about every twenty seconds and followed each look with a sigh that seemed to come all the way from his toes.

One of the teens staggered a bit and bumped into Emily. His short friend growled at her as if it were her fault, but the one who had stumbled put out his hand to calm him down.

"Sorry," he said to Emily with a thick accent. "Is no fun standing line."

He had a mop of dark hair that his camo cap did very little to keep under wraps and dark eyes that seemed to have no bottom.

"It's not fun, is it?" Emily said.

The eyes went from Emily to Ethan and back to Emily again. "You come here vacation? Holiday?"

She nodded. "Only, we didn't get any holiday. We saw the earthquake warning and are checking to see if we can move our tickets and leave... earlier." She didn't want to say that they'd only gotten there about two hours ago and hadn't even left the airport yet.

The boy laughed. "Is very smart. Soon the big one, yes?" He began shaking around like an extra in a Star Trek episode with the ship under fire.

Even Ethan began to chuckle as the line moved forward a few inches. Emily said, "Is that why you're leaving, too?"

He translated that to his buddies, who scowled and turned away. "We from Ecuador," the boy said. "Our holiday over. We go back to Ecuador army now."

"You're in the army?" she said, hoping she didn't sound as impressed as she actually was.

"Sí," he said, and flashed a bright smile at her. "They call us back yesterday in case problem with earth shake."

"Really?" she said, checking to see if Ethan was listening. He was. "It's probably a good thing we're going, then."

"Very smart girl," the boy said, tapping his temple. "But last time nothing happen. Maybe this time nothing happen again."

Emily thought about that all the way up to the counter, where, it turned out, the airline was filling up the return flight. They would have to stay for a few hours in the airport, but then they could get onboard and head back to the US.

She hoped that the boys behind them—well, just the one, actually—would be able to take an hour or so and show them around the country while they were waiting, so they could at least say they'd been there and done something with their time. As it turns out, his flight was only an hour away and already boarding.

Emily said goodbye with a handshake, maybe slightly longer than custom demanded, and lounged around the airport with her brother until the flight was ready to take off. Ethan called Mom and Dad from one of the phones in the lobby and explained the situation.

"We saw the earthquake warning, too," Dad said. "It seems pretty serious. This doesn't sound like the usual attempt to make news out of nothing."

"That's what we thought," Ethan said, but he didn't sound happy about it. "There are a lot of people here trying to get out of the country. If we hadn't rebooked when we did, I don't know if we'd have been able to get a flight."

"Smart move then," Dad said. "Although I'm sorry about your trip. After you worked so hard for it, too."

"Yeah. Well, the ruins aren't going anywhere. We can always come back after we win the lottery."

Ethan said goodbye, and that was that. Mom had sounded happy to get them back sooner.

"We're doing the right thing," he said to Emily, but she could tell he was trying to convince himself more than anyone else.

The plane ride home was awful. Neither of them wanted to say a word. All they could think about was the money they'd worked so hard to save only to have it flushed away on a trip they decided to end early.

At least they had gotten a passport stamp and had seen another country—albeit for a very brief time. They hadn't wasted everything.

But it felt like they had.

Continue to next page...

Afterward

As it turns out, an earthquake did strike Allqukilla shortly after Ethan and Emily left. It was a small one, only 4.3 on the Richter scale. There was minor damage to the city, a few power lines downed, and a water main broke, flooding part of the downtown area. But no lasting damage was done. The ruins were unaffected, and business in the country carried on as usual.

Almost.

The country's already large amount of debt made it difficult for them to pay their bills. Their central bank used the earthquake as a reason to create more money out of thin air. It was like watching an old newsreel as the saladera spiraled out of control. Inflation hit 25%. 40%. 110%. 1,000%. People carried satchels full of cash to pay for a simple meal. It reminded Dad of hyperinflation in Germany after World War I when people would carry cash in wheelbarrows to pay for basic items.

The twins watched the news feeds from the country every chance they got, watching the country's currency become less and less valuable, until it was almost worthless. Things got very bad in Allqukilla.

Maybe one day the twins would get another chance to go. At least it'd be a lot cheaper than their first try.

THE END

"I think there's a bench over against the wall you can lie down on when we get tired," Emily said. They trudged over to the long wooden bench, dragging their luggage with them.

Through the long, long night they took turns trying to get some sleep and watching over their baggage. But around three in the morning, Emily couldn't last any longer and drifted off. Fortunately, their bags were untouched when they woke up. Emily apologized to Ethan, but he was too heartsick to care very much.

"It's only five," she said. "You want to get some more sleep?"

"I *want* to. I haven't slept very much, though. The bench digs into my back. I think I'd like to get up and walk around." He stood and stretched, and looked down at their little area. "We can't leave our bags here unattended. I guess we'll have to drag them with us."

It was Emily's turn to stretch, and precisely at that moment the ground shifted violently under their feet. Emily fell on her side with a cry. Behind them came a grinding crash. A row of lockers to their left toppled over and smashed against the floor. Goods from the broken doors spilled over the floor. The ground wouldn't hold still. The walls swayed and pictures fell, sending glass shards like heat-seeking missiles skidding across the tile. People went down like dominoes.

This was nothing like the first earthquake. This was the real thing.

Ethan and Emily crawled under their bench, using it as protection. They took each others' hands and stared in horror as the airport fell apart around them. "We should have left last night," Emily shouted over the noise.

"We didn't know," Ethan shouted back, suddenly hoarse. "What are we going to do?"

It seemed to take an hour, perhaps two, before the ground stopped shaking. Tiles continued falling from the ceiling, smashing on the floor. People slowly began to crawl out from underneath their shelter as sirens wailed in the distance.

An elderly lady had fallen to the ground nearby, lying in the dust and smoke. Emily dashed over to help pick her up. All around were people who had been knocked down by the force of the earthquake and were struggling to get to their feet. Staggering across the floor, they headed for the airline counters, but the lights flickered and went out. Ethan crawled out behind Emily. The only light in the airport came from the outside windows.

"Do you think the airplanes can take off okay if the airport doesn't have power?" Ethan asked.

"I guess the earthquake could take out the power, but wouldn't they have backups?" Emily asked. Off to the left, walking slowly toward the front windows, a couple spoke quickly back and forth in heavily-accented Spanish. Ethan and Emily listened closely, but their speech was hard to make out. They were clearly local to Allqukilla, and they seemed very alarmed.

Ethan nodded as he tried to listen. "They say the backups are only for emergencies, not air traffic. And nothing could knock the power out except losing the dam," Ethan said.

"I'm sure there are power lines between here and there," Emily said. "Perhaps one of them got cut."

"That's possible," Ethan said, "but either way I don't think this is going to be a good place to be for some time."

A groan came from a nearby wall, and a crack snaked up the face of it.

"We have to get out of here," Emily said.

"We can't carry our luggage. Outside could be even worse than here in the airport," Ethan crouched, scanning the ceiling, and took a deep breath. "Well, one way or the other, we've got to go now."

"We can't even call Mom and Dad until they get power back—and my guess is that this isn't the only place in the city where it's dark." Emily kicked aside a chunk of debris and held out her hand for Ethan.

People huddled together in the darkness. "I'm not sure if we should go somewhere or stay inside," Emily said.

"All I know is, there aren't big steel beams to fall on you when you're outside," Ethan said. "Let's go."

The twins worked their way across the floor. A line of people paraded behind them, following their path. "Tell me that in your emergency planning you have marked where the embassy is," Emily said.

"Of course I do," Ethan said. "The problem is, it's on the other side of town."

"That's a long walk."

Ethan nodded grimly. "I feel like we're probably in for a long walk no matter where we go."

Outside, the sirens closed in.

Dust rolled through the lobby of the airport, pushed by an unseen wind. Something farther inside the airport had collapsed. Ethan and Emily covered their mouths to keep from breathing in all the dust.

Security personnel with brightly colored uniforms poured from every door, shouting at people in Spanish to get out of the airport. "You've got to move," a uniformed man said in Spanish to the twins, grabbing Ethan by the arm. "Out the door and into the parking lot."

Emily cast a longing look back at their bags but did as she was told.

"You must move right now!" the security guard said, unnecessarily, shoving them forward.

The front doors were only ten or twelve feet away, but the press of people being shoved ahead kept them from reaching it. The security men acted as human bulldozers, shoving the group ahead of them.

No bags, Emily thought. All their clothing, most of their money. "My passport!" Emily said, her gut shrinking in horror. She shoved back in a futile attempt to get back to the bags, just for a second, but it was too late. There was no getting to it.

Ethan grabbed her hand. "We'll make it work," he said. "I still have mine."

They were forced forward. The clear glass door at the front of the airport showed the dim light of very early morning. The sun had not yet risen over the far peaks. Only a soft glow diffused across the eastern sky. It should have been beautiful. Instead, people screamed and wept, some clutching each other. The crowd was relentlessly forced farther and farther away from the airport by security personnel. Sirens, once distant, drew ever closer.

The air was better here. Emily inhaled raggedly, blew it out, inhaled again. Right at the front of the airport, a concrete overhang showed cracks that had not been there the day before.

"Farther!" the policemen shouted. "Farther out into the open area."

Beyond the concrete overhang, the large open area formed a traffic circle. It had been decorated with flowers and a sign that said "Welcome to Takewawa." The sign had fallen, crushing the native blossoms. More sirens blared as police cars and an ambulance came roaring into the parking lot, narrowly missing the group the twins were a part of. A thousand or more people were squished into the garden area in front of the airport, spilling off the concrete ring and into the roundabout. Babies cried and children wailed for their parents, looking around frantically, hoping to catch sight of them. More people kept streaming out of the airport, pushing the group farther and farther into the garden area. Security people kept everyone away from the front of the airport.

Ethan saw the frantic look on Emily's face. He knew he had to say something. "At least we are together," he said. "We'll work something out. I've got most of my money."

Emily looked miserable. "Most of mine is back in my bag," she said, "along with my documents. I shouldn't have put them in there but we were just going to get on an airplane! I didn't think I'd need them again."

"It's okay," Ethan said. "We won't be the only ones in this kind of trouble."

Indeed, in the thousand or so people congregated in front of the airport, there were plenty who were obviously not locals, and many of them were also without their luggage. All of that was lost inside the airport. Two long buses started loading people on. The security guards shuffled people onto the bus as if they were raking leaves. Many of the passengers did not want to get onto the bus, and it was clear that the security guards were going to force them to do so.

"We have to get out of here," he heard one of them say to an airport worker. "There is trouble with the dam." If that was true—and, judging from the scurrying about and shouting, it easily could be—Ethan knew things were going to get very bad very fast. The airport sat on a plateau just above a riverbed. The Takewawa River flowed past the airport and out toward the sea. Damming the Takewawa formed the reservoir that provided the entertainment for the tourists at Ychu.

The dam also supplied hydroelectric power to most of the city, including the airport. If that dam burst, the city would likely never get its power back. It wouldn't be a matter of power lines you could put back up in a few days. It would be a matter of years to replace the infrastructure that was destroyed. Worse, the riverbed would become a raging torrent. Who knew how long the airport would even be above water? The flooding could be catastrophic.

Another squawk from the walkie-talkies. A van disgorged another fifteen policemen, gimlet-eyed, tapping their machine guns, and hustling people into every conveyance that could roll down the road.

"We have to get on the bus," Ethan said, grabbing Emily's arm. *"Right now."*

Turn to page 121.

In the morning, Ethan knew the right thing to do without even thinking about it. He stood and stretched, his feet warm on the tile floor, watching Emily sleep, her hair splayed out on the pillow just like at home. Ethan let her sleep and went to take another shower.

When he emerged, pink and glistening, with a towel around his waist, Emily was sitting up in bed.

"I don't think I'll ever take a shower for granted again," Ethan said.

"Maybe I should see if I will," Emily said, yawning and rolling out from under the sheet.

"Don't be too long. I used up most of the hot water, I'm sure."

"Silly," Emily said. "In this place? It's geothermal. You'd have to cool down the core of the planet before we'd run out of hot water."

"How do we have running water here, when all the other places around are missing their top floors?"

"Beats me," Emily said. "Maybe you should ask Pietro."

"Well water," Pietro said. "I bought this place because my dowsers told me there was a spring underneath it that I could tap. And I did. Presto, unlimited water."

Ethan goggled at him. "*Dowsers?* As in, with a forked stick and all?" His face said volumes about what he thought of that.

Pietro seemed not to notice and tucked into his eggs. "Actually, coat hangers work better. But essentially the same principle."

Having no idea what to say to that, he said, "We're going back to the embassy after all." He'd come down while Emily was still in the shower. He thought it might be easier this way.

Pietro took a bite of toast as if he hadn't heard. "Travis will be here in a few minutes, and you guys can get on your way."

"You didn't hear me. We're going back. We're not going with Travis."

"Deal's done. Money exchanged hands. We have an accord."

"We don't. No deal. We're walking out the front door and up the hill, and we aren't coming back."

"It's a shame," Pietro said, but made a gesture as if wiping his hands clean. "Nobody takes a contract seriously anymore. You are in breach, so I don't have to return your money."

Ethan swigged back his orange juice. It was thick and pulpy, just how he liked it. "I'm not asking you to. I knew you'd try to keep it anyway."

"I'm not a thief," Pietro said, "just a businessman. But I'm also not a kidnapper, so you do what you want. Take some snacks, too. I can pretty much guarantee you they won't have anything like them at the embassy." Pietro stood up and wiped his mouth with a napkin, setting it back on his plate. "And, if I may be serious about this for a moment, don't forget what I told you about money. Where you're going, money could come in a number of different forms. Like, for instance, those Cheetos there. Don't underestimate what people will be willing to do for salty snacks."

Ethan stood up. Emily walked in, still squeezing water out of her hair. "Did you tell him?" she said.

Ethan squinted at her. "Tell him what?"

"That we're going back to the embassy."

"Yes. But... how did you know I was going to tell him that?"

"Twin telepathy," she said, picking up a roll and the butter knife. "Or maybe you talk in your sleep. I'm trying to decide which will drive you the craziest."

Turn to page 267.

Turn to page 267.

People under stress go for money, Ethan thought. *It's a comfort to them.*

"Reminds me of that scene from *It's a Wonderful Life*," a woman said from his left. Her curly, grey hair peeked out from under her old-fashioned nightcap, and her eyes, like his, were pinned to the scene at the ATM.

"What's that?" Ethan said.

"Over there. Only they're not queuing up at the Bailey Building and Loan, and there's no George Bailey to talk them out of trying to get all their money at once."

"What if they did?" Ethan said. He did vaguely remember the movie, something about a "run on the bank," whatever that was.

"You see those piles of cash in their hands, don't you? Where do you think that money is coming from?"

The obvious answer—the ATM–wasn't what she meant. "From overseas, bank accounts and such."

She shook her head. "Not ultimately. Originally, probably—these sure aren't locals—but ultimately it comes from some bank here, playing the market against itself. You think they have unlimited cash?"

Ethan realized they probably didn't.

"That's right," the woman said. "They don't. And what happens when the banks run out of money?"

"They're not going to run out just because of tourists," Ethan said.

"No, but you think the tourists are the only ones pulling money out of the banks right now? Remember Mr. Potter? He had cash. He gave it to the bank in exchange for taking ownership, and he would have done the same to the Building and Loan, but George told his people where the money really was—out in the economy. If they could hold on, use what cash they had, and rely on their resources, they didn't need to pull out all their cash. It kept his business alive, but a lot of other banks failed in the crash. People demanded money the banks didn't have, because they'd loaned it all out. They don't keep it in a safe in the back, you know."

Ethan said, "Do you think this is serious enough for banks to fail?"

She shrugged. "Probably not. That wasn't a big earthquake. But if there's a bigger one? Who knows?"

"It's worse than that," Ethan said. "If all this money is spent up, it could make prices go up like crazy."

"Hadn't thought of that," she said. "Good thing we're keeping our heads," patting Ethan's tenderly.

Ethan touched his pocket where some of his own money lay deep down inside. It was a comfort to him, too, but in his pocket were mostly dollars. The ATM here would produce nothing but saladera. Still, people were gobbling it up.

Ethan had already seen that when people are in stressful or difficult situations they didn't reach for saladera, because it was losing value every day. They wanted something more solid. What made a dollar more solid than saladera, he didn't know. He resolved, however, to hang on to as many dollars as possible.

Ethan realized he needed to keep some other things as well. He thought about what would have happened if the hotel had been seriously damaged. *How much good would dollars have done? Perhaps we need to make sure that we have other things besides just money*, he thought.

Perhaps they needed to make sure that they had tools, or food—things they might need in case of a real emergency. He thought of the snacks stashed in their bags in the hotel room. Perhaps they should be slightly less excited about just eating whatever they wanted and make sure that they had reserves for the rest of the trip.

Around the lobby, chatter spread about an earthquake in the center of the country, 4.3 on the Richter Scale. In one corner a small television blared a newscast. It was not a significant earthquake, and there was only minor damage to buildings and very few injuries, according to the broadcast. Emergency crews were out looking for problems, but they weren't finding much. Apparently the worst of it was over. Hopefully.

The couple came back to stand by Ethan. "We're going back to our room," they said.

Ethan decided to do the same. They were smiling broadly, "Looks like that was the earthquake," they said.

"So much for the giant earthquake warning everybody was so concerned about." He looked over at Ethan, "Are you here to see the ruins?"

"Yes," Ethan said.

"We're going up tomorrow. How about you?"

"We're not supposed to be there for another two days," Ethan told them. "It was nice to meet you."

The gentleman stuck out his hand. "It's nice to meet you as well. I hope that the rest of your trip is not as exciting as this."

"Oh, it's already been fairly exciting," Ethan said, "but I'm looking forward to just the normal excitement of looking at some very interesting old buildings."

The couple left and went off toward their room. Ethan climbed the stairs and headed back to his room. He rapped softly on the door and Emily opened it right away.

"I was worried about you," she said. "I couldn't sleep not knowing what was going on."

"It's fine," Ethan said. "The hotel thinks the worst of it is over and it doesn't look like there was much damage. I met a couple from Southern California and they said this kind of thing happens all the time there."

Emily closed the door softly. "Doesn't seem to have been so bad, then. Maybe the worst is over?"

"I don't know," Ethan said. "That might have been it, or it might just have been a little bump that sets us up for the big one, but I sure hope not. But I still don't want to go home. Do you?"

If you think the twins should find a way home as soon as possible, turn to page 256.

If you think they will be fine, turn to page 40.

The sunlight filtered down through the trees, making dappled patterns on the path.

Ethan kept watch behind them, and Thon in front of them, in case they ran into more of the banditos that they had just escaped from, but the rest of the path downward was uneventful. It would even have been quite pretty, if they had been able to forget that they were almost caught. But the memory wouldn't leave them, and the awful feeling in the pit of their stomach stayed all the way down the path.

The rest of the mountain and into town, Emily stayed close to Ethan, often taking his hand, which Ethan ordinarily would have found annoying, but he completely understood in this situation. In fact, it made him feel a little better.

"We need to go to the center of town," Thon said.

It was gathering dark now, the light fading as the sun set behind the western peaks. Sapallu looked to be in fairly good condition. There were houses that had not done well, especially on the outskirts. But there were no people homeless in the streets. Civil order seemed to have been maintained, or at least restored.

"I don't see any police," Emily said. "I would have thought that the police would be out keeping order."

Thon shook his head. "Not in this town. It's not a large place. Nearly everyone knows everyone else. If you went out and looted, you'd be stealing from people you know. Father Augustin has been the town's priest for 30 years. He knows everyone in town and maintains order and discipline much better than the authorities do, even among those that aren't part of his church."

"He'll be too busy to deal with us, then," Emily said.

Thon laughed out loud. "I have never known Father Augustin to be too busy to help *anyone*," he said.

So it proved when they arrived at the church in the center of town. A pair of ladies stood on the front steps. Behind them sat bags of groceries, water, clothing, and other supplies. One of them jerked up her head in surprise when Thon approached. "Why," she said, "It's Thon! What brings you here? Your village isn't in trouble, is it?"

"No, no," Thon said, "it's not my village that brings me." He motioned to the two Tuttles standing behind him. "These are my friends, Ethan and Emily. They are American tourists who got stranded at the Ychurichuc ruins in the earthquake. I took them to my village, and we have just come down out of the hills. We only just got away from the bandits."

"Bandits?" the woman said. "You don't mean the White Guard, do you?" She said it the way most people clear their throat to spit something nasty.

"No," Thon said. "We know about them, too. They stopped us from coming by car. Then we had to travel overland, and when we did, we ran into a group of bandits in the hills. I wouldn't be surprised if they came from here." And he related their entire experience in the mountains.

As she listened, the woman's face hardened, until her mouth was set in a line like a carving in granite. "Just a moment," she said, and went into the church, returning a moment later with a small man in his fifties, graying at the temples, with a look in his face that told you he had seen almost everything there was to see.

"Father Augustin," Thon said, bowing. "My friends and I have some things to tell you."

"Come in out of the night," the priest said. "If what Annabella tells me is true, you have more than one thing to relate to me."

Father Augustin sat at a long wooden table that looked as if it were older than the Inca ruins. But it was a relief to sit anywhere, and the father had food—hot soup and bread—brought to the hungry and weary travelers. When he had heard their tale, he said wearily, "I will have a group go up into the mountains and discuss the freedom of our town with these banditos. It makes me sad that things like this should happen, but I suppose it is human nature. We will simply have to preach harder and show forth more good works, so these kinds of things don't happen anymore."

"I would have thought you would go up and shoot them," Ethan said, still fuming over having been chased off the mountain.

Father Augustine simply shook his head sadly. "These are children of God, too," he said. "They are scared and hungry, just like so many others. Forcing them to do what I want is not going to make things better. But it is possible that they can still be persuaded to come back to the right path. You said one of them was named José?" The three of them nodded. "I think I know where there is someone he will find most persuasive. Annabella, will you go and fetch Consuela to the church, please?"

Annabella's granite face softened, but retained a hint of something that made you want to find somewhere else to be. She looked like a housecat sitting outside a mouse hole.

Father Augustin pushed himself away from the table and wiped his face with a napkin. "And now I have other duties that I must attend to," he said. "You will stay here tonight, of course, and in the morning we will see what is to be done. I have contacts in Ecuador, who may be able to get you out of the country and to the airport there where you can get a flight home. Oh, and one more thing," he said, making a beckoning gesture to someone behind him. "This is Rosalia," he said. "Rosalia, will you take my young friends here to the phone?"

Turn to page 101.

The azure sky arched bright and blue over their heads. Birds called to them as if to say, "come on, what are you waiting for?"

"It kind of depends on how much he wants," Ethan said. "But I would like to take it if we can, especially if it's not part of the regular tour."

"Ordinarily, I would be totally in agreement, but like I said, this guy gives me the creeps." Emily wasn't thrilled with the idea.

"Um, sure. Me, too," Ethan said. "But Em, what could happen? It's a tour add-on, not a walk down a dark alley."

"Fine. I suppose we can do it," Emily said.

"Unless you tell me you definitely don't think we should," Ethan said.

"No," she said. "I think it will be fine. We just have to be careful."

They marched back across the parking lot, gravel crunching under their feet. The air smelled musty, as if the jungle around them was a room that hadn't been cleaned in some time. Bright birds flashed over their heads and sang tunes nothing like those sung by the birds at home.

When they reached Jorge, he had their tickets in his hand. "All set," he said. "What have you decided?"

"I think we're going to take the special tour," Emily said. "How much?"

"Just $25 each," he said.

"That's not so bad," Ethan said, and pulled saladera out of his pouch.

"Dollars only," Jorge said, shaking his head.

Ethan frowned and checked Emily with a sidelong glance, but she was turned elsewhere as if this was none of her business. "Okay," Ethan said, stuffing the Allqukillan money back in his pack and drawing out a fifty. Jorge's smile lit up again and the money vanished into a pocket of his jacket.

"It will only be us today," he said. "There was another family, but at the last minute they decided they would go home, probably because of the earthquake."

They got in line to go through the main gate into the ruins.

"Do you have earthquakes down here a lot?" Ethan was trying to be friendly to pass the time.

"Happens all the time. We have a small one like that every few months. I don't see what everyone is so excited about." And then the short line disappeared, and it was their turn. They were almost at the gate. Ahead of them at last was the object of their last two years of planning.

The stairs in front of them were worn with the passage of many thousands of feet. "I don't think these here are original," Emily said. She pointed off to the side. "Over there. Those stones are significantly less worn."

"Good eye," Jorge said. "These stone steps were put in for the tourists. The ancient ones were stolen or destroyed by the Spanish. When the conquistadors came, they destroyed as many of the access points to temples as they could, trying to stamp out the native culture and religion in favor of Christianity."

"Why do conquerors do that?" Emily said.

"Control, mostly." Jorge glanced over to the gate, and let his eyes linger for a moment. He turned and spat into the bushes at the side of the stairs. "If conquerors destroy people's connection to their past, they can more easily shape their future. The Spanish controlled god. That gave them power over the Inca. Today, governments do the same thing, but they control the money."

Emily crouched on the first step and placed her palm flat on it. "It's softer stone. They replaced the original with softer stone. That's why it's worn so differently." She stood up and brushed her hands together. "It looks the same, but it isn't."

Light green grass grew at the edge of the stones, waving gently in the light breeze, scraping their tips across the gray of the stone. Finished with the preliminary look, he took hold of Emily's hand. It seemed appropriate for them to enter this fairyland together.

Jorge strode out ahead, unable to see the magic around them.

And they were through the gate.

The air instantly felt different, as if it were infused with a spectral energy. A yellow and green bird floated down on the breeze and alighted a few steps in front of them. It cocked its head from side to side, as if asking them a question.

A dark-skinned young man standing nearby said, "I think he wants something."

"I don't have anything to give him," Ethan said.

"I have a piece of our roll from this morning," Emily said, and pulled it out of her pack. She tossed it in the bird's direction. The bird launched and caught it in its beak in midair, flying off towards the canopy of trees.

"I'll bet one of the Inca children did that very same thing," Ethan said.

"I guarantee it," the young man said. "It's good luck, too. My name is Thon. I *am* one of those Inca children. If you need something, I'll be here."

"That's a good omen, then," Emily said, shaking his hand. watching the bird until it vanished from sight against the forest.

Jorge said, "We should get going."

Off to the south, above one of the nearby peaks, a tendril of smoke rose into the sky.

"What's that over there?" Ethan said.

"It's nothing," Jorge said. "There are a lot of little camps and villages in these mountains. Most of them aren't really a part of the system; they seem to resist being integrated into the modern country and the world."

They climbed the stairs, each step bringing them nearer to the flat plane at the top of the hill. Before they reached it, the point of a tall stone pillar rose steadily above them. It leaned slightly to the left, as if it were in the process of falling over, but stood steadily enough.

Ethan's face broke into a broad smile. "I know that spire," he said. "I never really thought I would see it with my own eyes." Then they were at the top of the stairs.

Around them, the foundations of low buildings lay somewhat tumbled-down and covered in moss. The central square was roughly circular with the spire in the center—the lower court. Straight ahead was a stone staircase with another to the right and to the left. It was something like standing at the bottom of a large football stadium.

Jorge said, "This is where I would show you the ceremonial burial grounds over to the right, and then going up to the left, the King's Palace, but I'm pretty sure that you know all about those things."

"We still want to see them," Ethan said.

"Can we go to the burial grounds first?" Emily said. "There's something there I want to see."

These stairs were very different from the others. Tourists milled about them, taking selfies or videos of everything. The twins climbed the stairs on the extreme right side, where the original stone was least affected.

And these were the original stone stairs, block after block of fitted stone set together so tightly that no grass grew between them. It seemed that even the moss would not intrude on the architectural genius of the place. The stones looked to Ethan as if they could have been laid down yesterday. The contrast between the jungle off to the edge of the staircase, and the staircase itself, was stark and felt to Ethan as if some sorcery was keeping the jungle at bay.

"These are the original stairs," Jorge said. Emily ignored him, absorbed in her observations.

Emily flicked open her small pocket knife and attempted to stick it between two of the stones, but found she couldn't.

"These stones have been here for at least fifteen hundred years," Jorge said, "and in all that time they haven't even shifted a quarter of an inch, even with all the earthquakes."

"How do they resist the earthquakes?" Emily asked. "It seems as if the Earth would shift and move the stones as well."

"No one knows," Jorge said, "but the ground here does not seem to be affected as much by earthquakes as the surrounding area. In fact, if you look back over there," he said, pointing back toward the gate, "you can see places where the ground *has* actually shifted. We even had small mudslides from the earthquake a couple days ago. But up here it looks as if nothing has changed."

Emily bent down and placed her hand on the stone. Once she looked very closely at the facing stones of the staircase she could see carvings that had been worn away by time and rain and wind. The young man, Thon, sat there like the incarnation of an Incan god, a crooked smile on his face.

"Unchanged for thousands of years," Ethan said, gazing back toward the central square, where the timeless obelisk stood pointing to the sky.

And as he watched, the great stone tipped a little more, and a little more, and with a groan he could feel through the soles of his feet, toppled over and thudded into the grass.

Turn to page 335.

Tendrils of smoke wafted across the square. Ethan and Emily sat morosely on the bumper of the truck. For a moment, Emily thought about Thon, their friend from the Ychurichuc ruins, and wondered how he was getting on. She stood up and looked back toward the hills where his village was. If there was smoke there, if there were ruined villages, downed houses and power lines, she couldn't see anything. But then the smoke from Ychu itself was thick enough that she could hardly see anything in that direction anyway.

Ethan unzipped his pack and pulled out a Ziploc container of beef jerky. He handed one to Emily.

"I'm not hungry," she said.

"It doesn't matter," Ethan said. "You don't know when you'll be able to eat again, so you eat now. You eat when it's time to eat. Not when you're hungry. That goes as long as we're still in this country, until we get home."

Dutifully, Emily put the piece of beef jerky in her mouth. Salty and peppery, it burned the back of her throat, but she found that she felt steadier after she had a couple of mouthfuls.

A minute or so later, Jorge came striding across the parking lot, pressing the button on his key ring, and making the truck chirp. "You two get tired of sitting inside the cab?" he said.

Ethan and Emily just kept chewing their beef jerky. Emily saw Jorge's eyes go to the bag of beef jerky and then to her face, as if he hadn't been peeping. He did that a lot, she thought, trying to look at something without appearing to be interested in it.

"I talked to my friend," Jorge said, smooth and casual. "His name is Anibal. He's the one with the track machine I told you about. He says he would be happy to take us down, but it won't be cheap. This vehicle also doesn't move particularly fast, so it's going to be a long trip, seven or eight hours."

"That's okay," Ethan said. "It beats walking."

Emily thought about their dwindling supply of cash, and wondered what Jorge meant when he said it would be expensive.

"So," Jorge said, "you guys have more cash or what?"

Emily said, "I'm assuming you don't mean this pile of saladera I have in my pack."

Jorge laughed, as if he weren't standing in the middle of a disaster area, with bleeding people littering the courtyard around him. "No, of course not that stuff. Since the earthquake, that stuff won't be worth anything anyway. Remember, its value is declining all the time, and that was before everyone in the country pulled their savings and started buying all the bottled water."

Ethan remembered the run on the ATM a couple days back. This quake would make that little riot look like a ballroom dance.

Ethan put his hand on Emily's legs and gave a brief squeeze. She took that to mean that he didn't want her to say anything at this point, and Ethan then said, "I have money—dollars. How much are we talking about?"

Emily watched Jorge's eyes dance right and then left as if he were calculating something. *They haven't discussed the price of this trip*, Emily thought. *He's making this up. I wouldn't be surprised if there was no charge at all, and Jorge was pocketing the whole amount.* She resolved to make sure that she asked Anibal about that when they all got together.

"I think a $100 apiece should do it," Jorge said. His voice had a little catch in it, as if he weren't sure that they had that much money.

Ethan squeezed Emily's leg again down low where Jorge couldn't see it. "I don't know if I have that much," Ethan said. "I think I only have a $100 bill left. Can you at least take us some of the way for the $100?" He put an uncharacteristic whining note in his voice. Ethan never whined about anything.

Jorge pretended to consider, rubbing his chin and pulling off his baseball cap and running his hands through his hair. But Emily could see he was going to take the money. "Well, I don't think Anibal will be very happy about that. Kind of a big risk for him to take, and a lot of gas and time expended to get you where you're going."

"He can have all of our saladera as well," Ethan said. "I'm sure it's worth something, even if not nearly as much as it was when we got here."

"How much of that do you have?" Jorge said like a fish snapping at a lure.

"A few thousand," Ethan said. "We changed money right before we went up to the ruins."

Jorge pretended to consider this a moment. "Okay. Hand over the money, and I'll work it out with Anibal. He's going to meet us out behind the bar in an hour."

Ethan had imagined that when the track vehicle arrived, it would look something like a backhoe. But when it finally ground its way to a halt in front of them, it looked much more like a snow cat than anything else, not that it would ever snow in this part of the world. A cabin for four or five sat like a crow's nest on top of four independent treads arranged where the wheels belonged, each tread in the shape of a triangle, with the drive gear on top. It sat up so high, Ethan could have crawled underneath without his back touching.

It might once have been white, this contraption, but the paint had mostly given out except where it clung stubbornly to the underlying steel like lichen to Andean rock. But the steel gleamed, and no rust marred the motley finish.

The driver looked as old as the vehicle itself. He jumped down however nimbly enough and greeted the Tuttles with a warm smile.

"*Me llamo Anibal*," he said, pumping their hands in a handshake. "I'm very pleased to meet you." His Spanish was accented with something odd, as if he were from somewhere else.

"Is that a Castilian accent?" Ethan said.

The man, if possible, brightened even further. "Yes," he said, "I was born in the old country in Spain, just outside of Madrid. I have had many passengers over the years, but very few of them have been able to recognize the high speech of the old country." He considered the twins' meager belongings for a moment. "This is all your luggage?" he said.

"Sadly, yes," Emily said. "We weren't able to get back into the hotel to get the rest of our gear. I guess it's going to be lost."

"And to think they just renovated the old girl two years ago," Anibal said. "Barring a miracle—and our miracles are needed elsewhere at the moment—that hotel will be bulldozed sometime in the next couple of weeks, and all of that lovely loot that people brought down here as tourists will go into the landfill with it." The thought seemed to bring him back to the present. "The important thing now is to get you guys home. Jorge told me about your near miss up top."

"Yes," Emily said. "As quickly as possible."

"Well, old Esmeralda here," he said, running his hand lovingly over one dirt-encrusted track, "she won't do much past 35 miles per hour, but she's as dependable as the day is long. She'll get you where you're going. Might take a while, but she'll get there."

Turn to page 77.

The three travelers stocked up on drinks and food, had their cooler packed, and were just starting for the back door when a violent banging sounded behind them. They dropped into a crouch behind a rack of very stale bread. The front door rattled.

Through the gaps in the bread, they saw a group of young men milling around on the sidewalk, looking up and down the street as if searching for something. One of them, a tall, thin young man with dark hair and a scar across his jawline, pounded on the front door and shouted at the storekeeper to let him in. He leaned in toward the glass, shading it to help himself see inside.

The storekeeper turned white. "It is El Chapo," she said. "He must have seen your car."

One of the young men watching the street pulled out a pistol and handed it to El Chapo. The storekeeper dragged her key ring from her belt and unlocked the door leading to the store room in the back.

"We can't go now," Travis said from down near the floor. "You're in danger."

The woman's hands were steady, though her face was white and her lip trembled. "He will not hurt me," she said. "I am, after all, his mother."

That explained why the shop hadn't been looted. The three of them slipped through into the back room. She tossed them the ring of keys.

"If I do not have this, I cannot open the front door. Perhaps I can get him to give up and go away or tell him that you have gone somewhere else."

"Thank you," they said.

Ethan reached up and handed her a wad of saladera. "This is probably not enough for what you've done for us," he said, "but it's all I have."

Without looking at it or counting it the woman stuffed it into the pockets of her apron. "It will do," she said. "This too shall pass, and when it does, I will remember you fondly. Now go."

She slammed the door shut, and Ethan shot the bolt. Emily took the ring of keys over to the exterior wall.

"If they've already come around," Ethan said, "we might have real trouble when we get through this door."

Travis's face was grim but determined. "We'll deal with that when we have to," she said.

Emily looked them each in the eye. "Ready?" she said.

"As I'll ever be," Ethan said. His face was white.

Emily fit the key into the lock and turned. She solemnly hung the key ring on a hook to the left of the door. Only the handle held the door closed now.

Travis turned it and the door creaked inward an inch. She put her eye to the crack and took a deep breath. "Let's go," she said, and flung the door wide.

They rushed through the doorway and out to the car, practically flinging themselves inside. Emily tugged the door shut and heard it click. Not secure, but closed, the best she could do.

Ethan screamed out, "Emily!" as two young men came around the corner and saw them. They raised their pistols and fired one into the air.

"Stop!" they yelled, but that was comical. Of course they weren't going to stop. Emily ripped the rear door open and threw herself across the seats. Ethan reached back and slammed the door.

The men shouted for more of their friends, beckoning them to come and block off the alley.

Ethan shot Travis a worried glance. "How are we going to get through them?" he said.

Travis's face had a little more color and a little more life. "Remember I told you that this car had surprises? It's time to show them a little bit of what she can do."

Her dark eyes narrowed in concentration as she reached under the dashboard and flicked a switch.

"Hold on to your hats," she said, turning the key. The car hummed to life. Her foot slammed down on the accelerator. The engine's whine dropped ten notches from alto to a thumping bass, like awakening a bear from a winter slumber a few weeks early.

The Sentra shot forward as if fired from a cannon. They roared down the narrow alley toward the two men. One of them, apparently with a death wish, stood his ground, levelled his pistol, and cracked off a shot.

It pinged off the windshield as if he had tossed a pebble. The car kept coming. Travis smirked. The would-be hero's eyes widened, and he threw himself to the side. The Sentra blasted by and the front bumper clipped his leg. His scream was barely audible over the howl of the engine.

They flew past the intersection and down another, even narrower alley. Ethan would have been staring at Travis if he hadn't been glued in terror to the blurring landscape ahead. Her face had a look as if she had never been fully alive until now.

"Holy cow," Emily breathed from the back seat.

The car zoomed down the narrow alley. Walls closed in, closer and closer, but Travis showed no sign of slowing down. There was no pavement here, just dirt, rutted and pitted, and the Sentra bucked over it like a wild animal. A couple of times Ethan would have sworn they were going to take flight.

From behind them, a whole group of young men rounded the corner, weapons leveled, and let fly volley after volley. But the bullets whined high or pinged harmlessly off the back window.

"What on earth is this thing made of?" Ethan said.

"It's just a car," Travis said through gritted teeth, "with some special modifications of my own."

"Like the Millennium Falcon?" Emily said. "How in the world can this car possibly be doing this?"

"She is . . . remarkable," Travis said. Her smile broadened as they put the young men in their rear view. "My only question is, where does this alley go? Although this car is built like a tank, it isn't one. A brick wall would end this trip real fast." As if she had called it into being, ahead of them loomed a brick wall, dusty and gray with soot. A tiny alley branched off to the right. Surely it was too narrow to squeeze into.

Travis hauled the wheel around as the car slewed sideways. It skimmed the wall, skidded. Somehow it managed to regain traction enough to get around the corner and, nearly leaving paint on the walls, shoot down the alley toward the main road.

Out of the path of the main alley, Travis exercised some caution, braking hard, shedding speed.

"We have a map?" she said.

"Not for this town," Ethan said.

"Well," she said, "I suppose the main road has to connect to the road that leads out of town, otherwise it wouldn't be the main road, right?"

She gunned the engine. They shot out of the alley and skidded sideways onto the main road. Ethan desperately hoped no one would be on it. No one was, except at the far end, by the church. The main road ran directly past it. "Isn't that the headquarters?" Emily said. "And aren't those the people who were trying to kill us?"

"They need to try harder," Travis said. "I haven't even had a workout yet."

Turn to page 317.

Ethan awoke, his nerves immediately on edge. The tiniest crack of light penetrated the curtains where they weren't quite closed all the way—just the glow of electric lights from the city. Emily breathed softly, apparently still asleep. There it was again—a slight jolting, an odd sensation of something not being quite right. He rolled over to check the clock on the nightstand, but the clock was no longer facing his way, as if someone had turned it in the middle of the night. His gut clenched. Had someone been in the room? Ethan's ears strained in the dark for any other sounds, but the room was quiet.

Outside, though, he heard a voice call out and another one respond. Curious, he rose from his bed and padded across the carpet to the window. He parted the curtains quietly and looked out into the night. Down by the water some neatly stacked canoes had fallen over and some men were struggling to put them upright again.

Behind him, Emily said, "Is everything all right?"

"I think so," he said. "Something woke me up."

"What time is it?" Emily asked.

From the window Ethan could see the clock. "It's two in the morning."

"I'm afraid I won't be able to go back to sleep," Emily said.

Ethan agreed. "That's what I'm thinking, too. I woke up as if someone had shaken me."

"It wasn't me," Emily said and rolled over, putting her face down in the pillow. "I sleep through everything."

Ethan looked down. Uniformed men came out underneath him from the lobby of the hotel and ran down to the beach. They grabbed the two men who were down there struggling with the canoes and pointed back over their shoulders towards the hotel in some agitation. All of the men ran back in the direction of the hotel.

"I'm going down to the lobby, I think something happened," Ethan said.

Emily sat up again. "What could have happened?" she said, yawning.

"That's what I want to find out. I think we may have had an earthquake," Ethan said as he grabbed his pants, wallet, and the key card for the room.

"I'll come with you."

"No, there's no need. I'll be right back."

Ethan went quietly out into the hall. There were no other people emerging in a panic, so whatever it was it couldn't be too bad. The hotel was quiet—no alarms going off, at least—and something undefinable told him that whatever it was that had happened was over now. He walked two flights down a carpeted stairway. On the second one he was joined by a couple he remembered from the bus. "Hey, did something wake you up?" Ethan asked.

"Yes," they said. "We had a nasty shock in our room. Our suitcase fell off the dresser and woke us up."

"That's terrible. What caused it?"

The man smiled, his mouth a tight line across his face. "Earthquake," he said, "just a small one. We're from Southern California and we get these all the time. We're used to them."

The lobby was clogged with people. Most of them pushed up against the check-in desk. Some of them shouted questions at the attendant there. Other hotel staff talked quietly with individuals about various things. Most of them seemed to have had things go wrong in their room or minor injuries from having fallen, or having something fall on them. Ethan didn't have anything like that to complain about, so he hung around the edges of the crowd and listened.

On one side of the lobby, people surged past him toward the desk, intent on a conversation with the attendants there. It was clear to him, however, that they had no more information than what the hotel guests already possessed—that there had been a small earthquake, not terribly serious; the hotel seemed likely to go on providing its comfortable services for the foreseeable future.

Another group of people, however, clustered over at the ATM and were furiously withdrawing money.

Judging from the piles passing by in their fists, the machine wouldn't hold out much longer. Sooner or later, it would run dry. Sooner, was his guess.

That money came from somewhere, too. A bank account or credit card, somewhere else. *This is probably happening in other places, too*, Ethan thought. *I wonder how much money is pouring into the economy because of it.* The ATM would run dry. But Ethan's bank account would do that, too, if he kept draining it for more local currency. Still, what if the earthquake took out the electricity? Wouldn't he need saladera then—especially if the ATM stopped working?

If you think Ethan should withdraw as much money as he can from the ATM, turn to page 73.

If you think Ethan should avoid using the ATM, turn to page 201.

Ethan said, "I know this will probably be unpopular, but I think we need to consider getting off this road."

Emily said, "I think that's a wise idea."

"Except I don't know about the off-road capabilities of this particular car."

Travis revved the engine. "If you had to guess, what would you think those off-road capabilities are?"

"Given what I've seen so far," Emily said, "I would bet heavily on them being exceptional."

"How right you would be." Travis turned halfway around, checking right and left for a way off the main street. More gunfire rattled the windows. Travis gave no sign she noticed.

Across from the alley out of which they had just come was another similar break between the buildings.

"Judging from what we saw of the town from up top," Travis said, "the whole place isn't more than a couple of blocks wide. If I remember from the one time I was here before, there was a road that leads up into the hills. It goes out to the east of town, but I'm relatively sure that it bears to the north at some point and connects with another road that we can use to get over the border. The question is, can we get to it before they shoot through the back windshield."

As a partial answer, another rifle shot cracked and the entire window shattered. "Shields at five percent," Travis said. She turned and slammed her foot down the accelerator. The Sentra shot backward up the street toward the knot of men in the intersection.

They dived out of the way. Startled, El Chapo's final rifle shot went high.

Travis whipped the wheel around and the Sentra did a three-quarter spin, leaving the nose of the car pointed east. Travis again tromped down on the accelerator, and the Sentra blasted into the small gap between the buildings.

It was a straight shot down the alley, but the road was so scarred and pitted that the Sentra had a hard time remaining engaged with the roadway.

Bucking like a bronco released from the chute, the car went rocketing between the houses and onto a dirt road that led off to the east. One more rifle shot tagged the back bumper of the car. Fortunately, El Chapo was not a particularly good shot.

"That was a close one, friends," Travis said. "Now the question is, can we get this little beauty far enough up into the hills that he won't try again?"

"We showed him up pretty good. He won't give up easily," Emily said.

The car kicked up so much dust that it was impossible to see behind them, but it didn't appear as if anyone was giving chase. Five or six miles later, with the car climbing steadily into the lush green hills, it became clear that Emily was wrong. El Chapo *was* giving up easily.

Travis flipped the two switches underneath the dashboard, and the car slowed to its normal pace: only slightly suicidal. Emily picked bits of safety glass from her clothing. Dust boiled in through the open rear of the car, coating everything.

Travis said, "I don't think we're going to have any more trouble with that group, so unless we run into bandits up here in the hills, now might be a good time to get out some of that excellent food and have a picnic."

"I assume you mean *inside* the car," Ethan said, unzipping his backpack. "No offense to present company, but the faster we get out of the country the better I'm going to like it."

Emily opened the cooler and shared out the food as Travis continued at a much more sedate pace up to the peak of the hill. When they reached a decent vantage point, Travis brought the car to a halt. "You might be in a big hurry, but I have to stand and, um, stretch. Over in those bushes, actually." Emily said she needed to as well. The three of them piled out.

Ethan could see to the north a fairly wide, well-used road.

Getting to it, however, might prove complicated. The road they were on had long since ceased to be much more than a cattle track. It was possible that it had been used by someone transporting sheep or goats, but not for a long time. The Sentra, however, proved to have an outstanding suspension, and its tires were far more robust than Ethan would have thought.

"Shall we try to cut a path cross country here and see what we can find?" Travis said, returning and buckling her jeans.

On this side of the hill, the land sat in the rain shadow of the mountains, so the brush was sparser and the trees were thin.

"I don't see what choice we have," Ethan said. "Does that road go to Ecuador?" He pointed off to the ribbon winding its way among the hills to the north.

"If the map is right, and if that's the road the map shows, then it does. But I'm pretty sure that any major road in this part of the country will go to Ecuador, or it will go to a road that does go there."

"Time to have another adventure," Emily said, and climbed back in the car.

Turn to page 277.

At the end of the first day in the stadium, the food arrived. It was mostly rice and beans cooked over an open fire in a big kettle and doled out on paper plates. Some meat had been added. Ethan could smell it cooking from across the way, and it made his stomach rumble. He wasn't the only one. There was nearly a riot when it looked as if they were going to run short of food, but in the nick of time, another truck pulled in with another big kettle and eventually everyone got something.

Ethan asked Emily if she had enough. She said she had. He didn't really believe it. He knew he hadn't had nearly enough to eat. His stomach growled from having had almost nothing in it all day. The plate full of beans and rice that he got tasted wonderful but did very little to assuage his hunger.

It was a long and somewhat chilly night in the high mountain air. The humidity was quite low and did not hold the heat very well. It seemed entirely strange that so much disaster could have been visited on the ground and yet the sky was still full of stars and the world continued to turn as if nothing had happened. Smoke rose continually from outside the walls of the stadium, and people milled about endlessly attempting to use their cell phones that were slowly running out of battery, trying to figure out what had happened to their friends, their family, their property, and sharing information about how to get home.

Cots arrived late in the evening. They were spread out across the south end of the field.

"I'm going to get us one," Ethan said, and marched off. In a slow-motion wave, the crowd rose, staring off toward the advancing line for bedding. But there couldn't be this many, could there? Surely there weren't five thousand. Not half that.

Yet the wave kept coming. Cots were passed from hand to hand. There was Ethan; he had one. Then he handed it on. Another came to him, he looked around, and handed it to an older man.

A cot would be handed up the chain, and someone would find a young child, or an old woman, or someone pregnant, and give the cot to them.

No one gave orders. No one organized it. The crowd, so destitute, so hopeless one minute, swelled into something quite different with this simple act of service. Smiles appeared. Laughter floated over the ground. Ethan hefted one of the metal-frame cots and trotted back toward Emily. At the last second, he slowed and turned aside. Next to Emily stood—only barely—a mother with a baby and a clinging child. Ethan erected the cot next to her and bowed. Grateful tears appeared in the eyes of the mother, who laid her two children on the cot and knelt beside them.

"Sorry, Em," Ethan said, wiping his brow. "That was the last one."

Emily gave him a quick hug. "I love this patch of grass," she said. "Let's see if I can find us a blanket."

The next morning, Ethan rose stiff and covered in dew, and thought it might be a good idea to take a run around the track to warm up and get his muscles loose again.

As soon as he started, he was joined by three or four other people, and during the laps they had an opportunity to talk. Two of them were from Takewawa, and one was an American tourist who had come for the sport fishing.

Ethan told them what he had learned from the guard the day before, that the American Embassy was setting up a temporary base.

"I wouldn't bother with that if I were you," the American said.

"Whyever not?" Ethan said. "Those are the people who are the most likely to be able to help us out."

"What kinds of resources do you think they're going to have that the people on the ground here don't have?" he said. "It's not like they have private airplanes that can fly out of some airport that's not the central hub, and no one's flying out of *that* airport for a while."

"But they're surely equipped for this kind of thing," he said.

"The small embassy they have here?" he said. "A couple of staffers and the ambassador and his family and that's going to be about it. They'll have some vehicles, probably," he said. "But what are the chances that you were going to be able to get on one of them? A teenage kid from somewhere in the states? Those vehicles are going to be reserved for important people and people who have enough money to pay."

Ethan started to say that he thought he had some money, but the truth of it was what was in his waist pack was small and surely wouldn't be enough to bid for a seat on a crowded SUV.

"What do you think we should do?" Ethan said.

"Well, what I'm going to do," the man said, "is try to get to a place where I can let my family know that I'm okay."

Ethan remembered that he had had no opportunity to do that and resolved to ask the officials about being able to make a phone call later that day.

"And then," the man said. "I'm going to get into a refugee train and get over the border into Ecuador. I'm pretty sure that once I get there I'll be able to get myself out and back to my family."

A refugee camp sounded like an awfully risky way of going about it, Ethan thought. But when he got back and found Emily sitting up and rubbing the sleep from her eyes, he thought it would be a good idea to talk it over with her.

"I'm not quite sure how we can do that," Ethan said. "It's not as if they're going to let us walk out of the stadium."

"No," Emily said, "but once we get out on the bus and they drop us at the temporary American Embassy, we can pretty much do what we want."

"It's something we need to think about," Ethan said. "I don't know how soon they'll get us out of here."

It turned out to be very soon indeed. Before the sun was even more than an inch or two above the edge of the stadium, a small bus pulled in with an American eagle on the side of it. An official started to load people in. The helpful security man that they had talked to before waved them over and found them a seat on the bus. Emily thanked him profusely and Ethan squeezed himself into a small space, making enough room for Emily to get there as well.

The bus circled the track and drove back out of the service entrance. For the first time the twins were able to see what happened outside the stadium, and they were immediately glad that they had not seen what it looked like the day before. People streamed along the streets, moving toward churches, toward restaurants, toward any place that was still open, any place that they could go. All about them were flattened rows of houses, debris on all of the side streets. Many appeared to be blocked by rock and rubble. There were fires everywhere. Sirens blared as emergency equipment and firefighters roamed the city looking for the hottest spots to put out, but there was no way they could tackle all of the fires that were burning. The earthquake had left many buildings unstable, and people were unable to inhabit them.

In the center of the downtown, tall office blocks had been roped off with orange tape. Security men around the outside still attempted to enter in small teams and find people and get them back out. Glass lay on the pavement everywhere, and everywhere they went people turned toward the sound of their vehicle and raised their hands as if seeking help. The driver set his face grimly and kept driving. What, in fact, could he possibly do?

A little while later they pulled into a small parking lot where a Quonset hut had the American Embassy seal on the front door.

"This is where we stop, folks," he said. "I've got to go back and pick up another group of people from the stadium. The guard outside will help you."

Turn to page 398.

Emily followed Ethan off the bus, dragging her suitcase, bumping and scratching down the aisle. When they reached the ground, the dust rose about them in the parking lot next to the small inn, where a few musicians were lazily playing in the shade. The sun had sunk somewhat past midway. Only a few hours of daylight remained. That would have been fine if they had still been moving along toward Ychu, but with the bus stopped, there was not much likelihood that they would be able to get to the small town and to their hotel that day.

She shaded her eyes to take in their surroundings. The inn did not look well-maintained. It also didn't look as if anyone there was surprised to see the bus had broken down in their parking lot. A rotund smiling man stood in the doorway, waving at the tourists who exited the bus.

"This sure isn't how I imagined the first part of our vacation going," Emily said.

Ethan tried to reassure her. "It'll be okay," he said. "I saw a video while doing my research where the guy talked about how his bus broke down, too, but he was able to catch a taxi into town."

"A taxi?" Emily sounded incredulous. "All the way out here? I don't know about that."

Off to the right of the bus stood two cars with swarthy men leaning against them. A man in a police uniform stood beside them, joking with the other men. They seemed to be reenacting a play from yesterday's football match. The cop looked up, laughed, and jerked his head back toward the bus, signaling the others. He sauntered off toward the tavern.

From over by the cars, one of the drivers saw Ethan and Emily and shuffled his way across the parking lot. "Hey," he said, "are the two of you headed out to Ychu? You're going out to the ruins, right?"

Ethan looked at him warily.

"Yeah, that's where we had planned to go, but the bus is broken down," Emily said.

The man smiled. He was missing a couple of teeth. "I have a car and I am headed in that direction. In fact I am going all the way to Ychu tonight, and I am leaving in a couple minutes if you want a ride."

Ethan said, "That's very kind of you, but we don't accept rides from strangers."

The man's smile widened slightly. "Oh, I'm a taxi driver." He pointed to the car, where there was an official-looking seal, although no other identification.

"Aren't you a little out of the way to be picking up rides?" Emily asked.

The man's smile cracked slightly. "It's my lucky day! I just happened to be here," he said. "Normally I would be driving tourists around Ychu. Lots of interesting ruins near Ychurichuc, not only the ones everyone talks about." His eyes twinkled. The twinkle reminded Emily more of avarice than fun.

Ethan said, "I think I need to talk this over with my sister for a minute, will you excuse us?" The man nodded and returned to his car.

Ethan turned to Emily. "This doesn't sound like a coincidence to me at all," he said.

"That's just what I was thinking," she replied.

If you think the twins should hire the cab, turn to page 164.

If you think the taxi driver is untrustworthy and the twins should stay with the bus, turn to page 127.

The sun beat hot on his back, but that was not what made Ethan sweat. This was uncharted territory, something he couldn't plan for. As they crested the top of the walkway over the huge highway, they could see down into the market, sprawling away from them at the foot of the walk. A riot of colors warred with one another, garish and blinding in the midday sun.

Ethan thought that *libre*, or "free," must have meant being able to sell whatever it is you want, and the Allqukillans had taken it literally.

"Is that a… dragon?" Emily said, pointing to the right where a metal enclosure held something green and scaly, with ridges along its back.

"Except for the fact that they don't exist, I would say yes, it is," Ethan said. "I'm not sure what the Spanish word for 'dragon' is. How are you on mythical creatures?"

She shook her head. "I figure I'll be lucky if I remember how to ask for *una naranja*."

"At least it looks like there are some of those," Ethan said. "Over there seems to be where the produce is. That's most of what we need to get." He consulted his list, which was written in English and Spanish, just in case.

"But I'm hungry, too. Maybe we could get something hot to eat." Two vendors had set up right at the entrance to the mercado, and their multi-colored carts steamed gently in the busy afternoon.

"From those carts? Is that safe?" Emily said.

If you think the twins would enjoy a meal from the food cart, turn to page 347.

If you think they should steer clear of the food carts, turn to page 294.

"The bottom line is," Emily said, "we have to find a way to get home. And we have to do it with people that we trust. I know that the government doesn't make the best decisions all the time, but I'm pretty confident that they are not going to drop us in some dead-end town somewhere with no money and no way of getting anywhere. They're not going to sell us into slavery or something like that. Maybe it takes a couple of weeks for us to get out of Takewawa, but that's the surest and safest way we can go," she said. "What do you think?"

Ethan sighed. "As much as I don't want to take that long to get home, as much as I want to be home tomorrow afternoon if at all possible, the truth is, I feel the same way. I just think we have to take the sure way, even if it's a little bit slower."

"Okay," Emily said. "If we stick together, then we're going to make it home no matter what we do."

"All right," Ethan said, and opened the door.

Pandora stood outside chewing on a piece of beef jerky. "You guys decide?"

"Yep," Ethan said. "I think we're going to wander back to the embassy here."

Pandora shrugged. "That's your choice," she said. "I think it's kind of a dumb decision myself, but then it's not my life, is it?"

They headed back to Pietro who was holding on the satellite phone with Mom and Dad.

"They're going back to the States their own way," Pandora said.

"No offense," Ethan said. "We just feel like the sure way is the safe way."

Pietro laughed. "Okay, Mom and Dad. I think you've already transferred all the money I'm going to need. I'll get your kids fed and get them back to the embassy, and then they're on their own."

"We'll contact you as soon as we can," Ethan said to Mom. "I'm sure they have a satellite phone at the embassy, and maybe we can get them to let us use it." The twins said goodbye to their parents with a little bit of catch in their voice. It was hard to know when they would hear their voices again.

Turn to page 267.

Emily looked at Ethan, eyes wide. Ethan looked back at Emily, spots of high color in his cheeks.

"This isn't exactly what we bargained for," Emily said.

"No," Ethan said, "it sure isn't."

Emily's face suddenly broke into a wide grin. "Which makes it awesome," she said. "Why not run the roadblock?"

"Because we'll probably die," Ethan said. Small-arms fire pinged off the back windshield. El Chapo reloaded the rifle. Travis paid no more attention than if a fly had landed on the hood of the car.

"Anytime now," she said.

"Why are we voting?" Ethan said. "You're the one driving."

"Yes," she said, "and I know what I want to do. But this is going to be a democracy, because you paid for it. I always try to give good value."

"Then I vote we don't go," Ethan said. "There has to be another way out of town that doesn't involve us running a pair of concrete barriers."

"Emily?" Travis said, Her voice as placid as a summer's day. The rifle cracked, but this shot caromed off the roof of the car. Behind them the men broke into a run, closing the distance.

"In for a penny, in for a pound," Emily said. "Maybe today *is* a good day to die."

"I knew you for a Klingon the moment I met you," Travis said.

She reached under the dashboard again and flipped another couple of switches. This time, when she stepped on the accelerator, it felt to Ethan as if they were having another earthquake. The car rumbled and shook like the space shuttle on the launch pad.

"I'm glad you're wearing seatbelts," Travis said. "I make no guarantees as to being able to stay firmly on the ground here."

"Now you tell us," Emily said, but her face lost none of its bright happiness.

Travis stood on the accelerator, jerking back on the steering wheel, and the car's tires spun like tops, spewing dust and rocks. But *forward*.

Ethan and Emily jerked toward the front of the car, straining against their seatbelts. The little Sentra, instead of running forward toward the roadblock, zipped backward in reverse, shooting down the main road back the way they had come, toward the men who were chasing them.

"What on earth?" Ethan said.

"I need more space to get a run up," Travis said. Her body twisted around to look back through the rearview windshield.

"I'm assuming none of those guys back there have any guts, or this could be a really bad idea," she said. The Sentra blazed backward the two blocks in about five seconds. Men dived out of the road like ninepins scattered by a bowling ball. Travis slammed on the brakes, and the car skidded to a stop.

Turning forward, she shifted the car into a gear far over to the right, where Ethan didn't think the stick had previously gone.

"You might want to cover your head," Travis said. "The airbags in this thing were removed a long time ago." Then she stepped down on the accelerator the same way Mission Control punches the button to launch a rocket. The effect on the Sentra was roughly the same.

If Travis had strapped Titan missile boosters to the back of the car, Ethan didn't think it could have gotten any more speed any faster. For two, maybe three seconds, the wheels just spun in place, vomiting rocks and dirt everywhere. Then they grabbed traction and the little car shot down the block like a missile, aiming for the gap in the concrete.

"Those barrels have to be movable, right?" Travis said. "Otherwise no one could use this road."

"No one *does* use this road," Ethan said, gripping the dashboard, his face drawn in terror.

Behind him, his sister began to laugh. "This is probably really stupid," she said. "But I don't care." The needle on the dashboard crawled past 50, then 60, then 70, with no sign of slowing.

Two blocks away, Travis flipped one more switch on the steering wheel. The speedometer needle buried itself on the right-hand edge. They were slammed back in their seats. Ethan barely had time to hope that Travis was an excellent shot.

She was. The Sentra hit the center of the barrier perfectly, with no more than an inch to spare on either side. The plywood, not having sufficient time to break apart under the impact, acted as a ramp, and the Sentra launched itself into orbit.

Mouths gaped as the sedan rose like a silver bird. How high they got off the ground, Ethan never knew, because it was over so fast, but at one point he was looking down on the heads of the men at the roadblock.

On the other side of the barrier, the road stretched out. This section of the road, for some reason, was paved. Emily screamed as they plummeted toward it. It was Travis's turn to laugh as the car slammed into the roadway as if it had been dropped from heaven. There was a sickening crunch, and Ethan thought for sure that the engine had dropped out of the front of the car and run away screaming. But the Sentra bounced once, twice, the engine whining and the wheels spinning in space. And then, impossibly, the tires gripped. The little Sentra shot up the road, away from town, and into the hills.

Travis had to haul back on the steering wheel and almost stand up in her seat before she could get the brake to engage enough to stop the car. They were two, maybe three miles out of town now, up in the hills again where they could look down at the village. No one appeared to be giving chase. Travis yawned and stretched and turned to Ethan and said, "I believe you have been given your money's worth."

Turn to page 277.

Ethan and Emily thought about all the work they had done to get ready for this trip. All the time they had put into planning all the things that they had dreamed about.

"We worked on this plan for so long. I don't want to leave," Emily said. "We've done so much work, but I have a really bad feeling about this." She sat down heavily on the bed.

"I don't know what to do," Ethan said. "I'm afraid that staying here puts us in real danger. That was only a little earthquake, but what if the next one is much worse? What if we couldn't get home tomorrow, but we can today?"

"I can't shake the feeling that something terrible could happen if we stay," Emily said, putting her arm around her brother.

"Well, I guess it's settled. We'll get back on the bus and head to the airport. It's probably the smartest thing for us to do."

Neither of them were able to sleep much that night, and in the morning they were both bleary-eyed and sleep-deprived, feeling down and sad about the whole situation. Ethan asked Emily if she had changed her mind, but nothing that had happened that night changed anything about the feeling in the pit of her stomach. It was a quiet and somber ride in a half-full bus. Several of the tourists at the hotel had decided to join them, but after talking with the few passengers, it became clear that each of them had already seen the ruins. None of them were leaving without having even had a chance to see the thing they had come so far to experience except Ethan and Emily.

Each mile of new distance between them and Ychu made Ethan sadder and sadder. So much work, so much time and effort, and so much money that they had spent, yet there was nothing to show for it. The countryside that he looked at could possibly have sustained the people who lived there, but in the event of a serious disaster, there was no way that two American fifteen-year-olds were going to be able to fend for themselves. It just wasn't smart to stay.

The bus crunched its way over the dirt and gravel and down into the dry, dusty capital city. It looked just the same as they had left it. There was no smoke from fires, no downed buildings or power lines, no flooding, no damage of any kind, really. The city looked entirely untouched.

Ethan, feeling a little silly, glanced at Emily who was staring out the window.

"It doesn't look like there's anything wrong, does it?" Emily said.

"But if there is, how do you know?" Ethan said.

"I don't," she said, and then sighed. "I just have a terrible feeling."

"I guess I'm kind of glad we're going back," Ethan said. "I don't like all this uncertainty."

"I'm sad we're leaving," Emily said. "But I can't shake the feeling that it's the right thing to do."

The bus let them off just to the side of the airport, which looked like everything else in town, perfectly normal. They walked their bags through the front doors and found a huge crowd packed up against the airline ticket counters. It seemed that tons of tourists were clamoring to get out. The line to reach the ticket counter stretched almost all the way back to the doors, and Ethan immediately knew it was going to take them quite some time to make their way up to the front where they could get some information and find out if they could change their flight. Most of the people coming away from the counter looked somewhat frustrated.

They waited for two hours. They were very hungry and very tired when they reached the front.

The lady who greeted them seemed even more tired than they were, which wasn't too much of a surprise.

"You already have a flight?" she said.

"We do," Ethan said. "It doesn't leave until next week."

"I only have two options for you," said the attendant, after clicking away on her computer keys. "One of them is to leave on the flight that takes off in three hours, but it doesn't go directly back to the States. You will have a stop in Ecuador, another stop in Mexico City, and you will reach your final destination sometime early tomorrow afternoon."

"That's thirty-six hours of travel," Ethan said.

"That sounds exhausting to me," Emily added. "What is our other option?"

"Your second option is, you can wait until tomorrow for the direct flight back to your final destination. I only have two available seats left right now, so if you want them you have to make the decision now."

If you think the twins should get on the earliest flight, turn to page 62.

If you think they should wait until the flight tomorrow so their trip is shorter, turn to page 303.

Emily gazed down the street toward the solar array lining the top of a squat red-brick building. The flat black panels looked like open arms, gathering in power. It didn't look too heavily damaged, unlike many of the other buildings in the near vicinity. It didn't look damaged at all.

"I wonder," she said.

"It's entirely possible it be could be the thing we are looking for. There's only one way to know," Ethan said. "But it is kind of a risk."

"I think," Emily said, "that we're at the point where some risks are entirely justified. We're going to need to start acting like we can depend on ourselves. If we wait around for other people to do things for us, this mess is only going to get worse."

"I'm game if you are." He gave her a smile and a small shrug. That was a big thing for Ethan, Emily knew. For him to take a chance like this was somewhat out of character. But she guessed there were going to be a whole lot of things out of character from this point on.

She swung up Ethan's backpack and put it on her own shoulders. "I'll carry this for you," she said. They started off down the street to the southwest, toward the building that they had seen earlier.

It wasn't taking long for people to start putting their lives back together again. As they walked down the street, they saw people moving bricks out of the roadway, picking up pieces of wood and parts of buildings that had fallen into the street, everywhere talking softly to each other. This didn't appear to be a residential block; most of these buildings were small restaurants, office buildings, and a couple of electronics warehouses. Those appeared to have come to the most harm as their glass fronts were shattered. In one building, the second floor had collapsed onto the first, smashing all the inventory inside. The shop owner stood outside the building, staring inside, with his hands on his hips and shaking his head sadly.

"There is a lot of devastation here," Emily said. "It seems like there should be a way for us to help."

"I think the best way we could help," Ethan said, "is to get ourselves out of here so no one has to feed us or take care of us. I don't know that there's a whole lot that we can do."

Emily led the way toward the building that was their target, with Ethan following along a pace behind her. They worked their way down the street, and it seemed that here the damage had not been quite as bad as in some other places in the city. As they neared the block where the building was with the solar array, the damage seemed less, until they got to the building that was the object of their search.

This building seemed almost untouched. Even the glass in the front of the building had resisted shattering.

Some of the upper-floor windows had been broken, but for the most part the building remained remarkably untouched.

"They knew how to build this building, at least," Emily said. The front of the building bore a sign that said, in Spanish, "Internet Cafe."

"This is exactly what we were looking for," Ethan said. "And they still have power. Look!" He pointed inside where a couple of incandescent lamps glowed. There were also a couple of computers they could see from the street that had their screens on, emitting soft glows.

"Bingo," Emily said.

"You said it."

Ethan put his hand on the outside door handle of the internet cafe. Despite the sun, the handle was cool. He wondered if that meant air conditioning inside and listened for the hum of an air conditioning unit but couldn't make one out over the din of the city.

He tugged on the door but it did not swing open. He could see through into the interior of the building. There were people in there, but they seemed uninterested in his presence and hadn't even looked up.

"That's weird," Ethan said.

"What, is the door locked?" Emily said.

"Yeah," Ethan said. He rapped on the glass. Still no one in the interior looked up. "Okay, that's even weirder. How do they expect people to come to their cafe if the door is locked?"

"Maybe you need to knock a little louder," Emily said, and stepping forward, she rapped on the glass herself, looking through the glass into the interior. There was no movement at all. Several people occupied computer desks inside, but they kept typing away over the sound of the knocking. Or maybe they couldn't hear it. It was possible that there was some kind of music playing inside or something, Ethan couldn't tell. "So what do we do?" Ethan said.

Emily thought for a second. She said, "Do you have paper in your backpack?"

"Of course I have paper in my backpack," Ethan said. "But I don't understand how that's going to help us."

"Just give me a piece of paper and a pen," Emily said. He handed over the paper and pen. Emily took it and said, "Turn around, I need some place to write."

He felt her scribbling something on the piece of paper she laid against his back, then she said, "Okay, let's try this."

She slapped the paper against the glass with the drawing facing in. Through the paper Ethan saw a large thickly colored-in dollar sign. This time Emily pounded on the glass with her fist, and she did it until somebody looked up, a man with a long, pointy beard and shocking red hair tied back in a bun. When he looked, she pointed at the piece of paper. The man's eyebrows raised and his face broke into a wide smile. He made a gesture as if to say "Why didn't you say so?" then rose from his chair and sauntered over to the front door. He pressed a button and the door popped open.

"Took you long enough," Ethan said, a little testily.

"Well," the man said, "at least you were clever enough to figure out how to get through the door. Not everyone can do that."

Ethan stepped inside. The place didn't just have power, it was *air-conditioned*. Cool air flowed down around him. The man pushed the door shut and locked it behind them by pressing a button. Ethan heard a clack as electromagnetic locks engaged.

"I don't understand why you have an internet cafe that you don't want people to come into," Ethan said.

The man pointed back through the window at the rest of the city. He said, "Ordinarily, I wouldn't care. But things have changed over the last 24 hours. Now, there are only certain people that I think it might be smart to allow into my building."

Emily and Ethan exchanged a glance. "But you're letting *us* in?" Emily said.

"Absolutely," the man said. "You said the magic word." He passed them toward the interior without offering them any explanation or even beckoning them to follow him. His bun bounced lightly behind him like a jogger on a treadmill. The place smelled vaguely of cinnamon.

Emily said, "I guess the magic word is money."

Turn to page 285.

Ethan held tightly to the leather strap and gazed out the window as the countryside fled by. It was dustier than he expected it would be. He had expected the whole country would look like the area in and around the ruins of Ychurichuc with its vines, jungle, and ancient trees, but this area looked much more like the American midwest—dry and hilly, with large mountains towering in the distance. The gray-brown ground was hard and rocky, as if it seldom rained, and the road was pitted and pockmarked. It felt like what he imagined it would be like driving through a war zone.

As the bus jounced and scrambled up the hills, the whine of the engine rose in pitch. On one particularly steep hill, Ethan was afraid the overloaded bus would fail to make the crest, but at the last moment it gave an extra lurch, heaved itself over the hill, and started down into the valley below. About half way down, however, the sound of the engine quit altogether and the driver looked up in alarm as he braked hard. The bus shuddered and slid sideways, barely missing an oncoming truck, then steadied and coasted to the bottom of the hill. Drifting to a stop, it gave a great sigh and sagged in on itself like a huge, exhausted ox.

The driver rose, opened the doors, and exited the bus. Hoisting up the hood, the passengers were treated to a steady stream of what the twins could only guess to be Spanish curse words. As the driver continued tinkering and banging, some passengers looked around in alarm, but most of the locals seemed untroubled by this display, whatever it was. After a few moments, the bus driver came back into the cabin of the bus and made an announcement in Spanish and in some other language that Ethan did not know. He looked over at Emily and her eyes were wide.

"Did he just say the bus is broken down and would not be able to be fixed?" she said.

"That's what I heard him say," Ethan said. "He said we can wait here for the next bus, or we can take the opportunity to go into the little bodega they have here."

If you think the twins should stay on the bus and wait, turn to page 276.

If you think the twins should get off and assess their situation, turn to page 243.

The twins hung out at the internet cafe for another hour or so fueling up on beef jerky and oranges. Pietro was friendly, if a little bit cool toward them, and after a while they felt like they should probably head back, in case their transportation to their temporary lodging was available.

When they opened the cafe's front door again, the humidity hit them like a wet rag in the face.

"Ack," Emily said. "The weather didn't get a whole lot better while we were inside." They trudged the five blocks back to the embassy. When they got there, the situation hadn't changed much.

They asked the guard, "Has the bus come by to take us to our hotel?"

"Not a hotel," the guard said. "More like, well, you'll see when you get there. But no, the bus won't be here for another hour or so."

They sat out front and watched the still-smoldering city fill the sky up with smoke.

Turn to page 338.

"I want to report him to the store, so they can keep a lookout for him." Ethan trotted off toward the cashier. He spent a couple minutes explaining what had happened. The cashier seemed entirely unsurprised.

"This happen all the time," the woman said in decent English. "You can tell manager, but he does nothing."

Still, Ethan wanted to try. A burning lump of injustice flamed in the pit of his stomach. It wasn't right that the man could do this and get away with it.

The manager's office was up a flight of grimy steps. Ethan knocked on the door. A moment passed, then he heard footsteps and the door unlocked.

"Hello," he said. "My name is Ethan Tuttle, and I was just robbed in your store."

The manager's shoulders slumped a bit, but he waved the twins inside and closed the door.

"Let me guess," the manager said, "Somebody bumped into you in the produce section."

"Your store doesn't really have a 'section,'" Ethan replied as the manager snorted. "Actually, it was by the cans of soup."

The manager leaned toward the windows. "Look out there," he said. "Most of the people in the store are tourists. I bet you are here for the Ychurichuc ruins, yes?"

Emily said, "That's right."

"Many of these people are as well. They come here loaded with American, German, English money, and the pickpockets know they will come to this store. They wait for them, and then they take their money. They are very good."

"Why don't you stop them?" Ethan said. "It seems wrong that they keep getting away with it."

"I can't stop them," the manager said. "It's never the same ones. The tourists are not around long enough to press charges, even if we could catch them, which we can't."

"The cashiers must see when it happens. They must know," Emily said, her eyes on the floor. The cashiers had a good view of the place where Ethan had his money stolen.

To her surprise, the manager broke out laughing. "They probably do. It wouldn't surprise me if they were working with the pickpockets."

Ethan clenched his fists. His voice rose a notch. "That's horrible! Why would they do that? It just takes money from the store."

"Yes," said the manager, "but not from *them*. They get paid the same either way. The store is owned by the government. We all work for them. We will get paid no matter whether you are happy or sad. Even if you lose all your money. And what if the pickpockets offer to split some of it with them?" He shook his head and suddenly looked very tired. "No. It is no good. I understand you are frustrated, but go, buy your things if you still can, and get to where you are going. I will watch from here and see that you are not attacked again."

Emily saw Ethan start to say something more, but then he turned and walked over to the office door. "Thank you anyway," Ethan said.

"Good luck, Ethan Tuttle," the manager said. "Young lady," he added, nodding his head to Emily.

The twins descended the stairs, somewhat less excitedly than when they'd come into the store. It took them only a few moments to get the items they needed. Every few seconds, Ethan touched his waist pack, making sure it was still there. Emily's hand never left hers, even after they'd departed the store and made their way back to the airport.

"That's a lesson I won't forget any time soon," Ethan said, unlocking their locker. "At least our luggage is still here."

Emily took the handle of her bag. Her grip made her knuckles white. "I'm not letting go of this thing until we get into our hotel room."

"Good thing the bus depot is just around the corner," Ethan said. "I'm looking forward to sitting and letting the adventure happen on the other side of the glass for a while."

Turn to page 111.

Emily proved to be right on with her prediction of what they'd find at the crossing. When they approached the border, rolling up slowly with thousands of others, they found the situation as chaotic and nonsensical as they had expected.

A series of guards came forward and waved their vehicle to a stop, never mind that it was almost stopped already. Travis assumed an air of great importance, despite the shabby looking vehicle that she was driving. Her paperwork seemed to make an impression on the guards as well, as she was continually told to drive farther to the left toward the lines that seem to be moving quicker.

The guards handed over forms for everyone to fill out, but the paperwork made no sense, and the process itself was riddled with needless complexity.

"This is a new one," Travis said, scanning the papers. "Never seen these before."

"Why couldn't we just cross normally?" Ethan said, furiously scribbling. "We would drive up, step out of the vehicle, hand over our passports—no offense Emily—"

"None taken."

"—and then they would wave us through, and out we would go."

One guard appeared to have been detailed to ask about currency. "Are you carrying any saladera?" he said. He looked specifically at the Tuttles.

"Yes," Ethan said, because even when he thought it was going to get him in trouble, he didn't like to lie. "I'm carrying several thousand saladera."

The guard frowned and made a note on his clipboard. "You will need to exchange that saladera here at the border," he said. "We do not allow people to take our currency out of the country."

Ethan said, unable to help himself, "That doesn't make any sense. If you have an inflation problem, where you have too much money in circulation, it would be smarter to let me take the money out of the country, where it will do me no good at all, than to make me exchange it before I leave."

The guard made another note on his paper and pointed to a different line. "You will take the car over there. Then you will climb out and go into the booth. They will take care of the exchange for you, and then you will be allowed to proceed further." He marched off as if dragging the weight of the nearby mountains behind him.

"Nice going," Emily said. "Even if you weren't going to lie, did you have to insult him?"

Travis laughed. "I'm relatively sure he didn't think he was being insulted. Guards just don't like being answered back. And you're right," she said, laying her hand on Ethan's arm. Ethan's ears began to burn. "They would be much better off just letting you take the money out of the country. In fact, they'd be better off holding a giant bonfire and having people burn all their currency in the middle of the square. But of course, people won't voluntarily do that. I suspect they're going to get rid of that extra currency eventually. But this has been the policy in Allqukilla for many years. They don't want people carrying the currency out of the country."

"But why?" Ethan said. "That doesn't make any sense."

"You told me that you had experience in dealing with governments," Travis said.

"We do. Oh," he said, realizing.

"Exactly," Travis said. "There's nothing for it now. We better go and do as they say." She cranked the wheel to the right and the vehicle rolled its way over to a line fronting a makeshift shack in which sat a harried official with a huge pile of saladera behind him in a bucket.

"I was told I needed to exchange money here. Sir," Ethan said, belatedly remembering his manners.

"How much do you have?" the man said.

"I have 11,300," Ethan said.

"11,300. What currency would you like that converted to?"

Ethan thought for a moment. "I suppose we will probably need Ecuadorian dollars," he said.

"Sorry," the man said, "I don't have any Ecuadorian dollars."

"Well," Ethan said, "how about US dollars?"

"No," the man said, "I don't have any American dollars either."

Ethan scroll through the other possible currencies Euros, Chinese Won, Japanese Yen, the man didn't have any of those currencies, either.

"What *do* you have?" Ethan said. He couldn't keep all of the annoyance out of his voice.

"I have Argentinian pesos," the official said, taking no obvious notice, "and Chilean pesos."

"At what exchange rate?"

"One peso to one saladera."

"That's insane! Pesos are worth five times a saladera," Ethan said, entirely forgetting that he was going to be polite. "That's totally useless. I might as well be exchanging it for that paper you're writing on."

"You can file a complaint with the ministry," the man said, as if he had said it ten thousand times that day.

Ethan thought he probably had. "And what will happen if I do that?" Ethan said.

The man looked up at him and said nothing for a long moment. Ethan nodded. "I suppose I might have known. Well," he said, "I don't want any of those currencies, so may I have my saladera back? At least it will be interesting souvenirs for the people at home."

"No," the man said, scooping the saladera off the table and depositing them in the bucket, "we must keep the currency here in our country. I'm sorry."

"But that's like $200!"

"Yes," the man said, "things are difficult everywhere. Your time is up. Next!"

Ethan left the shack fuming. The two ladies leaned against the car, in the bright sunshine, and chuckled to themselves.

Travis swept her dark hair back over one ear. "I take it that didn't go well," she said.

"You take it correctly," Ethan said. "That was not just pointless, but also humiliating."

"Yes," Travis said, "but now the government is $200 richer, so there's that. I take it they were all out of any currencies you might have been interested in exchanging for."

"Yes," Ethan said, "how did you know?"

"Pretty much just math," Travis said, jerking her head over her shoulder at the endless line of cars behind them. "We aren't the first group to come through here in the last couple days. We're not even the first group of refugees. Heck, we're not even the first people in the last hour. Do you really think that even if they had any of that money on hand at one point, by now they would have any left?"

Ethan slumped his shoulders. "No, I guess not," he said. "This whole trip has sure been an education in finance."

Turn to page 176.

Ethan looked over the passengers of the bus. Some tourists got up to get out, but the locals showed no alarm that the bus had broken down. It seemed to Ethan that they had seen this before and perhaps there really was no cause for alarm. Through the window, Ethan saw the tourists milling about, looking askance at the tumbledown inn whose parking lot they were using for repairs. Some pointed at the local bodega. Out front, a stout smiling man waved at them, beckoning them to come over, presumably for a drink or possibly for a room for the night. On one edge of the parking lot, newer cars sat like dominoes. A group of raggedy men leaned against them. They reminded Ethan very much of the taxi drivers he had seen in the center of town.

Emily shot her brother a nervous glance. Ethan sniffed at her, and wrinkled his nose. "You smell awful," he said.

"You don't smell like *eau de cologne* yourself. Apparently, no matter what we do, we're doomed to smell just like everything else in here."

They spoke in English, hoping they would not be understood, and it seemed that they weren't.

Turn to page 362.

Ethan was almost hopeful that they would get another chance to show off the little car, its amazing abilities, and the no less incredible moxie of its driver. But sadly for him, the rest of the trip was relatively uneventful. There was only one other incident of note and that involved actually getting across the border when they reached it.

The mountains outside St. Lucia left them still several hours drive on the pitted, dirt roads of the Allqukillan backcountry. It allowed Travis to show off her little Sentra's additional off-road capabilities, but it wasn't anything like the sort of drama they had faced before. Fortified with their food from the mercado, they were able to keep driving deep into the night.

Travis kept the nose of the little car pointed toward the Ecuadorian border. "There's a little shack here," she said, pointing to the map, "that I think will make a good place for us to cross."

They had seen very little in the way of refugee traffic. One other little town had come and gone, where they had obtained the news that the government had declared a bank freeze, locking down all currency deposits and withdrawals.

"Even if we had cell service," Ethan said, "we still wouldn't be able to withdraw money." The phone networks were still down, and even if there had been power, the machines were unable to access the central system. Still, they hardly needed it. All that they really needed was in the car with them. Or perhaps lost under the floods of the Takewawa Dam. Time would tell.

"I would like to have another few thousand saladera," Ethan said. "You never know when that might come in handy."

The border crossing was staffed only by a single guard, in the shack Travis mentioned, shivering and bored. The barrier over the crossing proved to be a wooden post that he turned by hand. There was no one on the Ecuadorian side at all.

They asked the guard about it. He laughed. "No one ever comes here," he said. "I'm only here because I live in the local village, and it's better than sitting in the house listening to my mother complain at me all day."

They shared some of their food with the guard. It was a welcome relief for all of them. He showed no interest in their paperwork or lack thereof. When they were done eating, he raised the wooden bar and waved them across.

Travis tipped her little Sentra across the border and down into Ecuador. It took another three hours for them to find a decent road, but once they did, they made good time into the capital city, where the United States Embassy was only too glad to have them arrive. The clerk at the embassy didn't seem curious as to how they had managed to get cross the border without an

Ecuadorian stamp in Ethan's passport or without Emily having a passport at all.

"We're in one of those times," she said, "where it doesn't pay to pry too deeply into things. You want to get home, and we want desperately for you to do that. The longer you're here, the more difficult the situation becomes for you and for us."

With access to the international banking system, they were able to have funds wired and purchase tickets to fly home within a day. Also, with the ATMs now working, they were able to get a little bit of Ecuadorian money that they used to treat Travis to a nice dinner before she went back.

"I think it will be much less of a hassle going in the other direction," Travis said.

"You two have had quite the adventure, with and without me. I hope that you'll remember us here when you get back to the States," Travis said.

"Suppose I were to send a postcard to the internet cafe," Emily said. "Will that reach you?"

Travis chuckled a little. "Eventually, I'm sure that it will. Especially if there is a tip involved for the delivery man at the cafe."

"We'll make sure we get Pietro a little something to grease the wheels," Ethan said. Travis hugged them both and climbed back aboard her Sentra. The twins watched it out of sight.

This was not how they imagined the return trip to the States. No luggage but Ethan's backpack, the backpack Emily liberated from Pietro, and hardly any souvenirs to remember their trip by.

"All we really have are memories," Ethan said, as they sat at the gate waiting for the airplane.

"Well," said a voice from behind them, "if it isn't our world travelers."

The twins whirled around and there behind them was their father. They threw themselves into his arms, and could hardly stop talking about how surprised they were that he was there and all the things that had happened to them.

"One at a time," Father said, "we'll have plenty of time for the whole story on the way home. I couldn't let you guys have all the fun. I'm glad that I got here to meet you. Your mother and I were terribly worried about you, and this time, we need to make sure that when you get to the airport, you actually get on a plane."

An hour later, they did.

The End

"Okay, Thon," Ethan said, "What do we do now?"

"The first thing we need to see is what your supplies are. You might have to live off them at some point," Thon said.

"Your village won't feed us?"

"Of course we will. But there aren't a lot of people your size in town. And even after we get to town, there's going to be a ways to go to get you back home."

Ethan swung his backpack around, hanging it off the front of him like a mother holds her child. He unzipped the main compartment and looked inside. "I think I have everything I need here. I mean, I would hate to lose our luggage and all the things that we have stashed in it. I especially would hate to lose the two books that Dad gave me to read on the trip, but I have the tour book about the Ychurichuc ruins, I have my toiletries, and I have a change of clothes. I have the right shoes on," he said, wiggling his foot in the air to demonstrate. "I have my passport, and all the other documentation that I think I will need. Most especially, I have most of our money. How about you?"

Emily performed the same trick with her backpack, but the look on her face told Ethan that she already knew what she would find. "I have the books," she said. Ethan looked at her with astonishment.

"What?" she said. "You never know when you're going to have a few minutes and nothing particular to do. I always have the book I'm reading and the book I'm writing with me at all times. You know that."

"But I bet you don't have a change of clothes in there, do you?" Ethan said.

Emily frowned. "No, I don't."

"Not even a change of underwear?"

"Not even a change of underwear."

"Good grief," Ethan said. "Mom made us bring like twenty pairs of underwear. You left all of them in the hotel?'

"Yes," Emily said, a little testily. "I was pretty sure I wasn't going to need to change my underwear at the Ychurichuc ruins."

From behind her, she heard Thon snort, as if he were trying to suppress a laugh.

"Anyway," she said, "I just didn't bring those things with me today. I do have my documentation, and I think I have a travel toothbrush stuffed in one of the side pockets. You know, just in case I…"

"Just in case you what?" Ethan said.

"Well," she said, "you know, just in case." And then, knowing she shouldn't, she tossed a glance back over her shoulder toward Thon.

Fortunately for her, Ethan wasn't paying attention. "Well, that means all your stuff is still at the hotel. We'll have to go back and get it anyway."

"No," Emily said. "I mean, I would hate to leave all that stuff. But I'm sure we can just wire the hotel and ask them to send it on to us. In the meantime, when Thon tells us he's our best bet for getting out of the country, I believe him."

Ethan was about to ask her why she believed this, when Thon step forward and said, "We better get moving if we're going to stay ahead of the weather." He tossed his head to the right toward the south, and Ethan saw a shadow building there on the horizon. Clouds coming up, dark ones.

"Oh, terrific," Ethan said, "What's that people always say about things can't get worse?"

Emily said, "Is your village close enough that we will be able to get there before the rain comes?"

Thon pursed his lips and said, "It's in the hands of fate. What I know is that if we don't start moving right now, we definitely won't make it. Any rain is going to be very bad for us and a lot of others. There aren't going to be a whole lot of people who have good shelter, if I'm any judge of how severe that earthquake was."

"Yeah," Emily said, "the hotel might have been damaged and we couldn't get to our luggage anyway. Look on the bright side," she said, punching Ethan in the shoulder.

"Yes," Ethan said. "Well."

Thon said, "I take it that you are ready to go."

"We are," Emily said, "there's nothing left for us here."

In response, Thon shouldered his own small pack, and began to walk back up the central staircase towards the main buildings of the Ychurichuc Temple.

"But we were just up here," Ethan said.

"I know that," Thon said. "This time we're not going to be stopping. We're going on through and off the back of the mountain. There's a fence, but it isn't a very sturdy one. We won't have any trouble with it."

"After that, how far is it?' Emily said.

"It's about three miles," Thon said. "But it's not the kind of three miles you would run in a road race. It's probably five or six if you take into account all the ups-and-downs we'll have to do."

Turn to page 28.

Emily supposed that having unlocked the door, the man figured he had given them enough of an invitation and didn't need to say anything else. He had gone back to his desk and was clacking away on his keyboard. She looked at Ethan and shrugged, then walked deeper into the interior. The overhead lights were off, but that didn't seem to affect the lighting of the interior. With the big windows facing out to the city and toward the sunshine, the place was brightly lit. Six or seven people were scattered around the floor with their faces toward computer screens. In the center was an open area and a table with a couple of laptops on it. The laptops were closed and the chairs were empty. In the middle of the table sat two cases of bottled water, and Emily immediately wondered if those were available for consumption. She was quite thirsty. And getting hungry again quickly.

Ethan wandered around the table, peering over the shoulders of people working on the computer screens. None of them looked up at him or paid even the slightest attention to his being there. Emily walked over to stand next to the man who had opened the door. "My name is Emily," she said.

"You can call me Pietro," he said.

Pale-complected, with hair that had hints of rust among the dirty blond, he didn't look anything like

Emily's image of either Allqukillan or Italian, if that was what kind of name Pietro was.

"I told *you* my real name," Emily said.

The man shot a glance up at her and went back to studying the computer screen. "That wasn't very smart," he said. "What use would I have for your real name?"

"I'm just being friendly," Emily said.

The man nodded, but didn't say anything.

"We need to contact our parents," Emily said, when no further communication seemed to be forthcoming.

"You came to the right place," Pietro said. "But I won't do it for nothing."

"We didn't really expect that you would," Emily said. "We have money."

The man cocked an eyebrow up at her and shook his head with a smile on his face as if he didn't really believe her. "I'm sure you think you do," he said. "The question is are you right?"

Ethan had moved over to stand behind Emily. He reached for his waist pack and unzipped the front of it, drawing out a hundred dollar bill. "I think this is what my sister is talking about," Ethan said.

The man turned his head, but didn't appear impressed. He went right back to typing on his computer. "That doesn't convince me," he said. "And what's *your* name, anyway?"

"My name is Reginald," Ethan said.

The man snorted and this time swiveled in his chair to look Ethan full in the face. "You learn fast. That's something. That money is fine," he said, pointing at the hundred-dollar bill. "But I need something more real."

Ethan held the hundred-dollar bill up to his face and then looked back at Pietro. "This is real," he said. "I wouldn't carry counterfeit money."

Pietro laughed. "That's not what I'm talking about," he said. "I would eventually spot a counterfeit, even if it was very good. But all paper money is a counterfeit of real money anyway."

"It is?" Emily said. "I don't understand."

"We understand why somebody might not be all that interested in saladera," Ethan said. "It seems to be losing its value every day."

"Losing its value every *hour*," Pietro said, and there was a hint of chagrin there, as if it were something he was sorry about. "Ever since the new administration came in a couple years ago, the government realized that it was going to have a difficult time repaying its foreign debt and started the printing presses right up. Now with everyone scrambling for their bank accounts, saladera will be flooding the streets before long, and things are going to get hairy. But that's not what I'm talking about," he said.

"Even this—" he said, reaching up for the hundred-dollar bill.

Ethan jerked it away from his fingers.

"I'm not going to *keep* it," the man said. "But you hold on to it for now anyway. Even *this*," he said, correcting himself and just pointing at the bill, "It may seem real, but it isn't real money. Do you know what money is?"

"Of course we know what money is," Ethan said. "It's the stuff you use to buy things."

"That's what most people think," Pietro said, with the satisfied nod of the teacher on a roll. "And yes, most people's connection with money has to do with buying things. Or at least, that's what they think of it. But money actually is significantly more valuable than just a means of purchasing things. It's also significantly more fragile than that piece of paper is. It isn't at all what people think."

"How can that be?" Emily said. "Everybody uses money all the time. You're telling me they don't know what it is?"

"That's exactly what I'm telling you," he said. Pietro reached into the pocket of his faded blue jeans and pulled out a coin. Shiny and yellow, it gleamed in the natural light from the windows. "See this?" he said. "This is gold. Surely gold is money, isn't it?"

"I can tell by the way you asked the question, the answer must be no," Ethan said. "But I would have said yes if you had asked me in a different way."

"Of course you would have," Pietro said. He spun the coin on his palm and walked it across his knuckles like a magician. Ethan wondered if he'd try to pull it out of someone's ear next. "Although I give you full marks for being able to take tests. The truth is, even though everybody for generations has believed that gold is money, it isn't money either. Or it isn't necessarily money all the time, I guess that is a better way to put it."

Emily eyed the water on the table and licked her lips. Pietro said, "Thirsty? It's Emily, right?"

"Yes to both questions," Emily said.

"So," Pietro said, "if I were to offer you this gold coin and ask you if you would rather have the coin than one of those bottles of water, what would you say?"

Emily looked at the coin and held out her hand. Pietro placed the coin in her palm. It was heavy, certainly not a pound, but more than a couple of ounces. "I would say thank you very much for the coin," Emily said.

Pietro smiled and held out his hand for the coin. Emily handed it back, a little bit reluctantly.

"I thought you would probably say that," he said. "Because you're not very thirsty yet." As if deciding to get really interested, he pushed his chair back a little bit so he could take in their whole appearance: very dirty, quite smelly, and obviously American. Ethan wondered what else those pale blue eyes were seeing.

"How did you get to the embassy? I assume you came down the hill from the Quonset hut they have up there."

The twins glanced at each other. "We did," Ethan said. "And we had a time getting there, too, I can tell you. Did you know they've got thousands of refugees in a camp in a soccer stadium?"

"The Alberto Garcia. I saw something about that on the news. It's been more than a day since the earthquake. How many of those people over in the stadium would rather have a drink of water than a gold coin right now?"

"Some of them," Ethan admitted. "Things had been getting pretty bad there."

"And what about all those people who are not lucky enough to get to the stadium?" Pietro said. "What about those people? Would they rather have a drink of water than a gold coin? This coin is worth about $4,000 American. But if the city is without water and power for another few days, this coin will be worth almost nothing. People would be much happier at that point to have one of these bottles of water." Pietro stuffed the coin back in the pocket of his jeans. "Money changes according to the value that people place on it. All money is a store of value. Sometimes you can store value in objects that have no intrinsic worth, like this coin. Or like your hundred-dollar bill. But sometimes, those things lose their value. And sometimes, they lose their value without a natural disaster, although those certainly don't make things any better."

"Like what's happening to the saladera," Ethan said. "It started losing its value because the government is printing them."

"That's right," Pietro said. "Because of that, I won't take saladera for anything right now. And I don't even want dollars. If you want to call your parents, I'm going to have to teach you about a different kind of money altogether."

Pietro swiveled his chair back around and hammered a couple of keys on his keyboard. The screen flickered, then brought up a website like the main page of a bank. It was no bank that Ethan ever heard of, though. Pietro typed a couple more keys, then lightning fast typed in a long string of digits and letters. It was a password of some kind. The website blinked a couple of times and changed to let him in.

"Have you ever heard of cryptocurrency?" Pietro said.

Ethan looked at Emily. She narrowed her eyes. Ethan said, "Wait, didn't we learn something about that a few years ago when we were reading about Jekyll Island?"

"You may have," Pietro said. "Bitcoin is a cryptocurrency. It's just one of dozens of different kinds of cryptocurrencies, which are money just like any other kind of money. The only difference is that the prices of those particular kinds of money can't be manipulated by governments."

"You mean there's no inflation?" Ethan said.

"Oh, there's inflation," Pietro said. "But it's not because of the money supply. More of the currency is issued as a way of making sure that there is enough of it to supply the demand for it, but that doesn't mean inflation, necessarily. But no government can print additional quantities just to get itself out of debt, which makes it a lot harder to manipulate for political purposes."

"No president can order a bunch of it to be printed so they can pay foreign debts, for instance," Emily said. She licked her lips again. Good conversation. Interesting theories. But still no water.

"That's right. Nobody controls whether the value rises or falls. The market handles that."

Ethan cut in. "But didn't I read somewhere about Bitcoin being volatile, like a stock?"

"In the international exchanges, that's true," Pietro said. "The value of the particular coin against other currencies goes up and down according to supply and demand, just like any other currency. But the currency itself does not inflate. It doesn't change value according to people's confidence in a particular government or the government's ability to deliver on its promises."

"Like the government of Allqukilla," Ethan said. "It made a lot of promises, took on a bunch of debt, and now has a country that is in some serious difficulties." As if on cue, the sound of a siren went rolling by on the street outside.

"You're catching on," Pietro said. "The only kind of currency that I will accept is the kind over which no government and no group of people has complete control. That means a cryptocurrency."

"But I don't have any cryptocurrency," Ethan said. "Can't I exchange my dollars for some?"

Pietro said, "Of course you can. And fortunately for you I happen to be a fellow who can make that happen." He tapped a few more keys and rolled over to a new screen. "You'll need to enter your information and open an account," he said, but then he paused and looked Ethan up and down. "But you're under eighteen, aren't you? I don't know that it will let you do that."

Ethan held out his hundred-dollar bill again. "If you let me make a call to my father, who is well over eighteen, I'm pretty sure he can set up that kind of an account on his end, and then you can get the currency transferred to you. If I let you keep this hundred-dollar bill for security, as a deposit against whatever charge you're going to make, will that work?"

Pietro smiled very big and stood up, his chair swiveling behind him. "Follow me," he said. "I have just the phone we need in the other room."

Turn to page 49.

The carts looked sketchy. The twins passed them and their stomachs growled noisily, but they kept on walking through the gates of the market. Just inside, a vendor was selling blankets, brightly-woven and made of soft, wool-like fibers. Emily ran her hands over them longingly, but there was no way she had enough money to buy one. That wasn't what they were here for anyway.

Each shop had something different, from carvings made from a soft orange stone to custom leather satchels. The food vendors seemed to be congregated on the outside of the market, and the farmers there had every kind of fruit and vegetable imaginable... and some that weren't. The twins quickly stocked up on delicious-looking fruit and vegetables they could easily pack.

The prices were excellent, too.

"How can they sell their fruit so cheaply?" Emily said, biting into a mango.

"No overhead. Or not very much. They don't have to deal with big buildings and lots of regulations. Remember how the taco trucks did it back home? They had an advantage, keeping costs low compared to the restaurants."

"That must be how this place works, too." Emily thanked the fruit vendor in Spanish. The lady only smiled and nodded.

"Probably doesn't speak much Spanish. I'll bet she speaks Quechua or some other Amerind language."

"It's a good thing we found this place. We got way more stuff here than we would have in the supermarket, probably for a cheaper price."

"Farmers market food is the freshest, anyway."

Their bags filled, the twins went back to the airport to retrieve their luggage before heading to the bus stop.

Turn to page 111.

"We can't stand here," Ethan said. "Is it hide or run?"

A rifle bullet pinged off a rock five feet up the path from them. "It's run," Emily said, and took off again. Ethan scrambled after her, losing his footing.

The recent rain had made the rocks slick, and even their fairly new boots could hardly find purchase. Emily slid sideways into the brush, and Ethan grabbed her hand, hauling her back out onto the path. They made one more switchback.

Rounding the corner, they slammed into two men. The twins crashed to the trail, bouncing off the men as if they were made of stone.

"Well, well," one of them said. "What have we here? Emily screamed.

One of the men clamped his hand over her mouth. She bit down and tasted blood.

Now *he* was screaming. The other one slugged Ethan in the stomach with the butt of his rifle, and Ethan went down like a sack of rocks. The man said, waving his gun in her face, "You'll get the same if you don't shut up."

Emily stopped screaming.

Her brother retched in the dirt path. He put a hand out as if to say, *I'm okay.*

The man questioned them in Spanish. "What are you doing here? What are Americans doing crawling around our hills?"

Emily and Ethan pretended not to understand.

"I don't speak Spanish," Emily said in English. "We don't speak any Spanish. I don't know what you're saying."

The men shouted at them louder, as if that was going to do any good. Emily just continued shaking her head and raising her palms as if to say, *I don't understand you.*

The men turned to each other and continued speaking in Spanish.

"What are we going to do with them?" one of them said.

"I don't know," said the other.

"This wasn't what I signed up for."

"Well, we can't just let them go," the first one said. "I suppose we should drag them back up the hill. We will let José sort it out."

He dragged Ethan to his feet and shoved him back up the path.

Ethan stumbled and almost fell, but caught himself. He caught Emily's eye, hoping the bandits didn't speak any English. "I'm okay. That was good thinking."

"*Silencio!*" one of the men yelled, and threatened to hit Ethan again. Ethan said nothing more. He just kept putting one foot in front of the other as they climbed the path. Emily caught his eye once or twice, as if to ask, "Where is Thon?" But Ethan said nothing and hoped that their friend had gotten away.

A hundred yards or so up the path, they met the group that had been chasing them.

These men were out of breath from running. They seemed oddly pleased. The one they called José said, "The boss will be really happy. We were hoping that when those idiots from the White Guard took over the road, we would start to get people coming up over the hills. It's quick work for some easy money." They stripped the backpacks from Ethan and Emily, and began to go through them.

Right away, they found the money.

Their talk got more animated.

"Hey, José. This is pretty good. He even has dollars."

"We need that, since we can't get into the bank anymore!" one of the bandits exclaimed.

"You have any more?" one of them shouted in Spanish in Ethan's face, but he pretended not to understand what they said.

After a while, they gave up and tied them to a tree with rough rope at their camp. The camp itself was small, with only a couple of tents, as if they didn't mean to stay there for very long. Judging by the smoldering fire, the dirty cookware, and the small number of tents, they probably had only just arrived. This appeared to be the whole group, unless they were sleeping three or four to a tent.

Thus began one of the longest days of the twins' lives. The men hooted and hollered over the snacks in the twins' backpacks, parceled out Ethan's clothing, and celebrated over the money. One of them said it was more than they had seen in quite a while. Ethan arched an eyebrow at Emily.

Every now and then he would whisper something to her in English, and she would whisper something back. "Where do you think Thon went?" Ethan said.

"I don't know," Emily said. "But if he ran away, I'm going to revise my opinion on the attractiveness of native teenagers."

Every now and then, one of the bandits would tell them to keep quiet, but it didn't appear that their heart was really in it.

"What are we going to do with them?" one of the men finally asked. It was later in the evening. The fire burned brightly and all five of the men had settled into the camp. José stirred the fire a bit without comment and finally said, "I don't think we're going to get much more out of them."

"I'm sure their parents are rich," the first one said, "or why would they be here?"

"We could hold them for ransom and get a lot of money!"

José shook his head. "Even if their parents are rich, how will they get the money to us? And we have to keep them here and feed them and make sure that they're still alive when their parents come for them."

"We can't just let them go," the first one said. "If we do they'll warn everyone in the town."

"How long are we staying up here anyway?" another one said. "I told my wife I was going for help, not up into the hills to rob unsuspecting tourists."

There was more mumbling at that and murmurs of assent. Apparently he wasn't the only one.

"Another few days," José said. "With the roads blocked, there'll be more people coming over, and maybe we'll catch some more fat fish. After all, this is only the first day, and look at how much we've made!"

This seemed to settle the argument, and after a while, four of them went back to their tents. The clouds had moved off, and the night sky glittered with stars.

It was very cold. Emily began shivering. Ethan called out to the men and asked them in English if they could bring a blanket. They just told him to shut up. His hands began to go numb.

One sentry sat by the fire, wakeful, watching them closely, for an hour or so.

But after that, his head began to droop. A moment later, he began to snore.

As soon as his eyes shut and his chin hit his chest, something tugged on Ethan's arms. He almost cried out, but a hand wrapped around his face and over his mouth. A voice whispered in his ear.

"Don't say anything. It's me."

Thon.

Ethan felt his hands come free. For a long moment he couldn't use his arms. No blood had been flowing properly down his arms for some hours now. Thon cut Emily's ropes as well. He reached his hand underneath her armpits and hauled her backward into the undergrowth.

Ethan, one eye on the sleeping guard, leaned back and dropped into the underbrush.

Turn to page 370.

Ethan looked at Emily for help, but Emily just shrugged. "It certainly doesn't sound like any fun having to change planes three times and then get home even later than when we would if we took direct flight tomorrow."

Ethan said, "I agree, although it's going to be a miserable night here."

"Wouldn't we go get a hotel?" Emily said.

"We could," Ethan said, "but it seems a waste of time and money, since we're going to have to be back in the airport tomorrow morning fairly early to check in anyway. We might as well stay. We'll find a place to sleep and save our money."

Emily knew he felt keenly that they had already spent a great deal of money without even achieving the purpose for which they had saved it.

"That's all right with me," Emily said. "We'll find a quiet spot and you can sleep first. I'll stay up and we'll swap."

Ethan turned back to the travel agent. "I guess we'll take the flight tomorrow morning."

"That would be my choice as well if I were in your situation," she replied. Her printer soon chattered and spit out two tickets. She handed them over to Ethan. "I'm sorry your trip didn't work out. I don't think the airport will be very comfortable, but if you're trying to save money, it certainly will be cheaper than any of the hotels around here. They charge high prices because they know people sometimes get trapped at the airport and have nowhere to go."

Ethan took the tickets and stuffed them in his bag. "We might as well go and find somewhere to sit down," he said.

Turn to page 191.

Ethan had just cinched up his backpack, checking the straps to make sure they were just right, when Thon knocked on the door.

Ethan marched over and flung it wide. "Come on in," he said, without checking to see who it was.

Thon took one step tentatively over the threshold, his face set in a calm mask that Ethan was pretty sure hid a significant amount of concern. "Are you guys ready?"

Since he could see that Ethan was standing there fully dressed and ready to go, Ethan assumed that he was really asking about Emily, which is what Ethan would have assumed he would do in the first place. "I am," Ethan said. "I think Emily is just putting the last of her gear into her backpack."

Emily, hearing this, came out from the back room, a bright smile on her face. "Here I am," she said. "I'm nearly ready, but I'm having a little trouble getting the straps just right." Getting the hint, Thon stepped over to her and hefted the backpack. She draped it over her shoulders and stuck her arms through the straps.

"It's not really quite right. Just here," she said, pointing to where the backpack rubbed against her back. Ethan rolled his eyes.

Emily had been wearing backpacks for more than ten years, and she knew how to put one on so that it would fit. Also, she was an experienced hiker and never needed any help getting ready to go out on a hike.

He supposed it was only natural, the attraction between a young American girl and this young man who was coming to their rescue. Still, it made him vaguely annoyed and a bit more testy than he would otherwise have been.

"C'mon," he said. "We don't have all day for this. You two can flirt on the trail just as well as you can here."

Emily jumped forward a couple of steps. "What are you talking about?" she said. "I'm just asking for help with my backpack."

"Right," Ethan said. "And I'm the king of France. We need to get on the road, don't we?" This question was directed at Thon, who reluctantly nodded.

"It's nice of your village to let us use the car," Emily said, "Although it seems to me that there's no need. I'm sure we can make the hike in a day or less."

"Probably so," Thon said. "You are a very good hiker." Emily blushed a little.

Thon went on, "But it's important that we get you there as quickly as possible, and there are other situations best avoided."

Ethan scowled. Thon had been talking about "other situations" and such like for an eternity now, but wouldn't elaborate when Ethan prodded him. Still, it was nice of the village to let them use one of their three cars to go over to the next town. This way, it should only take an hour and a half or so for them to get there. As the crow flies, the distance was not terribly great. But of course no car could go as the crow flies, and even though the road wound back and forth around mountain passes and up and down fairly steep gorges, it was still faster than having to hike up the steep peak to the north and back down again into the town in the next valley.

When it pulled up in front of their house, however, the car did not look to be in any great shape. It was a very old Ford Escort, a model that Ethan hadn't seen on the road in the States for some years.

It was clean, but streaked with rust, and although the tires were new, the suspension creaked ominously when they stepped into the car. "She's not much," Thon's father said from behind the wheel. "But she will get us where we need to go. I have fixed her myself many times. We should be ready even if something goes wrong."

As they drove out the main road of the village, people came out to line the streets.

Thon's father guided the car slowly so that the twins could wave out the windows and exchange farewells with people that they had met.

More than once, Ethan heard himself say that they would be back. He had no idea when that might be, but he had to admit that the peaceful village had done a world of good for him. If it hadn't been for his sister mooning about over her wannabe boyfriend, it would have been one of the most relaxing times in his life. He

had enjoyed the couple of days he'd been in the village. Still, in the back of his mind he remained concerned about not being able to make contact with their parents to let them know what was going on.

Today would fix that. They would be able to get to a satellite phone to report back to their parents and get counsel on what it was that they should do.

For the first half hour or so, the road was very good. It had been well-maintained, and even though here and there rocks had fallen off the hillside and smashed into the roadway below, they had been mostly pushed off to the side where they would not obstruct traffic.

"Someone's done a very good job of clearing this road," Ethan said. "I wouldn't have expected the government to be quite so efficient out here." Thon's father laughed heartily. He flexed a bicep and pointed.

"This is the government right here," he said. "Way out here in the countryside, we don't expect the government to help us. This road is our lifeline; we have to be able to use it to get to neighboring villages."

Forty-five minutes out of town, the road descended in a treacherous switchback into a valley with a thin, trickling river running along its floor.

Thon's father took the road slowly, shifting to a lower gear to keep from having to constantly use the brake. "Otherwise, the brakes might overheat," he said at the bottom of the gorge. A narrow, one-lane bridge stretched across it, and the road continued on the far side in similar switchback fashion.

At the edge of the bridge stood a man in military fatigues, his rifle slung across his chest. He waved for the car to slow down and stop.

Thon's father exchanged a glance with his son.

Ethan wondered what that was about. It was almost as if they were expecting some-thing like this to happen. Thon's father rolled down his window.

"What is the meaning of this?" he said, his head half into the outside.

"I am headed to San Gabriel," answered Thon's father.

"No one goes to San Gabriel," the man said. "This road is under the control of the White Guard."

"The white guard?" Thon's father said. "I've never heard of that."

The man looked offended.

"Well," he said. "You will hear a lot more about it in the near future. You can't go this way."

"But we have to go this way," Thon's father said. "We have . . ." he began, and stopped.

"You have . . . ?" the man said, showing some interest for the first time. He took two steps toward the car. His index finger tapped the trigger guard of his gun.

"Important things we need to do in San Gabriel," Thon's father finished. "Isn't there some way you can allow us to use the road?"

"You cannot pass," the man said. He always came back to that, like touching base in a game of tag.

"We would be happy to pay you," Thon's father said, "if you will let us get to Sapallu where we can get to the bank."

"Won't do you any good," the man said. "The bank in Sapallu is closed. All the banks are closed by order of the government. In retaliation, the White Guard has seized the roads. We will give them back only when the government opens the banks up again."

Emily leaned over and whispered to Ethan, "I'll bet there was a run on the bank when the earthquake hit. I'll bet this is that hyperinflation we were warned could happen in the event of a catastrophe." Ethan nodded, keeping his eyes glued out the front window on the man and his weapon.

"But if the bank is closed," Thon's father said, "how are we supposed to get to our money?"

"That's not my problem," the man said. "My problem is making sure that these roads are not used except by people who are members of the White Guard."

Thon's father said, "We don't have anything to do with your fight with the government. Can't you please let us by?"

The man didn't respond to that, except to move back to his position by the bridge.

Thon's father tried one more time. "What do I do? How can I get to Sapallu? It really is most important that I arrive there."

The man might have turned to stone. Ethan thought he was probably breathing, but it sure didn't look much like it.

Thon's father rolled his window up and motioned for Thon to do the same. "It doesn't sound like we'll be able to get past here," he said. He laid his hand on his son's arm. "I think you may have to walk."

Emily was first out of her shock. "We're going to have to *walk*?" she said. "We're seriously going to let this guy push us around?"

Ethan punched her in the shoulder, still staring out the front windshield. "He's carrying a gun. We don't have to *let* him push us around. He can do it whether we like it or not."

Emily humphed, but there really was nothing to be done. The man wasn't going to budge. At best, if they angered him, he'd take the car and then they'd all be in trouble.

Thon's father backed the car onto a little patch of grass at the side of the road, almost facing back the direction they had come. He turned around in his seat. "I'm very sorry, Ethan and Emily. It looks like this is as far as I can take you. Unfortunately, this is only about halfway to Sapallu, and we haven't really gained you very much time."

Thon rolled his window down, shinnying out so he was sitting on the door. His head swiveled back and forth for a minute. Then he slipped back inside the car. "I know where we are," he said. "We're just over the hill from the village. We can get to it in a few hours. The climb will be hard, but not any harder than it was getting from the Ychurichuc ruins to my village."

Ethan thought for a moment and said, "*This* is why you had us take so many supplies in our backpacks. It wasn't because of the trouble that might be happening in Sapallu, was it?"

Thon shook his head. "I didn't want to worry you, but sometimes, when there's trouble, we do get bandits in the hills. There was a chance that something like this might happen. I just wanted us to be prepared."

"Well played," Ethan said. "I'm a big fan of preparation."

"I have a backpack, too," Thon said. "It's in the trunk. I'll get it out and then we can start hiking. We can get there before nightfall if we hurry." They piled out of the car.

Looking anxiously at the sky, which had begun to cloud over, Thon's father said, "It won't help if it rains. I will pray that it doesn't."

"Thank you, Father," Thon said. "That's about all any of us can do at this point."

"You will be protected," Thon's father said. "And I pray you will make good time. I will head back to the village and wait for you there. I will expect to see you by sundown tomorrow, and no later, or we will come out to find you."

Thon nodded and embraced his father. Then Ethan, Emily, and Thon shouldered their backpacks and began trudging back up the road a little ways to where a hairpin bend led back to Thon's village. Thon's father walked with them to the edge of the gravel.

"Here is where we depart from the road," Thon said. He pointed up to the peak above them. "We climb this mountain and then down the other side is Sapallu."

Ethan swallowed hard. "That looks fairly difficult," he said.

Emily shook her head. "I wouldn't have chosen this way, not on a bet. But you're right, it doesn't look much more difficult than the hike that we did from Ychurichuc. We can do it. If it doesn't rain. Or there aren't more of him," she said, jerking her thumb over her shoulder at the goon.

"There's a path," Thon said. "It's been worn over hundreds of years. People used to come this way all the time before the road."

"You won't be stopping on my account," Ethan said. "I'm ready to go."

"You may have worse problems than a difficult hike," Thon's father said. "If this man is right," he said, speaking as if the man weren't standing right there, "the situation in town may be very difficult. If the banks have shut down, you will have a very hard time getting access to money. That might make getting out of the country more difficult."

"Why would they shut the banks now?" Emily said.

"Sometimes, when there is a crisis, as in this circumstance," Thon's father said, "people will run to the banks to get their money out because they fear that they won't be able to do it later, and they will need to have cash on hand when they don't have access to the broader financial system."

"I saw something like that happen in the hotel lobby," Ethan said. "You know, right after the small earthquake just after we got here?" he said to Emily. "People in the lobby were hitting the ATM pretty hard. When people are under stress or things are difficult, they always seem to reach for money as a way to make themselves feel better."

"That's right," Thon's father said. "I'm not surprised. The people will have certainly gone to the bank and tried to get all the money out that they can. If enough of them do that, the bank won't have enough money to give them, which will just panic people even more. If that only happens in one or two places, it's not that big of a deal. But if it's happening all over the country, then there can be real trouble, as the entire banking system might be affected. That would lead the government to shut the banks down, rather than risk having all of them fail for not being able to meet their depositors demands."

"But if that happens," Ethan said, "How do people get money?"

"They don't."

"And when all that money suddenly comes out of the banks and goes into circulation, doesn't that just make the inflation problem worse?"

"Certainly does," Thon's father said. "We already have inflation of more than twenty-five percent. It's one of the reasons that our village hangs on to hard assets—water, crops, and even gold and silver—because it allows us to maintain the value of those assets even when the financial system is in crisis, like in this circumstance."

Emily snapped her fingers and wheeled on Ethan. "Wait," she said, "this was why we talked about keeping as much of our money in dollars as possible, right?"

"That's right," Ethan said. "Why does that matter?"

"Don't you see?" Emily said. "Because you kept your money in dollars, we still have hard assets that matter to people. We have currency that people will be interested in, even if the saladera has completely collapsed."

"I'm very pleased to hear this," Thon's father said. "I didn't know that you had kept dollars. Most tourists exchange their money either by withdrawing it at ATMs, where they only get saladera, or exchanging more dollars than they will actually need into the local currency. You didn't do that?"

"No," Ethan said, "I didn't. I brought a fair number of dollars into the country, not knowing for sure how the system would work, and whether I would be able to exchange my dollars for a good rate here. I wanted to make sure that if there were some kind of a crisis, that I had access to multiple kinds of currency, just in case one of them turned out to be better than the others."

Thon's father nodded appreciatively. "My son tells me that the two of you are very smart and very resourceful. Now I see he is right. Go with God, children. And come back safe."

Turn to page 66.

Down at the western edge of the church stood two thick concrete traffic barriers, six feet long, separated by a gap less than five feet wide. In that gap the thugs placed two barrels, metal, undoubtedly filled with something heavy, like water or oil. Rocks, maybe. Against those barrels leaned two thick slabs of plywood, painted with symbols that probably meant something to the people of the town, or at least to El Chapo's gang.

The part of the gang that hadn't come chasing after them congregated there, smoking, holding their guns as if they were extensions of their arms.

"All small-caliber weapons," Travis said. "If they had a proper big rifle, they could be a problem."

"The problem's behind us," Emily said, facing out the back. The chasers knew where the Sentra had to go, and they ran out into the road, cutting off the rear. These bandits weren't waiting for the travelers to decide what to do any more; instead they were pinging away for all they were worth, but the bullets made no more impression this time than they had earlier.

Then the group parted and El Chapo appeared. In his hands he carried a long rifle. He leveled it at the car and let fly. The bullet slammed into the rear window and a thin spider web of cracks appeared in the upper left corner.

"Darn," Travis said. "They got smart."

Another bullet cracked the window on the other corner. "So, my friends," Travis said. "It appears we have a decision to make."

The third bullet hit with an ominous crunch. *Time's up*, Emily thought.

"What's it going to be, my young friends? Do we run the roadblock, or do we head back the other direction and try to get out of town another way?"

If you think the twins should find another way out, turn to page 232.

If you think the only reasonable option is to run the roadblock, turn to page 251.

Stop. Go. Stop again. Go another few feet. Stop.

"We're in line. Or in a traffic jam," Ethan said.

Emily swayed, unsteady on her feet with the extra weight of the child.

"I could help hold Maya for you," Ethan said. He felt the child clench, shrink tighter against his sister. "Okay, maybe not."

"It's okay," she said, her voice filled with weariness, and something else—tenderness? It reminded Ethan of how their mother talked when she was tending them and they were sick. "I can hold her. If we're in line, we must be close."

Ethan would have given a finger for a window or some source of light. Not seeing out—not even seeing *in*—was maddening.

The van shuddered to a halt and the engine shut off. A grinding screech sounded as the door opened and bright sunlight poured in, blinding the passengers. Ethan put his hand in front of his face to shade his eyes.

"Vamos," a voice said, and the refugees—*That's what we are*, Ethan realized—poured out like gravy breaking through mashed potatoes.

They stood outside, blinking in the sunshine, while uniformed men grabbed their arms and shouted at them in Spanish. Some groups were shoved one way, some another. Ethan's eyes adjusted. They were in a vast bowl, a stadium, on the floor. Around the edge of the field ran a rubberized track, an athletic track—*Great, I can get some training in.* In the center lay a carpet of grass. It was on this that the refugees mustered. Beyond the unloading zone, a tent city sat like gopher mounds. Sad knots of people milled about back there.

A guard came toward the twins, an annoyed look on his face. "This your kid?" he said.

Ethan cocked an eyebrow. "Seriously?"

The guard scowled. "She not with you? Then she comes with me."

Maya tried to burrow into Emily. The guard grabbed Maya's spindly arm and hauled on it. Emily staggered. Ethan clutched at his sister, holding her up. "Hey, dude," he said. "Careful. The kid doesn't want to go."

The guard tugged harder and fumbled in his belt for his nightstick.

Emily cried out, "Don't! She's scared. She's bleeding. She wants to stay with me!"

Over the din, a scream rose into the air. Ethan, Emily, and the guard froze, but Maya's head popped up and swiveled from side to side, seeking the source.

The character of the scream changed, from despair to shock, and then as they listened, to a kind of hysterical joy. Maya squirmed like a butterfly wriggling from a cocoon. Emily was forced to let her go, and the moment Maya's feet hit the ground, she took off like a bullet toward the sound.

Ethan turned and there stood a woman in a light brown dress, her arms wrapped around Maya as if she would never let go. Nearby a man raised his arms to heaven and shouted something that sounded like a prayer.

The guard stood there with his clipboard, face blank. *No blanker than mine, I bet*, Ethan thought.

"Well," Emily said, a huge smile on her face, "I guess we're ready to go now. Where do you want us?"

Turn to page 158.

Travis arrived right on time, just before lunch. At least, Pietro told them it was Travis. Ethan had in his head the image of a large man, rough-and-tumble, the kind who would make long overland journeys with the entirety of the Allqukillan police in hot pursuit. The person who showed up was about as far from that as it was possible to imagine.

Pietro took them out the back of the internet cafe, one floor down from where they had come in. "It's an underground parking garage," Pietro said. "It comes in handy periodically."

In the garage Pietro had stashed several vehicles of various kinds, many of them clearly adapted to run on

alternative fuels. Ethan examined the bulging back end of one, trying to figure out what sort of retrofitting had been done.

Pietro smiled, something like a mother when someone admires her newborn baby. "You like that, huh?" he said. "I'm rather fond of that adaptation myself. I can pour straight grain alcohol into the back of this baby, and she'll run like a dream, getting something like sixty miles to the gallon."

In the center of the garage, stopped in a kind of aisle between rows of cars, stood an aging, decrepit Nissan Sentra, dull gray and streaked with rust. Leaning against it was a petite woman, slim and slight, with dark hair to her shoulders and skin so creamy white it was difficult to believe she had ever been outside. Her khaki shorts were covered with pockets, some of them obviously full, and her shirt was one of those safari-type numbers, and so fresh it might have been ironed and starched. With fancy mirror shades on her face, she let a tiny smile flit across her mouth and disappear as if it were afraid to be seen.

"This," Pietro said with a flourish and something not unlike a bow, "is Travis."

Travis nodded at Emily, whose pace had faltered just a bit. "Yes, I get that a lot. My parents wanted a boy and couldn't give up the name when I disappointed them."

"Travis is jealous of my fleet of vehicles, especially that one back there."

She shook her head as if she had heard it all before. "You're always saying that," she said, "but I've never seen that car moved from that stall."

"That's only because I take my lady friends out in other vehicles," Pietro said.

Travis rolled her eyes. Ethan liked her at once.

"We don't have a lot of luggage," Emily said, hanging back a little, which he thought was somewhat uncharacteristic of her.

"That's good," Travis said, "because although my car has many adaptations, and there is far more to her than meets the eye, one thing she does lack is significant cargo space."

Pietro said, "Which means the car actually has significant cargo space, but it's all being used for other things at the moment."

"I can neither confirm nor deny," Travis said. "Backpacks?"

"Yes," Ethan said, "that's about it. Oh, and this box of snacks that we liberated from the pantry in the cafe."

Pietro took a step forward and peeled back the top of the box, looking inside. "Mm," he said, "a fine selection. Some salty, some sweet, and a sizable amount of liquids. Obviously, the two of you have had some experience with emergency backpacking."

"Not as much as we're likely to have," Ethan said. "And nowhere near as much as we think we need. But then, we were expecting to be staying in hotels and having access to everything in our luggage. We're kind of having to make do on the fly," he said to Travis.

"Making do on the fly is one of my favorite things," Travis said. "But that's only when one of my plans go sideways."

"Plans?" Ethan said, handing over his backpack.

"Plans, absolutely," Travis said. "I don't do anything without a plan. Planning is essential."

Pietro laughed. "And yet plans themselves are useless."

"That does not invalidate the truth of my first statement," Travis said, flipping open the trunk of the Sentra and depositing the backpacks in the surprisingly small empty space back there. "I think it would be best for us to get on the road as quickly as possible," Travis said. "Emergency vehicles are out in force today. Having now moved most of the people, they can get back to hassling the rest of us."

"We're not doing anything wrong," Emily said, "are we?"

"Absolutely not," Pietro said.

Emily shot him a glance as if she wished he hadn't spoken. Travis saw it and gave a tight smile. "I think they want to hear this from me," Travis said. She put down the box and squared herself to Emily. They were almost the same height, but there wasn't any question which of them was in charge.

"No," she said to Emily, "we are not doing anything wrong. There is a 'voluntary' ban on travel, meaning that you can certainly drive your own vehicle anywhere you want in the city, as long as you have permission from the people who will impound it if they stop you."

"And we have such permission?" Ethan said, though not as if he believed that any such thing was possible.

"Of course we do," Travis said. And she smiled brightly enough to light up the whole garage. "If, however," she said, "you wish me to explain to you how I have come by such permission, I'm afraid I will develop selective deafness."

She slammed the trunk and sashayed around to the driver's door.

"How are we going to arrange the seating?" Travis said. "Ethan, do you want to ride up front with me? Or is that Emily's job?"

"No," Ethan said, "I'm the navigator."

Emily opened her mouth as if to say something, and Ethan gave her a surreptitious kick in the shin. "I mean, I'm the one with the map. I'd like to follow along where we go."

"Suits me," Travis said. "I'm not really into playing chauffeur. Besides, we'll have plenty of opportunities to switch, because this is going to be a very long drive, no matter how we do it."

"Ecuador did look like a long way on the map," Ethan said.

"It's a long way, all right," Travis said. "And that's even when the roads are clear, which they will not be this time around."

"Many thanks," Travis said brightly in the direction of Pietro. "I'll report back when the journey is over," she said. "Don't expect to hear from me for at least a couple of days."

"That suits me fine," Pietro said. "It's not like I'm going to hang out on my roof with my satphone waiting for your call."

"That's exactly why we've never gotten together," Travis said. "You just don't take care of the little things that make a girl feel special."

Pietro laughed at this, but Ethan thought that there was at least a little bit of chagrin in it. He waved as he walked back across the parking garage, stopping to caress one of the vehicles on the way. He disappeared through the door back into the internet cafe, and his own private kingdom, without a backward glance.

"All aboard," Travis said. "We had better get going if we're going to stay ahead of the weather."

Ethan climbed into the front seat and found it surprisingly comfortable. The seats themselves were leather, a little wider than normal, and filled with extra padding.

Travis saw Ethan bouncing up and down on it, checking out the accommodations. "Made for a long journey," Travis said. "I go back and forth quite a bit, often carrying passengers. I find that we do much better if people's buns are not numb a half an hour into the trip."

"I wish they made all car seats like this," Ethan said.

"They don't make *any* car seats like this," Travis said, turning the key and starting up the engine. Just like the seats, the engine sounded of substantial modification. The growl of it was audible, and Ethan thought surely some upgrades had been done to that part of the vehicle as well.

He raised an eyebrow in Travis's direction. She flashed one of those dazzling smiles, tossed her head slightly. "Spared no expense," she said. "You never know when you're going to need a little extra power." But the car rolled sedately up the steep ramp, a thick steel door descending behind them.

At first, Travis drove with confidence, even though by the map you could tell they were taking a mostly circuitous route.

"We will head to the freeway," Travis said, "although I don't expect that to be a successful way to go. Normally when you get a disaster situation like this, the freeways are the first things to be rendered impassable."

Emily leaned forward to put her head in between Travis and Ethan's. "Is that because they fall down more easily, or because everyone tries to take them to get out of town?"

"A little bit of both," Travis said. "In this case, most of the freeway is not elevated, so it will probably have done pretty well against the earthquake. The problem is, neither Ecuador or Allqukilla are particularly wealthy countries, and there isn't a lot of traffic over the mountains between the capital cities. That means that the road is narrow. In a lot of places, it's only one lane in each direction."

Ethan and Emily exchanged a glance. "Seriously? In the States, we have at least two lanes in each direction even between our smaller towns."

"As you may have noticed," Travis said, her arm taking in a half-circle of rubble-strewn scenery, "this is not the States. Those kinds of roads cost a great deal of money, not to mention the fact that these roads are going over very steep and difficult terrain. That multiplies the cost. The government is already struggling to keep its currency value up, and doing a pretty poor job of it. Where would the money come from to make wider roads?"

"It seems to me," Ethan said, his brow furrowed, "that they could make parts of the road, especially the difficult parts, into toll roads, and let private businesses fund those. That would let them build many more roads without having to expend any public money."

Travis took her eyes off the road for a moment and gave him an appraising glance. Ethan felt himself blushing a little bit. "It's too bad they didn't have you around when they were doing their planning," Travis said.

"That's the kind of thinking they could really have used. But unfortunately, no one here seemed to think of that, or, more likely, they just didn't think it would work."

"We've seen it work," Emily said. "Both in the positive and the negative," and she took a few minutes to tell Travis the story of how they had seen the effects of local versus government roads and how businesses were impacted by government planning of infrastructure.

"Very interesting idea," Travis said. "In a few minutes we will find out whether the government roads have managed to survive at all."

They reached the freeway on-ramp a couple of minutes later. The sun was approaching its peak for the day. The smoke in the air had dissipated some, it now having been a couple of days since the earthquake. Most of the fires had burned themselves out or been extinguished. The number of people in the streets, however, was much larger. They weren't driving around, but walking back and forth; picking up debris; wheeling barrows full of crushed concrete, ruined brick, and splintered wood, adding to the debris piles on almost every block.

"How are they going to get rid of all this stuff?" Emily said.

"It wouldn't surprise me if no one knew the answer to that," Travis said. "Somehow or other, they will have to do it. I imagine there is some sort of plan, but you know what they say about plans."

Ethan scowled. He hated this quote. But he said, "No plan survives contact with the enemy."

Again Travis shot him a glance, this time with a wink to go with it. "That's what people like to say who don't do much planning," she said. Then she shrugged. "But it does have a great deal of truth to it. You probably had a plan for how this vacation was going to go. How is that plan holding up?"

"Absolutely swell," Ethan said. "We had the earthquake calendared for the fourth day, but otherwise..."

Travis laughed.

"Obviously not very well," Emily said, scowling at her brother. "It's been a little more eventful than we would have liked."

The freeway on-ramp was open, and Travis took it at a moderate speed. Once on the freeway, however, the problem became apparent. It was as Travis said it would be, with cars lined up to the horizon. Some sat with their engines off. Whether they had run out of gas or simply given up on the prospect that they were going to move forward, they couldn't tell.

"Hold on a minute," Travis said, putting the car into park and opening her door. "Since we're not going anywhere, let's see if I can get some information from the locals here."

She slammed the door and jogged forward to a rusty pickup truck just ahead of them on the freeway. She knocked on the window of the orange truck and motioned for the driver to roll his window down. They had a brief conversation, with Travis pointing forward and making a motion to the right. Then she nodded, clearly said thank you, and jogged back to the car.

She climbed in, slammed the door shut, and gave an ornate sigh. "Well, this is the news. Our friend," she said, waving in the direction of the pickup, "has been sitting here for around an hour and hasn't moved fifteen feet. He doesn't know what the holdup is, whether there's a problem with the freeway up ahead or if there's just too many cars trying to get north into Ecuador. Either way, although I can absolutely sit here and idle my vehicle much longer than any of these people, this is your call. You want to stay here, or do you want to try another way?"

If you think the twins should stay on the freeway, turn to page 124.

If you think they should try taking another route, turn to page 384.

Emily sat down on the suitcase, not wanting to be any closer to the towering man than she had to be. The bus rounded a sharp corner at a speed that was far too high for the suspension, and she felt herself tossed from the suitcase into the lady with the basket of chickens. Bird poop splashed out of the basket and onto the front of her shirt, thick and viscous, smelling of ammonia. The man above her laughed as if he had never seen anything so funny in his life. Despite the laughter, he extended his hand out to Emily, pulling her back up to her feet.

"I'm sorry," he said, "It's just so funny to watch what happens to tourists when they sit down on their luggage instead of standing up and holding on to something secure."

"Well, you might have told me," Emily said, brushing herself off, but it seemed to only make the mess worse. The stain covered her from neck to navel. She smelled like a barnyard.

"I would have told you," the man said, "but we don't get very much entertainment on this bus ride. It's funny to see what happens."

Emily stewed in her chicken dung adornment as the bus chugged slowly up into the hills.

Turn to page 265.

Emily couldn't actually see the earth rolling, but it felt very much as if she could, as if the ground were coming up to her in waves. She had already been crouching when the first wave struck, and the shaking rolled her over on her right side. At first she wondered who had pushed her, and she glanced around only to find that Ethan and Thon had also fallen over and were struggling to stand up.

She felt that she should be able to get to her feet, that there should be a way for her to do that, but every time she put a foot into the ground and began to push off it shifted on her, and she fell over again. The third time this happened, she lay there and watched. They were halfway up the staircase with a couple of hundred tourists below them in the central bowl. All of them had fallen to the earth and were milling about on the ground, as if they thought they might be able to get to their feet. They were having no more success with that than she had.

Over the rumbling of the ground, she heard the screams begin. All the people, all of the tourist signage, everything that man had put up, all of it had fallen to the ground.

And the obelisk. It had stood for centuries. This was just one push too many.

The ruins themselves appeared unaffected. Perhaps the Inca had built them so well that the stonework was a part of the earth itself. Regardless, they appeared entirely unbothered by the rumbling ground and waves of earthquake.

Emily's eyes went wide and she reached for her brother's hand. Ethan took it and locked eyes with his sister.

"I guess we know whether there's going to be a major earthquake," he said. "Because that was *definitely* a major earthquake."

Emily had no way to know for certain, but she guessed it was at least a 7, possibly as high as a 7.5, on the Richter scale. It would surely do major damage to the capital—and it would probably be very dangerous for Ychu as well. Emily had a fleeting image of the dam holding the water back in the reservoir.

But there was no time to worry about that now.

Emily waited for what seemed like an hour. Finally, the rolling of the ground stopped, and people were able to at least get to their knees. The screaming tapered off, as people realized that they were not seriously hurt. The obelisk's fall had been slow enough that the nearby tourists had escaped its massive bulk. Unfortunately, the obelisk itself had not fared as well. A massive crack split the ancient stone in a ragged black line from side to side.

Out came the phones. There was frantic dialing. All of the people looking at their phones kept taking them away from their ears, looking at their screens, and putting them back up to their ears. But no one was connecting.

Service is out, Emily thought. *That's not a good sign.*

Thon crawled over to Emily rather than trying to stand. "Are you all right?"

"I'm fine," Emily said. "Never felt anything like that before."

Thon nodded, his eyes wide. "This is the strongest one I've ever felt."

A man with a bullhorn came up the lower staircase from the parking lot. He thumbed a switch. "We have suffered an earthquake," he said unnecessarily. "We are asking all tourists to evacuate the ruin site at once. Transportation will be made available in the lower parking lot. Everyone please gather in the central square and come down the main staircase into the parking lot." Most of the tourists began moving that way.

"You okay, Ethan?" Emily said.

Ethan dusted himself off. "Yeah. I think so." He nodded toward the obelisk. "I think my heart is broken, though."

"Where's our tour group?" Emily said. The three of them scanned the lower bowl. No trace of them there.

Without a word, Emily and Ethan dashed down onto the bowl and ran up the stairs toward the central temple, where the tour guide and his group had disappeared.

Turn to page 45.

The front of the temp-bassy was not much for entertainment.

They killed time by playing various guessing games. They talked about what they thought their parents were doing at home. They talked about the kinds of things that they would tell their friends when they got home, what they would say at school about their vacation. But hanging over the entire thing was an impending sense that their marvelous vacation had already come to an end, and without much of the "marvelous" part. It was as if their trip to Disneyland was accompanied by all the rides being closed. And torrential rain.

Eventually, about the time the sun got to the horizon, the bus showed up, an ancient school bus with grimy windows and torn up seats. It ground to a halt in front of the embassy, and the twins packed themselves onto the conveyance along with forty or fifty other American tourists. The bus groaned under the weight and staggered out onto the nearby streets. Everything they passed showed the results of terrible devastation. People watched the bus with dull eyes as it passed by, some of them reaching out halfheartedly, as if any transport to anywhere would be better than staying where they were. One group of children stood on a street corner watching them as they passed, and Emily threw her water bottle out to them. Before she could see if they managed to get it, the bus rounded some debris and they were lost to view.

They found themselves in a white field, with a number of canvas tents set up.

"You've got to be kidding me," Ethan said to Emily.

"I don't think anyone is kidding about this," Emily said. "But at least we know that they won't fall down on us and kill us in the middle of the night."

A thin, tired-looking young man came onto the bus as they arrived. He carried a clipboard, leafing through it as he spoke. "When I call your name," he said, "please get off the bus and you will be shown where to go."

The first group did not include the Tuttles. They were in the second group, assigned to the green company over on the north end of the field. Their eight-man tent was shared with three other people.

Emily poked her head inside. "At least there are two separate cabins," she said. "We can get dressed in private. I mean, we could if we had any clothes."

At first, the tent smelled a little musty, as if it had been in storage in a damp place for a long time. After two days the musty smell went away and was replaced by something even less pleasant. After a week, Emily dearly wished for that musty smell back again. Their tentmates were relatively nice, a couple from Florida, and a woman from North Carolina with a thick accent and very little patience for South American countries.

They did get fed, but it was poor food, mostly beans and rice with no meat or vegetables. Ethan wondered about the quality of food those stuck in the city were getting, if this was the best the embassy had to offer them. After ten days or so, they started to receive a little bit of fruit and some flatbread to go along with it. The water was flat and stale-tasting, smelling of chemicals, but it kept them alive, and a little at a time people left the refugee camp and never came back. A bus would come once a day and take twenty or thirty people and their luggage off to Ecuador. Two buses made more or less constant round trips back and forth to Quito to put people on specially-commandeered aircraft and take them to an embarkation point in Dallas.

In the meantime, while the twins waited for their turn, there was nothing particular to do. It was easily the most boring time of their lives.

Eventually, when it seemed that the refugee camp had been turned into a ghost town, their names were called by Paul, the attache responsible for getting people on the buses and transporting them to Ecuador. Ethan gathered up his belongings into his bag. It took less than five minutes.

Emily dearly wished that she had a change of clothes or some of her belongings, definitely by now lost forever. Paul pulled her aside before she got onto the bus and handed over a sheaf of papers.

"This will do as a temporary passport," he said. "This should get you into Ecuador without any trouble,

and then from Ecuador back to the States. You'll want to get a permanent passport when you get there, but this should do until then."

"I'm very grateful," Emily said. "You've been very nice in difficult circumstances."

Paul grimaced. "There's not many that think so," he said. "And truthfully, we wish we could have done a lot more. But at least things should work out for you."

The bus ride was one of the saddest the twins could remember. The road to Quito was a sixteen-hour drive. Most people on the bus were very grateful to be leaving the refugee camp, and the twins were as well. But they knew they were leaving behind a country they had always wanted to see, without ever having really seen very much of it at all. They would take home their memories and a few less pounds than they had arrived with, but not a lot else.

At the airport in Quito, they were on the tarmac within a few minutes of arrival to the airport and boarding a plane. A number of other people were on the plane as well, mostly people who had been in Ecuador, but there were a few people who had been in Allqukilla when the earthquake struck. They told horrific tales of their time on the road, always in the hot sun, and always with no food and too little fresh water.

"It was a horrible time," one of them said. "I never expected to be in a refugee camp as an American." And that was the biggest thing the twins could take away from the experience. So many things had happened that they never expected. They would need to be much more vigilant the next time and prepare better for various eventualities. But at least they were going to get home.

Their parents were waiting at the airport.

THE END

"There's no sense in it, but my gut tells me Thon is our best bet," Emily said. "I can easily imagine getting stranded out there someplace and Jorge abandoning us because we ran out of cash. You have to admit, Thon is a lot less likely to do that."

"Especially with you around," Ethan said. Emily arched an eyebrow, but Ethan looked away in the direction Thon had gone. "We better hustle. Up for a run?"

"Always," she said.

Ethan jogged over to Jorge. "I think we're going native. Sorry. Nice to have met you. Maybe we'll get another chance at this down the road."

Jorge scoffed. "You're making a big mistake, but it's no skin off my nose. More room for other fares." Without another word, he turned and stormed off.

Emily cinched up her backpack and started off at a healthy clip toward the cemetery. Ethan stayed a couple paces behind her. Below them, in the bowl, tourists were still vainly trying to get cell reception. Ethan blew out a breath. "That's bad," he said.

"I think we're going to find out how bad," Emily said.

They reached the top of the cemetery stairs, and for a moment Ethan thought Thon had already disappeared. Emily, though, called out for him, and his dark head bobbed into view at the far side of the circle.

"You coming with me?" he shouted.

"Will you take us?" Emily called back. In response, Thon waved at them to come on.

On the other side of the cemetery, Thon sat on a rocky outcropping and waited for them. When the twins jogged up, he said, "That was quick. You changed your mind in a hurry."

Turn to page 281.

"Why not?" Ethan said. "We're here to try new things, right?"

"Right," Emily said, "And they smell delicious."

Empanadas and street tacos were being sold at the first cart they came to. The second had rice and beans with shredded pork and chicken.

"This one sounds good to me," Ethan said. Emily thought she'd be better off with the first one until she could get into the farmer's market and get some fruit.

Ethan got in line behind two other people and watched the vendor dole out generous portions of meat and beans to the man at the front. He felt, rather than saw, a man come up behind him, but he couldn't miss the vendor's reaction.

"Hey," he suddenly shouted, "You! Get out of here!" The vendor pointed at the man behind Ethan. Ethan thought for a minute he was pointing at him, but he moved aside and the vendor came out from behind his cart and advanced on the man standing just behind Ethan in line.

He was short, with greasy hair and a stained t-shirt. His beady eyes fixed on the vendor and he backed slowly away, his hands up.

"Did he touch you?" the vendor asked Ethan in excellent English.

"I... don't think so," Ethan said.

The man jabbered at the vendor in rapid-fire Spanish, pointing at the cart and talking about beans, as far as Ethan could tell.

"You don't want any beans," the vendor said, slowly enough that Ethan could follow. "You want this kid's money. Get out of here and don't come back."

The man had enough and took off running.

The vendor turned to Ethan. "Vultures," he said, switching back to English. "They see you come over from the airport, and they follow you."

"What for?" Ethan said.

"To rob you, of course," the vendor said, and got back behind his cart. He served the fellows in front and then started on Ethan's meal. He took a wide flatbread and sliced it down the middle to make a pocket. He began heaping rice and beans into it.

"You're from America?" the man said.

"Yes," Ethan said. "Thank you for saving me from being robbed. I don't think he could have gotten my money, though."

Emily wandered over from the other cart with a bag full of tacos. "What happened?" she said.

Ethan told her. When he finished, she said to the vendor, "That's very nice of you, but why do you care? I mean, why not just let him take our money?"

"If he takes your money, how can you give it to me?" He handed over the huge pita stuffed with meat and beans. "That's 200 saladera. Unless you want to pay me in dollars. I would take two dollars instead."

"Two dollars?" Ethan said. "But the exchange rate is around sixty to one right now. You're giving me almost double that."

"Kid, the exchange rate doesn't matter. What is true on the street is what I have to live with. Your dollars are better—I don't care what some banker or politician says about how much the money is worth."

"Good enough for me," Ethan said. "Here's two dollars."

Emily glanced at her watch, suddenly getting nervous. "C'mon, we've got to get some food and grab our luggage before the bus arrives!"

Turn to page 111.

"I know I was talking big about leaving, but the truth is I think staying here is safer, surer, and better," Emily said. "But that's me talking. You have a plan for everything. What do you want to do?"

"My plans usually have one thing in common: they involve sticking close to people who are already trying to help us. That means here."

"You sure you don't want to strike out into the unknown?" she said, throwing a thumb over her shoulder at the building with the solar array.

Ethan took a long look down the street. "No," he finally said, though he didn't look happy about it. "I'm not sure. But I'm tired of adventures. I didn't come here to take a scenic tour of Takewawa, even before the earthquake. Now, I just want to get home. These people," he said, waving at the marines, and behind them the Quonset hut housing the American diplomatic personnel, "tell us they're going to get us home. I think we should let them."

Emily folded her arms across her chest and tilted her head to the side. Her face wore an expression of mild amusement. "Does this mean we're developing wisdom?"

"Foreign travel broadens the mind."

Emily laughed.

Turn to page 338.

"There's a village up here not too far," Travis said. "It's not a big thing, but it should have some supplies, and maybe we can get out and stretch our legs a little bit."

Four hours in the vehicle so far, and as far as Ethan could tell from the map, they weren't dramatically closer to the border than when they had begun. Up in the countryside, many of the roads had been washed out or made impassable by rockslides. A couple of times the road that had showed on the map, or that Travis remembered from having taken this route before, simply didn't exist anymore, as if someone had reached down from the sky and erased them.

The weather had been beautiful, sunshine streaming down from the sky and virtually no wind, but somehow that had made the entire trip a little more surreal. It was as if the sky and the earth were disconnected; terrible things were happening on the ground, and the sky was blissfully unaware.

And of course, Emily thought, *that's the truth, isn't it? The sky doesn't actually know anything about what's going on down here.*

Topping a rise, the car wound down into a valley unlike what she had expected. The valley was dry, with none of the lush greenery that she would have expected from the mountains.

She made a face. "I don't understand why the valley is so dry," she said.

"It's rain shadow," Ethan said, pointing to the hills. "None of this area is getting any rain at all."

"It's a trick of atmospherics," Travis said without taking her eyes from the road. "The clouds break and divide in this area of the country. It's like this all the way to the Ecuadorian border. Once we get there though, it's green and glorious, like Dorothy coming out of her ruined house into the magical land of Oz."

The twins laughed.

The road—little more than a mountain track, really—looked down on the quaint little village of St. Lucia nestled against the dry hillside. Terraces of field and garden lay against the mountains, radiating out from the village like ripples from a pond. The road wound down across a thin river that trailed away over the plain into the distance. Smoke rose from a couple of the buildings and drifted over the scene, a gray screen over the brown.

Travis frowned. "I don't like the look of that," she said.

"The look of what?" Emily said. As far as she could see, it looked like any other sleepy Andean village.

"The smoke," Travis said.

"Shouldn't there be smoke?" Ethan said.

"Yes," she said, "there should be. But it shouldn't be coming from the church."

The Sentra drifted into the town, with Travis's head on a swivel, as if she were looking out for something. The streets of the central town were not empty, but they had an eerie feel to them, as if the people were apprehensive about being seen. They glanced at the car as it rolled by, obviously concerned about who might be inside, but when there was no one that they knew, they turned their eyes elsewhere. Some got off the street before the car passed, peeping at them from doorways.

Everyone was in a great hurry. No one lingered. There were no groups chatting away. Solitary figures darted to and fro.

Travis's frown deepened. "I don't like this at all," she said. "Ordinarily, there are groups of people on the street, playing music, talking with each other, the way things happen in small towns everywhere. This has a completely different feel than it did the last time I was here."

The closer they got to the church in the center of town, the more obvious it became that disaster had struck there, too. The cloud of smoke rose higher into the mid-afternoon sky, malignant black, like the things that were burning were things not meant to be on fire.

"There's only one store here," Travis said. "But I think we should be able to refill our stock of water and maybe grab something hot to eat."

"Sounds good to me," Ethan said. "I could do with something more than beef jerky and Coke."

"It's right down here," Travis said, somewhat un- necessarily, because the town appeared to have just one main street.

No one, however, was on it. They pulled up in front of the mercado, with its barrels of goods show- ing through the window. The sign on the door said *cerrado*—closed.

Travis looked at her watch. "That's impossible," she said, "this store has never been closed at this time of day in living memory."

"It's closed today," Ethan said. "Maybe we should try somewhere else."

"There *is* nowhere else," Travis said. "There's one store in town, and it's the only town for fifty miles in any direction. We either get our stuff here or resign our- selves to eating beef jerky the rest of the trip."

"And getting thirsty," Ethan said, sighing. Would nothing go right on this trip?

"How long will 'the rest of the trip' be?" Emily said.

"A hundred and ten years, judging by how fast we've been able to go so far," Travis said, smiling grimly and shrugging.

"I admire your precision," Emily said. Travis started to say something, and Emily stopped her with a hand. "No, I get it. There's no way to know."

"Exactly," Travis said. The Sentra jerked to a stop and the three of them climbed out of the vehicle.

"Does this remind you a little bit of the internet cafe?" Ethan said.

Emily nodded. "That one said it was closed as well, but all it took was a little money to open it up."

Travis said, "Then let's hope this owner is persuadable by the same means Pietro was." She marched to the front door and peered inside. "I don't see anybody," she said. "But I'm sure they're in there." She pointed up to the second story where windows overhung the front door. "They live up there, I'm sure. That means they're here, unless . . ." She didn't finish the sentence, but made a quick glance up at the smoke-filled sky.

Travis rapped on the glass of the front door, but there was no response. Ethan and Emily milled about on the sidewalk for a moment, gazing up and down the now-deserted street. With nothing to see, they went to look through the front window into the shop. Rows of shelves stood against the walls, making narrow aisles. The lights were off, which was to be expected, but there was enough light streaming in the window to tell the place was deserted.

"There's nobody here," Ethan said.

"So I see," Travis said, "I wonder where everybody has gone."

Just then, there was movement from the back of the shop. A shadowy figure made frantic gestures with her hands, as if shooing them away. Travis reached back and ripped velcro, pulled a 5,000-saladera bill from one of her pockets and slapped it against the front window. The waving of the hand continued, but the woman's head swiveled from side to side as if she were checking to see if she was being observed, even though she couldn't possibly see very far down the street from where she stood.

Not enough inducement, then.

Ethan drew a 5,000-saladera bill from his own pocket and placed it on the glass above Travis's. Emily noticed that this allowed him to drape his arm somewhat across her shoulders. She thought that was at least part of the appeal, not to mention that he got to be something of a hero. Now the shooing hands went away, and the woman scurried forward and unlocked the door.

Emily said, "That seems to be the key all over the place."

The woman whispered something quickly under her breath in Spanish, too low and fast for the twins to catch.

Travis nodded and turned to them, her face set hard. "She wants us to come in, but as quickly as possible. And she wants me to move my car around to the back."

Emily and Ethan slid through the narrow opening in the door to stand in the dim interior. "I'll be right back," Travis said. She jogged the two steps over to the vehicle, cranked it up, and pulled it down the street and around the corner of the building.

The woman scurried toward the back of the building. She was a heavy-set lady in her late 50s or early 60s, in a shapeless floral dress that made it look as if she were wearing a beach tent. She glanced over her shoulder, saw the twins were still standing by the front door, and with terror-filled eyes, waved to them to come and follow her.

"We speak Spanish," Ethan said, and the woman relaxed a fraction.

"That's something, anyway," she said, a little slower so it was easier for them to understand her. "But it won't do you any good if you're standing by that front window when El Chapo comes by."

"El Chapo?" Emily said, already moving away from the front of the store.

The woman just shook her head and tisked. She went through a wooden door in the back wall and held it open for the twins to go through. When they had done so, she closed and locked it behind her.

Ethan held out the money. A deal was a deal, after all.

She turned her nose up at it as if it were rancid. "Keep it," she said.

"I thought that was what got you to open the door."

She gave a short bark of derision. "What got me to open the door was the growing evidence that on the street were three stupid Americans who were going to get themselves killed."

Their eyes adjusted to the dim. They were in a long, narrow storeroom, about ten feet wide, that ran the length of the rear of the store behind its back wall. Set into the cinderblock exterior wall was a gray metal door with two businesslike deadbolt locks. The woman unlocked them with a thick brass key and drew the door open a crack. A moment later they heard the sound of the Sentra's high-pitched whine creaking to a stop outside. The woman beckoned frantically for Travis to join them.

Her khaki shirt and pocketed pants slithered through the cracked door and the woman slammed it shut after her. She turned a couple of heavy-sounding bolts and relaxed a tiny bit.

"What's all this about?" Travis said.

"Since the earthquake," the woman said, very quietly, in a voice that would never have carried outside the room, "the town has been somewhat cut off."

"We noticed that," Travis said. "It was nearly impossible to get here."

"Some people have taken advantage of that time," she said. "There has been looting, and some, uh, abuse of the citizens." Emily thought the woman looked ashamed. *What does she have to be ashamed of?*

"Abuse of the citizens?" Travis said. "That sounds like something you say when you don't want to tell anyone what's really going on."

The woman swallowed hard, but said, "Things like taking food from us. Breaking into shops and taking things. The rest of us are being as cautious as possible. These are not good men."

"Is this the El Chapo that you were talking about?" Ethan said. The woman nodded miserably.

"He's a young man that grew up in this town. We all thought we knew him. But as soon as the mayor and the police chief left to get emergency help, he and his gang started terrorizing the town."

Not too much, Ethan thought. *Wouldn't this be the first place someone would break into?*

"What's up with the church?" Travis said. "Is it on fire? Why doesn't someone put it out?"

This got a very different reaction from the woman. From shrunken and embarrassed, she drew herself up, standing taller. Emily saw that she was actually somewhat younger than she had supposed, maybe not out of her forties. Misery had made her look considerably older, but now she was angry and some years dropped away.

"The church was damaged in the quake," the woman said. "El Chapo and his gang set up their camp there. They keep feeding wood into the fire. They keep it lit at all times."

"That's a lot of wood, then," Ethan said.

"I believe they are burning the hymn books and pews." She gritted her teeth and her eyes flashed.

Messing with the town was one thing. Desecrating the church was clearly something much worse.

"We need some supplies," Travis said, "We don't intend to stick around in town very long."

"That's wise," the woman said. "Are you headed for Ecuador?"

"We are," Travis said.

"I have some things I can give you. What do you need?"

"Water. Food, especially hot food if you have any."

"I have some hot food," the woman said. "I stopped cooking a couple of days ago when I wasn't sure that the gas was still safe, but I have had few customers."

"You have no power, either?" Travis said.

The woman shook her head and unlocked the door back into the main body of the store. She stuck her head through and apparently was satisfied with what she saw. "The water is over here," she said.

"Do you have anything we could eat in the car?" Ethan said. "I'm getting a little tired of beef jerky."

"I do have a couple things," the woman said. "They're a day or so old, but they'll give you some variety." She went to the wall against the back of the store, where there were two pots sitting on what resembled a camp stove. She pointed at plastic containers to one side. "Take a couple of those," she said. "I'll fill them for you."

The pots proved to be full of soup, a rich cream-based broth with potato and chunks of pork and beef floating in it. It smelled heavenly.

"And we will pay you," Ethan said. "This is very kind of you."

The woman let a small smile drift across her face. "We have to take care of each other when times are bad," she said. "Our little village is better off than most."

"That's true," Travis said. "Takewawa has been hit pretty hard."

Over the next ten minutes or so, the three of them filled her in on the conditions in the capital city. The woman's eyes were wide the whole time, and she shook her head, muttering things like "*Madre de Dios*" and other Spanish prayers.

"I am glad I live here," the woman finally said. "As bad as things are with El Chapo, he won't be in charge for long. Soon the villagers will get sick of his shenanigans, and we will throw him out on his ear."

Turn to page 223.

A woman sitting near Emily turned to her and began babbling something in a language that sounded very unfamiliar to Ethan.

"I'm sorry, I didn't understand that," he tried to say in Spanish, but she didn't seem to understand him.

Someone tapped Ethan on the shoulder. Standing behind him was a man about Ethan's own height with long, dark hair and a hooked nose that looked like it had been broken more than once. "She doesn't speak Spanish, or English, either. She is Quechua. She only speaks the language of the Inca."

"You look as if you can tell us what's happening," Ethan replied. The man laughed, but it didn't sound like he thought it was very funny.

"The bus has broken down to let some of these tourists off so that the innkeeper can get some of them to stay for the night."

"Won't there be anyone along with another bus?"

The man shrugged. "Sometimes they bring along another bus, sometimes miraculously the driver is able to fix it. Either way, I think you will probably make it to Ychu tonight, but most of the tourists will be out of sight before either of those things happen."

Ethan smiled triumphantly at Emily. "I thought so," Ethan said. "It seemed awfully convenient."

Emily said, "Those people leaning on the cars over there, who are they?" She pointed across the lot.

The man said, "Those are taxi drivers and some people who used to work for the taxi companies. They will get your friends there, and probably faster than we will, but they are going to take quite a bit of their money before they do."

Ethan thought for a moment about both the desire to get to the hotel quickly and the amount of money he had in his pocket. "We're going to stick it out," Ethan said. "But why doesn't the policeman put a stop to it? I mean, this is a kind of a scam going here, isn't it?"

"But it doesn't really hurt anyone—at least," the man said, looking a little sheepish, "it doesn't hurt any of the people who are from here. No offense."

"None taken," Ethan said. "Aren't the tourists in more danger riding with those guys?"

"Not at all. If the taxi drivers ever laid a hand on one of the tourists, the police would come after them, and they'd lose their licenses and go to jail. What good would that do them? They don't want to rob the tourists at gunpoint. Why would they? They can rob them just as easily with a smile and taxi fare."

The twins were astonished at how much sense the scam made. It was well-orchestrated and clearly worked.

"Besides," the man said with a wink, "the policeman probably gets a piece of the action, just a little something in exchange for turning a blind eye."

The smells of the country rose around the twins, pungent and strong. For the next fifteen or twenty minutes the tourists were picked off like wandering sheep by the entrepreneurs outside. They disappeared to refreshment in one direction and out of the parking lot by taxi to the other. Ethan stewed in the sweltering bus and wondered if he had made the wrong decision. The driver's tinkering did not alter in pitch and there was the occasional outburst as he whacked his hand or his head on something underneath the vehicle. No sign appeared of a miraculous fix.

Despite being packed nearly to the rafters, the bus was oddly silent as the passengers either dozed or gazed lazily out the window without apparent curiosity. The only sounds were the buzzings of flies—there was plenty of that—and the occasional cluck from one of the chickens. Emily appeared to doze off at one point. Ethan's legs cramped, so he decided to take a couple of laps around the bus. No one approached. Ethan looked with longing at the bodega. He bet they had water in there. It'd probably cost a thousand saladera a bottle.

As the sun descended to the point where Ethan was sure they would be spending the night on the bus, the hood came slamming down and a sweaty but pleased bus driver clambered aboard. The engine fired for the first time in hours. The passengers audibly exhaled as the bus at last trundled forward, pulling away and starting for the mountains again, toward Ychu.

Ethan thought this stinking afternoon would ruin anything that came later. Nothing could make up for the putrid torture of the long bus ride.

He was wrong.

The travel brochures said Ychu was a beautiful little town tucked away in the Andes mountains, but all the accolades did it no kind of justice. As soon as they crested the hill and started into the green valley, even the native passengers sighed, oohing and ahhing as they pointed down at the picturesque little town. A network of grid-like roads crisscrossed the village. The layout was obviously of Spanish design, despite its position in a place that the Spanish were never able to permanently conquer.

The lake sat like a sapphire jewel with a gently curving village hugging the shoreline. At the far end the huge dam that supplied power to the capital city rose up out of the water, a majestic sight from any vantage, but especially impressive as they trundled down the suddenly well-maintained asphalt into the Ychu valley.

"It's even prettier than I thought it would be," Emily said cheerfully, elbowing her brother.

Ethan had been standing for the last four hours, and sweating for the last three. But seeing these spectacular sights seemed to erase his memory of the discomfort and bad smells. "I can't wait to get there," he said, "get into our hotel room, and start planning how to get out on that lake."

The pig squealed off to his right.

"You said it, piggie," Ethan nodded to the beast. "The sooner the better."

Turn to page 27.

Emily decided that perhaps shifting her weight and herself around until she and Ethan were face-to-face, where they could protect each other, would be a better idea than squishing up against whatever bloody thing was there in the dark.

Back toward the rear a woman began to scream. Calm voices attempted to find out what was wrong with her, but she didn't seem to hear them. She just kept screaming in a language Emily didn't understand. It might have been Quechua. She didn't speak enough of that to be able to tell. Neither, apparently, did anyone else.

The bus lurched around a corner, slamming everyone against one wall then back the other direction. The woman's screaming intensified and other people cried out in obvious pain. The ride couldn't last much longer. Ethan imagined this must be what it had been like to be carried away from a bombing zone in World War II. Or moved out of imminent danger in Puerto Rico after the floods of the summer of 2017.

Fortunately, the bus ride didn't last much longer. Ethan and Emily kept their arms wrapped around each other, giving them a more stable platform. People bumped into them, but they didn't sway nearly as much. Whatever the bloody thing was that Emily had come in contact with before didn't reappear, or if it did she couldn't feel it through her jeans. The bus slammed to a stop, throwing everyone forward like luggage tumbling around on its way to the belly of an airplane.

Emily thought she would be glad to ride in the belly of an airplane if she just had an opportunity to do that. Wherever they were going now surely was farther and farther away from any chance of getting home.

The metal door groaned and spread wide at the rear of the cargo van and a different kind of uniform greeted them as a soldier with a weapon slung across his back beckoned to them to come out of the van.

They were in a large arena. The bus had come in through one of the service entrances out onto what was a soccer stadium floor.

A track for track and field events—there was the sandy pit for the long jump, off to the right—circled the entire lower bowl. The van was one of several in the process of disgorging passengers onto the green field, which was slowly being turned into a brown one by the churning mass of humanity.

Thousands of people could fit on the floor of the arena. Some people were making their way into the seats. Policemen tried half-heartedly to hold them back but there weren't enough for the job. Pretty soon the entire stadium would be filled. There were more vans behind them waiting to let people out. The airport couldn't possibly be the only place that they were being evacuated from.

As she disembarked, she looked around to see if she could figure out the source of what had been bumping into her and saw a small child, no more than seven or eight, wiping its nose. Dried blood painted both arms up to its elbows. The child looked at her with alarm and scurried off in another direction. Emily couldn't be sure that was what she had felt in the van but she hoped it wasn't. She would like to have done something to help.

Turn to page 158.

Ethan hoped that with the guard asleep, and everyone else in their tents, there would be time for them to get away. They crept as quietly as they could through the underbrush, but it was inevitable that they would knock loose some rocks and step on some dead twigs. It seemed to him that they had gone only a few yards before there was a shout from the camp behind them.

Moving as quickly and as quietly as possible, the three of them made their way down the hill. It was very slow going. The thugs cut them off from the road and stayed in that area, patrolling it. They knew that if their fugitives were able to get to the road they could make much better time.

The rest of the night passed almost in a dream, moving for a moment, then stopping for what seemed like hours. The chill soaked through their clothing. There was no preventing it, and no change of clothes available. All their gear was back in the camp.

Thon did the best he could to keep up their spirits. "We have friends in the village," he said. "When we get there, we will be able to chase these guys off and get you some fresh clothes."

But as the night lengthened, Ethan was sure they would never make it. His hands had gone numb again, this time from cold. When the sky began to lighten in the east, he almost didn't believe it.

Emily was in no better shape, he could tell. She huddled close to Thon as much as she could, and this time Ethan only envied them. He tried to stay as close to them as possible as well, but inevitably they got separated, trying to hide in the thin undergrowth all night. They waited for the shot that would say that they were discovered, that their luck had run out, but as the first rays of the sun topped the mountains to the east, the pursuers gave up and fled back to their mountain camp.

The last few hundred yards, Thon and the Tuttles were able to use the path. It led right down to the outskirts of the village. Being able to run a little heated them back up slightly, and Ethan felt that he might not actually die. Still, he had developed a rattling cough overnight, and he knew that he was going to need serious rest and possibly even medical attention. Thon saw it and Emily wrapped her arms around her brother and half carried him along.

"We've got to get him warm," Emily said. Thon nodded.

"The church in the middle of town. That's where we need to go. The father is a friend of mine, and he will take care of us." Thon was as good as his word. The priest took one look at the shivering, sopping wet teenagers and whistled for help. They were babied, dressed in warm clothing, and put to bed. Their exhaustion was so deep that Ethan hardly remembered falling asleep.

He woke, disoriented, to a bare room with white plaster walls. He was in a soft but small bed that his feet overhung just a little bit. On the wall over his head was nailed a wooden crucifix but no other decoration. He turned his head, and there sitting at his bedside was his sister.

"Hello, sleepyhead," she said.

"Hello yourself," he said, and managed a small smile. "What time is it?"

"It's about 4:00 in the afternoon," she said.

"Four in the afternoon?" Ethan said, alarmed. "We have to get moving."

"Whoa, cowboy," she said, pushing him back down onto the bed. "You're not going anywhere. It's 4:00 in the afternoon all right. But it's 4:00 in the afternoon a whole day after we came down out of the mountains. You've been asleep for 33 hours."

The effort to sit up caused Ethan to begin coughing again, a hacking, dry cough that he felt would shake his bones apart.

"That," Emily said, "and you are in no condition to be moving anywhere. I'll tell Father Augustin that you're awake."

Turn to page In the 402.

They spent the remainder of the evening and most of the next day at Thon's house with his small family. Thon was the youngest of three children, and the last one remaining at home. That meant that there was an available room for Emily and Ethan to use.

Thon's father was away in the neighboring village, but his mother welcomed them with open arms.

Suspicion about his sister and their guide had been nagging at Ethan all along their journey to the village, but now that they had arrived, his suspicions grew into full-blown certainty. Emily would start to speak, then flush in the face, and stutter to a stop. This happened especially often when Thon paid close attention to the things that she was talking about. Ethan was used to an Emily who babbled on without stopping, who always had a great deal to say. He didn't know this tongue-tied, shy, teenage girl, who didn't seem to be able to stop tripping over her own tongue.

Dinner that night was grilled chicken with beans, cultivated, Thon told them, from their own patch along the hills and back of the house.

Ethan, used to the normal noises of suburbia, found it intensely peaceful to be in the small village, where there were hardly any mechanical noises at all. This is not to say that there was no power or no modern appliances. The village had its share of those powered by the solar array, which stuck up out of the forest like strange invasive trees.

"The problem was that being surrounded by so many mountains," Thon said, "we only get a certain amount of sunlight everyday. Even though we are very close to the equator, and the sun is very high here, the height of the mountains, and how close they are to our village, means that our sunlight is quite restricted. We have to be very careful about our power consumption."

Emily said, drawing a little bit on the back of her hand, "I would say you get seven, maybe eight hours of sun a day here. Does that sound right?" She looked up at Thon.

"That's about right," Thon said. "It's enough to power critical appliances, medical equipment, lights, and so forth. We can charge small electronic devices, laptops and such, but of course, access to the internet is very expensive. Mostly, we make do with electric lights and copper wire telephone systems. Those do hook into the central grid," he said.

"We really need to call our parents," Ethan said. "They'll be very worried about us."

"I'm sure they'll figure that we are fine," Emily said, as if something else was on her mind.

"And they'll be right," Ethan said. "That doesn't matter. We need to let them *know* as soon as we can. We also need to figure out what we will have to do to get out of the country. Now that we've moved away from the capital city, we're outside the US Embassy's power structure, and they won't be able to help us as much, if at all."

"I'm sorry. Of course you're right," Emily said, shaking her head at herself. "Mom will be frantic enough to charter a plane. So what's the plan?" Emily said.

Thon said, "We don't have a satellite phone in the village. The closest one is over the ridge in Sapallu. It has a satellite phone and good internet connection. It would take us most of the day to get there."

"We'll want to go tomorrow," Ethan said. "As much as I would love to spend time in this village, I think it's unwise for us to do that. We need to start working out how to get home."

Turn to page 305.

Emily sighed. "I don't trust Jorge. But he does seem to know what he's doing. And right now, heading back to civilization is the only real option." She unzipped her backpack. "Here's my fifty. You got yours?"

Ethan did. They walked back over to Jorge. "We'll stick with you," Ethan said, handing over the cash.

Jorge tucked it away so fast it seemed to vanish. "We're pressed for time," he said. "The longer we wait, the more difficult this is going to be." He turned and began jogging toward the entrance to the ruins.

"We can do the first leg in my truck. Once we get back to Ychu, you two will be able to connect with a friend of mine who has an even better vehicle to get you around the lake and across the dam. That's going to be the easiest way to get you back to Takewawa," he said.

"Won't we want to go back the way we came?" Ethan said, hustling after Jorge.

He guffawed, his laugh harsh and unpleasant. "That road is hopeless. I'm sure you saw how steep it was when you came in. There'll be rock slides and mud slides all over it, and it wouldn't be surprising if it took them a few weeks to get that cleared. Seen it all before."

They walked across the central plaza and started descending the stairs to the parking lot. The birds had resumed their chattering and other animals were growling in the trees even louder than they had been before, as if making up for lost time.

"Are people going to be trapped in Ychu?" Emily said. "If that road doesn't go back to Takewawa, how are they going to get out of the city?"

Again, Jorge shrugged. "I don't know if they are," he said. "But that's not our problem. Our job is to get you to where you needed to go, so that you can get out of the country and back home. There's another road, understand. Might be open. Certainly going to be less choked with stalled traffic than that main one. Besides, I can get places other people can't."

It was a good offer. He hadn't said anything out of line. But watching him march across the green, Emily couldn't help wondering what was in it for him. It was a sure bet there was something, and that he was already working out how to get it.

Jorge led them across the parking lot, through groups of milling and increasingly hysterical people, to a large 4 x 4. It had an extended cab and a large bed, and it looked as if it had seen some use. The tires were fat, though, and fairly new, with excellent tread.

"This is the old girl that will get us over the first leg of the journey," Jorge said, with obvious affection in his voice. "I've had her specially modified, so she can take a heavy load and a lot of pounding."

"It looks like she's already taken some," Ethan said.

Jorge laughed. Ethan thought it was the first genuine laugh he had heard from him the entire morning.

"Yeah," Jorge said, "She has been through a few things with me. We've done some good work together."

The twins clambered up into the cab, both of them on the bench, with Jorge over on the driver side. A couple of the tourists broke away from the crowd and came jogging over.

"They're going to want to ride," Jorge said. "Are you okay with a couple of additional passengers?" he said.

Ethan look at Emily and she shrugged. "Why not?" Ethan said.

Jorge started the engine and rolled down the window. "You people looking for a ride?" he said.

"We sure are," the man said. "We need to get back to Ychu so we can work out how to get out of the country."

"Lot of that going around," Jorge said. "But I don't take people for free."

"We have money," the man said, "It's back at the hotel in Ychu."

Jorge grimaced and shook his head. "I'm sorry, that's not good enough. You'll just have to find another way to get back." And before the tourist could make any further objection, Jorge was rolling up the window and putting the truck in gear.

Its tires ground over the gravel of the pavement, and headed out onto the road leading back to Ychu. A couple of tourists tried to get in the way of the vehicle, but Jorge just kept rolling and eventually, of course, they had to move or be run over. They all moved.

Emily gripped Ethan's hand and gritted her teeth. This was not at all the way she hoped that this would go and not at all how she thought a gentleman should behave. But it had been clear from the beginning Jorge was no gentleman.

Still, had he done anything wrong? He had a truck and he was willing to use it, but he wanted to be compensated for his time and gas. That was the market, wasn't it? What was wrong with that?

At the edge of the parking lot, two uniformed policemen held up hands for them to stop. Jorge did, rolling down the window. Clean-scented air flooded the cab, and Ethan realized how stuffy it had been.

"You can't go," the policeman said. "The road is blocked."

Jorge tipped down his shades, showing the man his eyes. "Carlos, hey, it's me."

Carlos the Cop grimaced. "You fall off the mountain, I'm not coming to the funeral. And who will take care of little Juanita's car payments without you around?"

"Hey, it's me," Jorge said. "You'll get yours the first of the month, same as always. And I think this earthquake might open up some more opportunities. We should meet later and talk about that."

Carlos clearly didn't like it, but he waved them on.

Emily and Ethan held a silent conversation while pretending to look out the passenger window. What was that all about? Was Jorge paying off the police?

The road was a mess. They pulled out of the parking lot and started down the hill, but they hadn't gone a hundred yards before there was a significant impasse. Rocks piled up ten feet and higher in a sloping pile, blocking the entire road. A couple of cars were stopped at the edge of the rock slide. Without hesitation, Jorge moved over into what would have been the oncoming lane, had there been any traffic, and cruised on by them.

People craned their necks to see what this truck was going to do, but Jorge hardly paused at the edge of the slide before rocking the gear shift into low and starting up the side of the rocks. The truck bounced precariously and once or twice Emily was sure that it would flip sideways and drop them into the ravine below, but

if Jorge was a nasty guy to deal with when it came to business, he certainly knew how to drive a truck.

The truck cleared every protruding rock and rumbled down the other side of the slide, finally making its way onto the road again. Even here, where the road was clear, the earthquake had cracked it in places, and it was obvious that the road itself would not be the same for some time.

With one thing and another, they managed to get through all of the obstacles and get back to the town. But as they approached, it was obvious that Ychu had taken severe damage from the earthquake as well.

A wave had come from the lake and swamped the boats and watercraft on the beach, tossing them into a wild jumble and carrying a bunch of them out into the lake itself. They bobbed there like stranded ducks.

The hotel had lost one wing—though not the wing where the Tuttles had been staying—and had sustained enough damage that it was clear it was not going to be open for business again for some time.

"Bad luck," Jorge said, pointing. "That's a nice hotel. I hope your luggage is in a different part than that one there that's collapsed."

"We're on the other side," Ethan said. "But if the whole thing is seismically unsound, there's no way they're going to let us in to get our gear."

"All we have is our backpacks," Emily said, "which is okay for now, but if we have to stay anywhere for any extended period, all our clothes and other kinds of things are in our room."

"Not to mention a good deal of our money," Ethan said.

Jorge shot a startled glance over to him, and Ethan made a fast motion with his hand as if to tell him to calm down. "We have plenty to pay your friend, don't worry about that," he said.

Jorge relaxed a little bit and ground his way over the damaged road into the courtyard in front of the hotel.

"I'm going to try to get in touch with my friend," he said. "He has a track vehicle that can go over obstacles even this little darling can't manage."

"Where will you find him?" Emily said.

"He'll be in the bar right over here to the west of the hotel," Jorge said. "That's where he always is this time of day."

The minute Jorge was gone, Emily said, "I really, really want to get our luggage."

Ethan said, "I may have lied about having enough money to keep Jorge happy. That guy can imagine quite a bit."

They sat there for a moment and stared at the hotel.

If you think the twins should go get their luggage, turn to page 128.

If you think they should wait outside, turn to page 106.

Ethan rubbed his eyes, as if trying to get rid of a headache. "We're going to have to find another way."

Emily looked behind her, down the still-empty entrance ramp to the freeway. "There's always reverse," she said. "Assuming this car can go in reverse."

Travis turned around and draped her arm over the seat so she could see out the back window. "She'll do reverse," Travis said. "Among other things."

Ethan tried desperately to keep up with their position on the map, but Travis didn't make it easy. She dodged down alleys, drove on small, almost dirt-track roads, all without consulting any kind of map except the one in her head.

Ethan thought he had a pretty good idea where they were, but he didn't like to ask, in case it appeared that he wasn't doing his job as navigator. He found he very much wanted to stay in the front seat next to this woman.

At one point, Travis rolled slowly down a particular block, then stuck the nose of the Sentra out into the intersection, craning her neck to peek around the side of the building, to see if there was anyone there.

Across the street from them, a police car rolled slowly by. Travis held her breath, and this compelled Ethan to do the same. Brake lights came on as the police car passed. Presumably recognizing who and what they were—civilians for certain—the lights on the top of the car flashed on, and the policeman parked and climbed out of the vehicle.

Travis gave an elaborate sigh and nodded to Ethan, "You're going to want to open the glove compartment in front of you," she said. "Take out pretty much everything that's there and hand it to me."

Ethan did this, pulling out a large sheaf of papers and handing them over. They were strapped with a rubber band and had an official-looking seal on the top of one of them.

Travis rolled down her window, letting in the smell of the city. The smokiness of the previous few days had substantially disappeared now, and it allowed them to breathe freely. Ethan rolled his own window down to get a cross breeze. Even though the city no longer smelled like a war zone, it still smelled nothing like it had.

The policeman walked slowly up, his hand on the butt of his pistol. He stopped in front of the vehicle and said, "Come out of there, and let me see you."

In response, Travis held her sheaf of papers out her window. The policeman scowled but edged forward and, without taking his hand from his gun, took the papers from Travis.

He spent a moment, presumably familiarizing himself with what he was looking at, and then unstrapped the rubber band and began to go through them.

When he got to the paper with the official-looking seal, he paused, unfolded the paper, and read it from top to bottom. Travis watched him with the ghost of a smile on her lips. The policeman's eyes widened, and he hastily stacked the papers back together, handing them back through the window. "My apologies, *señorita*," he said. "I had no idea."

"It's quite all right," Travis said, in a slightly foreign accent she dug up from somewhere. Apparently it wasn't just the car that was full of surprises.

"Please carry on with your mission," the policeman said.

"I will," Travis said. "Thank you very much for your cooperation."

"It's my pleasure," the policeman said, sketched a bow, and went back to his police car. He drove out of there rather more hastily than he had come in.

Travis handed the sheaf of papers back to Ethan, and waved at him to put it in the glove box. Emily stared at Travis, mystified. "I'm afraid to ask," she said.

"Don't be afraid to ask," Travis said, brightly, "but that doesn't mean I'm going to answer."

"However," she said to Ethan, blowing out a breath, "I am hoping that your map extends outside the city of Takewawa. We are going to get to the edge here pretty soon, and when we do, I'm going to need a little bit of help."

Turn to page 351.

Turn to page 351.

Emily felt like she had to drag Ethan around the store. He acted like he'd broken a leg or something, hanging back, looking nervously at everyone who came close. A blonde woman in line smiled at him, and he smiled nervously back.

She said, "Are y'all from the States?"

Ethan's face brightened a little. "Yes, we are."

"We're here for the ruins," Emily said, relaxing just a little for the first time in a while.

"We're going south, along the old Inca road," the woman said. "We saw the ruins last year."

Her purse was loosely dangling from one arm. "Be careful," Ethan said. "We just got robbed by a pickpocket here in this store. Make sure you keep a close eye out."

The woman's eyes widened. "You didn't! Here? You poor dears. Tell me the man didn't get all your money."

"He didn't. Just enough to teach me to be a lot more careful," Ethan said.

The cashier began ringing up the woman's items. "I would have thought produce would be cheaper," the woman said to the twins, thinking the cashier wouldn't understand her.

"They all say this," the cashier replied in decent English. "You should go to the market over the street. Much cheaper."

Emily said, "Why would you tell us that? You work here. Don't you want us to shop here?"

"I don't care." The cashier shrugged. "I get paid by him," she said, pointing up at the windows looking down over the registers, "and he gets paid by the government. You come, you don't come, I get the same. This big tourist store. Much money from other country. You pay. You don't care. So it cost more."

Ethan shot a look at Emily. He looked embarrassed. "I should have thought of that," he said. The blonde woman had paid and left, and now it was Ethan and Emily's turn to pay their bill.

"You can't think of everything," Emily told her brother. "In our country, the government doesn't own stores like this," she told the cashier, who shrugged again. It seemed her favorite way of communicating.

"This not your country," she said, and gave them the total bill. Emily unzipped her pack and paid out, getting some coins as change. They left in a hurry, not wanting to spend another minute in the ABC.

Ethan got some cash from the ATM, scowling the whole time, while Emily stood guard. They kept a steady watch on everyone in the airport lobby while making their way over to the lockers. Fortunately, nothing had happened to their luggage locker.

"I'll watch for thieves while you open it," Ethan said.

Emily tugged out the key and fitted it in the lock. "Let's get to the bus," she said. "I think I'd like to get away from the city as soon as we can."

Turn to page 111.

"There's only one way to eat a really good tamale," Travis said. She hung her elbow out the window and let the juice drip down from her hand and across her forearm in a bright streak like orange blood.

Ethan and Emily devoured their tamales with similar relish. "This is just about the best food I've ever eaten," Ethan said. "I can't believe we had to find it on the freeway out of the country."

Travis waved her finger, driving with her knee. "Don't minimize that," she said. "Some of the best things you're going to find in your life will come to you while you're looking for something else."

"They call that serendipity," Emily said, her mouth full of tamale.

"I've heard it called a lot of things," Travis said, "but serendipity will do."

The traffic jam had broken up almost without warning. One minute all the cars in the world were stopped dead on the freeway between Takewawa and Quito, and the next moment all the traffic was rolling. A few minutes later, it was almost up to freeway speeds.

"Only for a few miles," Travis said, as she braked and began to slow again, "But that was a darn good couple of miles. It always refreshes me to put a couple miles under the wheels, especially after we've been stopped as long as we have."

"It's very nice of you to take us all this way," Ethan said. "I can't think this was what you had planned for the day."

"It was not," Travis said. "But once again, it sometimes happens that you find the thing you're looking for on the road to something else."

Turn to page 271.

Ethan said, "I really think our best bet is to get back to civilization as quick as possible. I know Thon makes it sound like his village is some kind of paradise, but the truth is I just don't believe it."

"You think he's lying?" Emily said, with some heat.

Interesting reaction, Ethan thought. It only increased his desire to head in another direction from the dark-eyed teenager from the local village. "I think he's unable to promise us an airfield. You see any other way we could get home?"

Emily opened her mouth, stopped, and closed it again.

"Besides," he said, "there won't be any communications equipment there, and there's no way for us to get a message to Mom and Dad that we're okay. They will be frantic, starting the second the Google alert hits their phone."

Emily gave in reluctantly, throwing a glance in the direction of their new friend. "I hate to say it, but you're right," she said. "Jorge doesn't seem like the kind of person we would normally be able to trust. But he is headed in a *direction* that I trust. So maybe we can go with him and be okay."

The twins marched back to the small group huddled in the center of the Ychurichuc main plaza.

"We are going to go with you," Ethan said, talking to Jorge. Jorge nodded. The beginnings of a small smile appeared on his face.

"I'm confident that my vehicle can get you where you need to go," he said.

Thon seem disappointed but not terribly surprised. He shook hands with the twins and said, "I guess this is goodbye. If I ever see you again, we will meet as friends."

"We sure will," Ethan said. "Take care of yourself."

Emily said, "We didn't get anything like enough time here at the ruins. We will try to come back, and when we do, I hope we have a chance to meet you again."

Thon simply nodded at this and struck off in the direction of the graveyard.

"Where is he going?" Jorge said.

"He lives over that way," Ethan said.

"It'll be quite a hike, I imagine, but he looks... fit," Emily said, tearing her eyes away from his receding back. "I'm sure he'll make it."

Jorge shrugged, as if it no longer mattered to him one way or the other. "Okay," he said, "first things first. This isn't a charity ride. I'll carry you down, but you'll have to pay me."

"I'm shocked," Ethan said.

Jorge did a double-take, then continued, "Well, anyway. I want fifty bucks, cash, each. And right now."

"Fifty bucks!" Ethan said. "That's twice what the tour cost, which, incidentally, we didn't get much of."

Jorge shrugged. "No refunds on that. But I promise that if I fail to get you to Ychu, we can work something out." He scanned the emptying ruins. "You have better options?"

"Not anymore," Emily said, fuming.

"I'm sure you have the cash," Jorge said. "This is the time to use it."

"Is it? It's not like there's going to be a lot more, not if communications are out. That will make the ATMs a little cranky, I bet," Emily said. "Will you excuse us for a second?" She hauled Ethan off by the sleeve.

"Sure," Jorge said. "You have one minute. Then this train moves on without you."

Emily hissed in Ethan's ear. "Now look what you've done."

"Me? I'm just trying to get us home. Yeah, this fellow is a creep, but he's also our best bet. Unless you want to chase down Inca boy."

Emily thought about it for a second. It was a terrible decision, one way or the other, filled with unknown risks. "We do have the cash," she said. "Just... It all comes down to which way would be best."

If you think the twins should stay with Jorge, turn to page 377.

If you think they should try to catch up with Thon, turn to page 344.

The twins skirted the tall concrete ramp leading to what looked like some sort of free-for-all farmer's market and took the broad sidewalk to the ABC. A brightly-lit interior beckoned them inside.

"Looks just like the supermarket back home," Emily said.

"That's why we choose places like this when we can," Ethan said. "We're going to get plenty of culture in the other places we go. I like to be safe when choosing my food."

They bounced across the blacktop to the doors, which shushed open in front of them. The smell of the place wafted out into the sunshine, but it wasn't at all what they were expecting.

"*That* doesn't smell like the supermarket," Emily said. "It smells like sour milk."

A few flies lazily floated in through the open door.

"Well, we're here—we better get to it," Ethan said, and walked into the store.

Crowds of people browsed the aisles, which were not arranged the way they remembered from the store back home, with produce in one section and bread in the other. Things seemed to be placed haphazardly all over the store.

As they passed an aisle, a man shot out into the passage and crashed headlong into Ethan. His basket of juice and bread skittered across the floor.

"*Lo siento!*" the man shouted, far too loudly. "I very sorry," he said, changing to English.

Ethan staggered to his feet and the man jumped at him, brushing him off and jabbering away in Spanish. Ethan kept saying, "It's okay. I'm okay." But the man seemed completely distraught and continued brushing dirt off him even though it was by now long gone.

"You're hurt!" the man said. "This is blood?"

Ethan twisted his arm to look. A reddish stain spread from his forearm to his elbow, flecked with a few seeds. Tomato. He'd squashed a tomato.

"No, no," Ethan said, his face bright red. "I'm fine. Nothing's wrong." He tried to explain to the man that he wasn't hurt, not even a little.

Emily gathered up the basket and put the scattered groceries back in, trying to ignore the dust clinging to the loaf of football-shaped bread. "Here," she said. "Nothing is missing."

"Except a tomato," Ethan said, pointing to his arm. The man stared for a moment, then a huge grin split his face, and he began to laugh.

"Yes! A tomato! I'm missing one!" He laughed as if this were the most hilarious joke he'd ever heard, apologized again, and took off at the same speed he'd arrived.

"Are you really okay?" Emily said.

"Yes, I think so," Ethan said, looking around for his list. Emily plucked it from under his foot.

"This what you're looking for?"

"Yeah," Ethan said, still checking himself as if he thought part of him might be missing. His hand went to his waist pack.

His face drained of color. "But now I'm looking for something else!" He whirled frantically, staring at the floor, peeking under the nearby display, patting his pockets.

"What?" Emily said. "What is it?"

"My money," Ethan said. "It's *gone*." He sprinted off in the direction the man had gone. Emily headed for the door, sure that if he was still in the store, he would come that way. Five minutes later, she was sure he was already far away.

Her suspicion was confirmed when Ethan came glumly down the final aisle, his shopping bag hanging limply on his arm. "He's gone," he said. "I looked everywhere."

"How did he get your money?"

Ethan tapped his waist pack. "When he was patting me down. Must have been. Old magician's trick—distract me with the tomato and unzip my pack while I'm concentrating on something else."

"Are your other documents still there?" Emily said, her hand on her own pack as if it might jump off and go running down the grocery aisle.

Ethan nodded. "He just got the money. Not even all of it—he left the dollars, but took all my loose saladera."

"Good thing you have that secret stash," Emily said. "Come on, let's get the stuff we need. I have the money for it. You can get more from the ATM before we go to the bus."

If you think the twins should go to the ATM for more money, turn to page 387.

If you think they should complain to the store manager, turn to page 268.

Passengers from all over debarked from their buses and vans. They queued up in front of a pair of security guards in front of the Quonset hut. One of the guards took passports and other forms of identification and checked them. The other guard examined the parcels, packages, and luggage the people in line had brought with them. It was almost like customs, Ethan thought.

"I need to see your passport," the guard said. Ethan unzipped his waist pack and handed over his documentation. The guard looked at it and checked carefully the stamp Ethan had gotten when he arrived in the country. He smiled a tight smile and handed the passport back. He looked at Emily.

"I'm sorry," Emily said. "I don't have my passport. It's been lost."

"We lost it in the earthquake," Ethan said.

"So neither of you have any luggage?" the other guard said.

"I have my backpack," Ethan said. "But outside of that, we only have the things that we have with us—the clothes on our backs and what is in my waist pack."

The guard mumbled something about being sorry before he let them in the door. He said, "I'm not sup-posed to let you in without identification. But it's pretty obvious that the two of you are brother and sister, so if one of you has proof of citizenship, I'm going to pretend like that works for both of you."

The interior of the Quonset hut was lit only by skylights. It looked as if the hut had been there for some time because of the wooden floor and decorations on the wall. But it was pretty obvious that it had not been a U.S. Embassy property, as the walls were filled with posters in Spanish talking about employment contracts and construction equipment.

There was a faintly musty smell about the place, mixed with the unmistakable scent of desperate tourists. It was very warm. The small windows at one end of the hut had been opened to their maximum which allowed a slight breeze, but it did almost nothing to cool down the inside of the hut, slowly baking in the afternoon sun. Ethan slowly sweated into his already very dirty shirt and wished for nothing so much as a bath and a good long sleep without interruption by an earthquake or by the need to make life-and-death decisions.

Behind two desks sat harried-looking embassy personnel, taking down names and phone numbers and looking like they had neither slept nor eaten in quite some time.

The twins had been waiting in line only a couple of minutes when an embassy official looked up at them and smiled.

"Where are your parents?" the woman said.

"They're back in the States," Ethan said. "We came on vacation by ourselves."

"We didn't expect to get caught in an earthquake," Emily said, "but we did the best we could to get out before it hit. But we weren't in time to get on an airplane to get out of the country."

"I've heard that story a lot," the official said. "Hundreds of people have more or less the same problem."

"We don't have any of our stuff, either," Emily said.

"Just my backpack," Ethan said. He held it up for inspection.

The woman did not inspect it.

They told her everything that had happened to them from the time that they arrived in the country. She made several notes on her clipboard.

"I can offer some assistance," she said when they had finished. "We have an American-only camp we've set up, and I can get you into that. It's not luxury, but it's a place to stay, which you don't currently have?" She checked their faces and saw she was right. "As for the rest," she continued, "that may be a little bit more difficult. I know you have plane tickets to get back out of the country, but those tickets obviously aren't going to be used. In fact, although you may not have heard this, the airport has been almost totally destroyed by flooding."

Ethan and Emily exchanged a glance.

She gave Ethan a tight smile. "The Ychu dam failed and most of the structures in its path were completely destroyed. No one will be flying out of that airport for some time, if ever again."

Ethan sagged. That was their only way out. Of course the water from the escaping lake would wipe out everything in its path.

"What we will try to do," the woman said, "is to find a place to link up with the American Embassy in Ecuador. We should be able to make contact with them and begin to move people into their jurisdiction, I don't know how long it will take, however. If I understand correctly, Emily here has no identification."

"That's true," Emily said. She felt the woman should have been able to do something about it.

But the lady didn't give them much hope. "We'll do the best we can," she said. "But in the meantime, things are going to be very difficult."

Turn to page 171.

Every day Ethan grew a little bit stronger.

The town proved to have a satellite phone, and although it was much in demand, the twins were able to get a few minutes on it to call home and let Mom and Dad know that they were OK.

Understandably, their parents were frantic; for almost a week they had had no way of knowing whether the twins were even alive. They were overjoyed to hear that they were alive, and that they were well, even after a number of amazing and somewhat terrifying adventures. Together, they planned to find a way to get over the border into Ecuador, so that they would be able to fly out of the Quito airport in the capital city. Father Augustin assured them that he would do all in his power to get them where they needed to go.

"My church has great influence in this part of the world," he said. "We are always engaged in humanitarian efforts, helping the children of God to support themselves and to have the necessities of life. Currently, I think one of the necessities of life is that we get the two of you back to the States."

He had even had Consuela organize a posse—what a thing in the 21st century—to go into the hills and root out the bandits, which they did with some ease. Allegedly a couple of the wives went up and returned dragging their husbands by the ear.

Ethan spent a great deal of time reading from the church's excellent library. His Spanish improved. Emily sat with him for hours a day, and they talked and read together. She also spent a great deal of time with the volunteers at the church, distributing supplies to people coming in to coordinate relief efforts. The church was at the center of all that activity in town.

Sapallu had been hit hard initially by the earthquake; its power was initially cut off, but most of the buildings were intact, and their food supplies, while sparse, were enough to supply the town for a few more weeks at least.

"The roads are starting to get cleared off," Emily said, after an excursion with a repair group. "The people here have done tremendous work, going up in the hills and clearing sections of road every day. Father Augustin organizes most of the activities, and has really done tremendous work in helping to put the town back together. And I have something to show you."

She handed Ethan a square piece of brown paper. On it was printed a black cross, a date, and a number. "What's this?" Ethan said. He paced a little around his bed, gathering strength. He'd be fully well in another few days, he thought. Then he would be able to travel.

"It's scrip," Emily said, as if he should know what that was.

He handed it back to her. "That doesn't mean anything to me," he said.

"Scrip is a kind of money," she said. "Because the banks are shut down, people here needed to come up with a source of currency that the townspeople can use until things are back to normal. People need a way to pay each other for food and shelter. The father had been reading some books on the subject, and he and one of his advisors came up with an idea to print their own money."

"The church is printing *money*?" Ethan said. The idea sounded ridiculous but also kind of cool.

"That's right," Emily said. "I'm not sure exactly how it works, but the church is the issuing authority, and they are the ones whose seal of approval is on the scrip. The townspeople are using it just the way they used saladera before. It seems to be working really well."

Ethan sat down on the bed, already winded just from walking around the room for a few minutes. At least he wasn't coughing any more. He ran his hand over the clean white sheets, feeling the smoothness of the fabric under his hand. Out the window, two bright yellow birds roosted in the tree.

"It always seems like there are more things to learn," Ethan said. "Everywhere we go, I think I want to get out of there as quickly as possible, and then when I find out what's really happening there, I never want to leave."

"I feel the same way," Emily said. "I've been here a week, and already I love these people like family."

"Like family?"

Emily laughed and patted his hand. "Don't worry, big brother by eleven minutes. I know the difference between a summer crush and wedding bells."

Ethan sighed and lay back on the bed. "I think I'm ready to have my adventures at home. Another couple of days," Ethan said. "The doctor says I'm strong enough to start walking around the town. If that's true, then no matter how great this country is, I'm ready to get back to ours."

Turn to page 101.

The Author

Connor Boyack is founder and president of Libertas Institute, a free market think tank in Utah. In that capacity he has changed dozens of laws in favor of personal freedom and free markets, and has launched a variety of educational projects, including The Tuttle Twins children's book series. Connor is the author of over a dozen books.

A California native and Brigham Young University graduate, Connor currently resides in Lehi, Utah, with his wife and two children.

The Illustrator

Elijah Stanfield is owner of Red House Motion Imaging, a media production company in Washington.

A longtime student of Austrian economics, history, and the classical liberal philosophy, Elijah has dedicated much of his time and energy to promoting the ideas of free markets and individual liberty. Some of his more notable works include producing eight videos in support of Ron Paul's 2012 presidential candidacy. He currently resides in Richland, Washington, with his wife April and their six children.